# INDIRECT CRIMINALISATION

This book presents the first detailed study of 'indirect criminalisation' (the legal treatment of antisocial behaviour through civil preventative measures such as the ASBO) in England and Wales.

Since the late 20th century many Western jurisdictions introduced a range of civil preventive measures in order to prevent and deal with various types of criminality. Although the stated objective of these interventions is the prevention of crime, their implementation can result in the imposition of restrictions akin to criminal punishment leading to the indirect criminalisation of certain kinds of behaviour.

Through the adoption of an interdisciplinary approach which combines criminal law theory and empirical criminology, this book engages with the phenomenon of indirect criminalisation using the legal framework on anti-social behaviour in England and Wales as a case study.

It engages with central questions within legal theory:

- What are the normative challenges posed by indirect criminalisation and mechanisms for distinguishing criminal from non-criminal rules?
- How can such questions be tested and applied empirically?
- Has the ASBO's successor been operating as de facto criminal measure?

# Indirect Criminalisation

## *The True Limits of Criminal Punishment*

Stavros Demetriou

•HART•

OXFORD • LONDON • NEW YORK • NEW DELHI • SYDNEY

HART PUBLISHING

Bloomsbury Publishing Plc

Kemp House, Chawley Park, Cumnor Hill, Oxford, OX2 9PH, UK

1385 Broadway, New York, NY 10018, USA

29 Earlsfort Terrace, Dublin 2, Ireland



First published in Great Britain 2023



A catalogue record for this book is available from the British Library.

A catalogue record for this book is available from the Library of Congress.

Library of Congress Control Number: 2022949267

ISBN: HB: 978-1-50994-143-8
ePDF: 978-1-50994-145-2
ePub: 978-1-50994-144-5

Typeset by Compuscript Ltd, Shannon

# *Acknowledgements*

I WOULD NOT have been able to complete this monograph without the encouragement, guidance, assistance and support of a number of colleagues. In particular, I am indebted to Dr Neil Partington (University of Sussex), Dr Kevin Brown (Queen's University Belfast), Dr Lucy Welsh (University of Sussex), Professor Colin King (Institute of Advanced Legal Studies, University of London), Dr Marti Rovira (University of Oxford), Dr Alessandro Corda (Queen's University Belfast), Dr Milena Tripkovic (University of Edinburgh), Dr Adriano Martufi (University of Leiden) and Dr Elina van't Zand-Kurtovic (University of Leiden) for their insightful and constructive feedback on earlier drafts of this monograph. Their invaluable comments and recommendations significantly enhanced the quality of this monograph. I also owe an enormous debt to Professor John Child (University of Birmingham), Professor Mark Walters (University of Sussex) and Laurence Koffman (University of Sussex) for their outstanding supervision during my PhD thesis (University of Sussex, 2017) which laid the foundations for this monograph. I must also acknowledge Professor Donald Mcgillivray (Head of Sussex Law School) and Professor Heather Keating (Head of Law, Politics and Sociology, University of Sussex) for their continuous support throughout this process without which I would not be able to complete this work. Moreover, I would like to express my appreciation to Elias A Stephanou and the rest of the team at Elias A Stephanou LLC for their assistance, encouragement and support during the final stages of this process. Furthermore, grateful acknowledgement is made to all of those local enforcement agents and their institutions for participating in the empirical study conducted for the purposes of this monograph.

Many thanks also go to the publishers and editors of the *Public Law* journal and the *Legal Studies* journal for granting me permission to use material from the following sources: (a) S Demetriou, 'Crime and Anti-Social Behaviour in England and Wales: An Empirical Evaluation of the ASBO's successor' (2020) 40 *Legal Studies* 458–76; and (b) S Demetriou, 'From the ASBO to the Injunction: A Qualitative Review of the Anti-Social Behaviour Legislation post-2014' (2019) (April) *Public Law* 343–61. I am also tremendously grateful to Katie Whetter (Senior Commissioning Editor) and everyone else at Hart Publishing for their professionalism, understanding and support during this process.

Finally, I would like to thank my wife Lyto, my daughter Maria, my parents Demetris and Elena and the rest of my family for their unconditional love, understanding, patience and support.

*To Lyto and Maria*

# Contents

# 1

# *Liberty, Security and the Civil/Criminal Law Divide*

## 1.1. INTRODUCTION

THERE IS GENERAL consensus in political and legal discourse that a key function of the liberal state is to 'protect and safeguard the lives of its citizens'.[1] For Mill, in a 'civilised community', the state can rightfully interfere with someone's liberty only if this is 'to prevent harm to others'.[2] Similarly for Hobbes, whose political theory laid the foundations for the modern liberal state, people agree to abandon their right of nature, that is their ability to exercise their powers as they wish in order to secure their own preservation, as a means of establishing and maintaining a commonwealth.[3] In return, those who enter this social covenant expect that they will 'be protected against other men' who might wish to unjustifiably interfere with their liberty.[4] On this view, the liberal state is an artificial entity created by individuals who abandoned their right of nature.[5]

Clearly, from a Hobbesian perspective, the liberal state is based on a trade-off between individual autonomy and security. Members of the polity accept that some limits will be imposed on their liberty with the expectation that they will be offered security that will enable them to realise their full potential. It is this prospect of security and self-realisation that incentivises individuals to enter this social covenant with others.[6] In order for this to be achieved though, duties are imposed on both members of the polity and the liberal state. Members of the polity do not just acquire a right to security. A duty is also imposed on them

[1] *A v Secretary of State for the Home Department* [2004] UKHL 56 [99].

[2] J Mill, *On Liberty* (New York, Dover Publications, 2002) 8.

[3] T Hobbes, *Leviathan* (Hertfordshire, Wordsworth Editions, 2014) 131.

[4] ibid 136.

[5] ibid 7.

[6] According to Hobbes, this social covenant is between members of the polity themselves rather than between each individual and the sovereign. The importance of this lies in the need for the liberal state and every contracting party to acknowledge others as equal members of the polity. See Hobbes (n 3) 136; S Demetriou and N Partington, 'Criminalising Hate: The Need for Rationalisation and Reform' (2022) 6 *Criminal Law Review* 448, 457–61.

not to *unjustifiably* interfere with the liberty of others. As far as the liberal state is concerned, a duty is imposed on it to keep its citizens safe while striking a fair balance[7] between individual autonomy and state control.[8] To this end, the state must call those who are suspected of breaching the covenant to account for their actions and if found liable to be punished for their transgression.[9] For Hobbes, punishing those who are found in breach of the covenant is an integral feature of the liberal state since 'covenants, without the sword, are but words, and of no strength to secure a man at all'.[10] As we shall see, though, striking a fair balance between liberty and security is a particularly complex process that raises many practical and normative issues. What might, for instance, enhance the security of a specific social group can, at the same time, undermine the liberty of another.

The liberal state has many tools at its disposal through which it can 'protect and safeguard the lives of its citizens'.[11] One of the most, if not the most, powerful weapons in the state arsenal for the protection of its citizens is the criminal law. Through criminalisation, the state can not only punish those who unjustifiably interfere with the liberty of others, but it can also prevent this from happening.[12] This preventive function of the criminal law is premised on the assumption that if the legislature determines, for instance, that the unlawful infliction of grievous bodily harm is worth criminalising, then there is reason to prevent this from happening in the first place.[13] In fact, from a Hobbesian perspective, if the liberal state is to uphold its commitment to offer security to its citizens, then it has a duty to prevent the commission of crime. The prevention of crime will not only assist the liberal state to fulfil its duty to protect its citizens

[7] A non-liberal state, such as a totalitarian regime, can be even more effective in safeguarding the security of its citizens. What really distinguishes a liberal state though from other political orders is its promise to limit state interference with personal autonomy to what is absolutely necessary for safeguarding the security of its people and for the maintenance of those conditions within society that will enable them to realise their full potential. See Demetriou and Partington (n 6).

[8] As we will see below, some legal commentators, such as Carvalho, Ramsay, and Ashworth and Zedner, argue that there is an inherent ambivalence that lies at the heart of the liberal state. According to them, while an integral feature of the liberal state is respect for individual autonomy, the ever-increasing pursuit of security led to the introduction of measures that undermine citizens' liberty. See H Carvalho, *The Preventive Turn in Criminal Law* (Oxford, Oxford University Press, 2017) 2–3; P Ramsay, *The Insecurity State: Vulnerable Autonomy and the Right to Security in the Criminal Law* (Oxford, Oxford University Press, 2012) 5 and 184; A Ashworth and L Zedner, *Preventive Justice* (Oxford, Oxford University Press, 2014) 257.

[9] Based on Hobbes's account, when men enter this social covenant, they also agree to abandon their right to punish others for wrongs committed against them. Simply put, they agree not to take matters into their own hands. Instead, the state is trusted to punish those who are found in breach of the social covenant as it deems 'fit, for the preservation of them all'. See Hobbes (n 3) 236–37.

[10] ibid 131.

[11] *A v Secretary of State for the Home Department* (n 1) [99].

[12] A Ashworth, 'Conceptions of Overcriminalization' (2007–08) 5 *Ohio State Journal of Criminal Law* 407, 409.

[13] As Duff puts it, it would be morally problematic if the state criminalises the unlawful infliction of grievous bodily harm, but fails to criminalise those who attempt to inflict this kind of harm on others. See A Duff, *Criminal Attempts* (New York, Oxford University Press, 1996) 134.

from any unjustifiable interference with their liberty, but it will also enable them to plan their behaviour without feeling insecure and therefore be in a better position to realise their full potential. It is for this reason that the criminal law of many Western jurisdictions includes an array of inchoate offences, such as criminal attempts, which enable the state to intervene prior to the commission of the principal offence in order to prevent future harm.[14]

Although the prevention of crime 'is a laudable and defensible role of the [liberal] state',[15] the ever-increasing need to manage future risks has,[16] since the late twentieth century, led to the proliferation of preventive criminal offences many of which extend the reach of the criminal law well beyond the ambit of traditional inchoate offences. These are called pre-inchoate offences since they allow the state to intervene well before someone's conduct reaches the threshold required to establish liability for an inchoate offence. These offences depart from the mainstream 'risk-based crime prevention [logic] by pre-empting incipient threats. By targeting anticipated crimes … as if they had already happened'.[17] This is not to suggest that the state's preoccupation with the prevention of harm is a new phenomenon.[18] Instead, what I am arguing is that some of the criminal offences introduced since the beginning of the twenty-first century in many Western jurisdictions are so *antithetical* to the values and principles underpinning a liberal society, such as the need to provide members of the polity with a fair warning about the kinds of conduct that might fall within the ambit of the criminal law,[19] that even a committed contractarian who believes that everyone has a right to security will feel unease about them.[20] Although the introduction of these pre-inchoate offences is often justified by lawmakers on the need to reassure members of the public about their safety and security,[21] my main argument is that we (as members of the polity on whose name these laws are enacted) should not lose sight of the impact that these offences might have on individual liberty and well-established principles of justice.

A particularly apposite and illustrative example are those pre-emptive offences targeting terrorism. In particular, many Western jurisdictions

[14] In England and Wales, for instance, it is an offence under s 1 of the Criminal Attempts Act 1981 for anyone to intentionally do 'an act which is more than merely preparatory to the commission of [an] offence'.

[15] Ashworth and Zedner, *Preventive Justice* (n 8) 82.

[16] M Feeley and J Simon, 'The New Penology: Notes on the Emerging Strategy of Corrections and its Implications' (1992) 30 *Criminology* 449, 449.

[17] J McCulloh and D Wilson, *Pre-crime: Pre-emption, Precaution and the Future* (Abingdon, Routledge, 2016) 1.

[18] Ashworth and Zedner, *Preventive Justice* (n 8) ch 2; Ramsay, *The Insecurity State* (n 8) 166.

[19] As Robinson rightly points out, providing a fair warning 'is a quality of special importance in criminal law, where a defendant's life and liberty are often at stake'. See P Robinson, 'Fair Notice and Fair Adjudication: Two Kinds of Legality' (2005) 154 *University of Pennsylvania Law Review* 335, 340.

[20] I elaborate further on some of the principles and values that are inherent to a liberal society in ch 2, section 2.2.

[21] Ramsay, *The Insecurity State* (n 8) 2.

have, especially after the terrorist attacks carried out in the United States on 11 September 2001, introduced a multitude of pre-emptive offences criminalising a wide range of behaviour while carrying lengthy custodial sentences.[22] At a European Union level, for example, through Directive 2017/541, Member States were asked to criminalise (if they had not done so already) various terrorism-related activities, such as providing and/or receiving training for terrorism. As far as England and Wales is concerned, reference could be made to section 58(1)(b) of the Terrorism Act 2000[23] which criminalises, inter alia, the possession, without reasonable excuse, of any document which can facilitate the commission of an act of terrorism.[24] This offence can be justified on the ground that, given the risk posed by terrorism, it would be unreasonable for the state not to intervene prior to the commission of a terrorism-related activity. Consequently, the section 58 offence allows the state to intervene well before someone has even reached the threshold required for criminal attempts. Pre-emptive criminalisation, therefore, 'facilitate[s] intervention at an earlier stage, with no requirement that the substantive harm results at all'.[25] The core of the debate in this area is to identify when conduct becomes sufficiently proximate (and therefore blameworthy) to the harm anticipated to warrant criminalisation.[26]

The introduction of pre-inchoate offences is often justified by citing the precautionary principle which dictates that the state should be in a position to punish people for crimes they *might* commit in the future.[27] Three points must be noted here about the use of the precautionary principle as a justification for the introduction of preventive-led interventions and the impact that this has on the relationship between the liberal state and its citizens. First, the ambit of pre-inchoate offences is extremely broad and ambiguous covering a range of behaviour that might otherwise be regarded as lawful. These offences, such as the section 58, do not punish people for causing some kind of harm to others and/or for behaviour that is inherently wrongful. Instead, these offences allow for the imposition of punishment on individuals who *might* cause harm to others

[22] For a more comprehensive analysis of the impact that the 9/11 terrorist attacks had on the legal approach adopted by many Western jurisdictions against terrorism, see C Walker, 'The Impact of Contemporary Security Agendas Against Terrorism on the Substantive Criminal Law' in A Masferrer (ed), *Post 9/11 and the State of Permanent Legal Emergency: Security and Human Rights in Countering Terrorism* (Dordrecht, Springer, 2012).

[23] Other examples include the offences under s 1(2)(b(ii) of the Terrorism Act 2006 and s 57 of the Terrorism Act 2000.

[24] For a more detailed analysis of this offence, see J Hodgson and V Tadros, 'How to Make a Terrorist Out of Nothing' (2009) 72 *Modern Law Review* 984.

[25] J Child and A Hunt, 'Risk, Pre-emption, and the Limits of the Criminal Law' in K Doolin et al (eds), *Whose Criminal Justice? State or Community?* (Hampshire, Waterside Press, 2010) 54.

[26] It is imperative to acknowledge that notwithstanding the normative and practical challenges posed by pre-emptive criminalisation, these offences fall within the scope of the criminal law and are therefore subjected to the same procedural and evidential rules as all other criminal offences.

[27] J McCulloh and B Charlton, 'Preempting Justice: Suppression of Financing Terrorism and the "War on Terror"' (2006) 17 *Current Issues in Criminal Justice* 397, 397.

in the future. The importance of this lies in the fact that very few constraints are imposed on the state's ability to interfere with the liberty of its citizens. To illustrate this further consider the following hypothetical scenario.

Suppose that there is intelligence suggesting that Sam might be a member of a terrorist group operating in the United Kingdom. The Secretary of State authorises, under section 32(3) of the Regulation of Investigatory Powers 2000, the police to carry out intrusive surveillance of Sam's residence.[28] Following further intelligence, the police manage to obtain a search warrant for Sam's property. The police found in Sam's flat what appears to be a shopping list containing several materials that can be used to make an explosive device. Sam was arrested and prosecuted for an offence contrary to section 58 of the 2000 Act on the basis that his shopping list 'contain[s] information which is, of its very nature, likely to be useful to a potential terrorist'.[29] As explained by the House of Lords in *R v G*, there is no need for the prosecution to prove that it was Sam's intention to use the information at hand for terrorism-related purposes.[30] Instead, the prosecution must only prove that Sam 'was aware of the kind of information which was in the document or record which he possessed'.[31] Moreover, although the Lords sought to limit the scope of the section 58 offence by pointing out that it would not cover 'information of a kind which is useful to people for all sorts of everyday purposes and which many members of the public regularly obtain or use',[32] the true limits of this offence remain unclear since it is up to the jury to decide whether the information 'would typically be of use to terrorists'.[33] What this means is that: (i) Sam faces a custodial sentence of up to 15 years and a fine simply for being in possession of information that *might* 'be useful to a person committing or preparing an act of terrorism'; and (ii) even if Sam avoids liability by providing a reasonable excuse for his conduct,[34] pre-inchoate offences allow the state to use a range of liberty and privacy invasive measures, such as intrusive surveillance and pre-trial detention, for conduct that is otherwise lawful and often far remote from the actual harm that these offences seek to prevent.[35]

[28] According to s 32(3) of the Regulation of Investigatory Powers 2000, in order for an intrusive surveillance to be authorised, the Secretary of State or the senior authorising officer must be satisfied that this is 'necessary: (a) in the interest of national security; (b) for the purpose of preventing or detecting serious crime; or (c) in the interests of the economic well-being of the United Kingdom'.

[29] *R v G* [2010] 1 AC 43 [44].

[30] ibid [46]–[49].

[31] ibid [47].

[32] ibid [42]–[43].

[33] Hodgson and Tadros (n 24) 988.

[34] Terrorism Act 2006, s 58(3).

[35] For Logan, criminalisation has both an expressive and instrumental function. As far as the latter is concerned, the enactment of a criminal offence provides law enforcement agents with the necessary powers and authority needed to intervene in people's affairs, such as by obtaining a search and/or an arrest warrant. Consequently, the more criminal offences enacted the more 'opportunities [are provided] for seizures of citizens by police'. Although Logan's observations relate to criminal offences enacted by municipal governments in the United States, his argument is readily applicable in the context of pre-emptive offences as well since the broader and more ambiguous the scope of these offences is, the more opportunities are provided to law enforcement agents to lawfully interfere

Second, although security has been traditionally presented as a necessary condition for the protection of individual liberty,[36] the proliferation of pre-inchoate offences in many Western jurisdictions during the last two decades blatantly highlights the paradox that lies at the heart of the liberal promise.[37] In particular, despite the fact that the introduction of pre-inchoate offences is often justified on the alleged need to enhance security allowing members of the polity to enjoy their freedom without any unjustifiable interference by others, as seen above, the measures introduced to do so appear to pose a threat to the very thing that they are supposed to protect, that is individual liberty.[38] As Ramsay puts it, the modern liberal state is so preoccupied with security that it is willing to do whatever it takes to address potential (and even unknown) risks regardless of 'the cost to the rights of the law's subjects'.[39] A possible explanation for this is the politicisation of penal policy which is often referred to as the phenomenon of penal populism. According to Garland, in an attempt to gain political capital, politicians attempt to introduce measures and policies (usually in response to trigger events, such as terrorist attacks) 'that will not be viewed as signs of weakness or an abandonment of the state's responsibility to the public'.[40] Security is inevitably used as a trump card for penal reform, such as the introduction of new criminal offences, that seeks to address newly identified threats to people's security. What is problematic about penal populism is that not only on many occasions political knowledge overrides penal expertise,[41] but also the fact that it generates more insecurity which in turn results in less liberty.[42] In an attempt to address existing sentiments of insecurity amongst society, Western states introduced, especially following 9/11, an array of emergency powers and pre-inchoate offences that have significantly expanded the net of social control. This resulted in the identification of new threats leading to the introduction of even more tools and powers. Concerns about the legitimacy of emergency powers are demoted while civil liberties 'tend to be sacrificed to the more pressing claims of security'.[43] The precautionary logic that is embedded in these policies allows

with people's liberties. See W Logan, 'The Shadow Criminal Law of Municipal Governance' (2001) 62 *Ohio State Law Journal* 1409, 1439–40.

[36] G Burchell, 'Peculiar Interests: Civil Society and Governing "The System of Natural Liberty' in G Burchell et al (eds), *The Foucault Effect: Studies in Governmentality* (Chicago, IL, University of Chicago Press, 1991) 139.

[37] Carvalho (n 8) 2–3; Ramsay, *The Insecurity State* (n 8) 5 and 184; Ashworth and Zedner, *Preventive Justice* (n 8) 257.

[38] Ramsay, *The Insecurity State* (n 8) 184.

[39] ibid 4; McCulloh and Charlton (n 27) 404.

[40] D Garland, *The Culture of Control: Crime and Social Order in Contemporary Society* (Chicago, IL, University of Chicago Press, 2001) 111.

[41] ibid 13.

[42] L Zedner, *Security* (Abingdon, Routledge, 2009) 11.

[43] ibid 45.

state interference with individual liberty well beyond what is absolutely necessary for the prevention of harm.[44] Liberty and autonomy are thus no longer seen as the cornerstone of a liberal society, but rather as an obstacle in the pursuit of security.

Third, although originally the precautionary principle was utilised to justify the introduction of pre-emptive offences targeting 'grave and irreversible harms, [such as those associated with terrorism,] the logic of precaution [spread] downward to provide a warrant for decision making in situations of uncertainty even where the anticipated harms are of a lesser gravity'.[45] The extensive application of the precautionary principle not only led to the normalisation of pre-inchoate offences (and other emergency powers),[46] but it has also resulted in the proliferation of various (supposedly) civil preventive measures. The proliferation of civil preventive measures, highlights a different facet of the rise of the preventive state since these interventions formally lie outside the ambit of the criminal law. They form the middle ground between the criminal and the civil law.[47] As we shall see, the stated objective of these measures is the prevention of certain types of criminality rather than to punish people for their past wrongdoings.[48] It is for this reason that these measures are labelled as civil rather than punitive. That notwithstanding, many civil preventive measures allow for the imposition of significant restrictions on the liberty of those subjected to these instruments. Restrictions that can be so severe that they can potentially amount to a form of *punishment* in their own right, albeit labelled by the legislature as civil measures. I argue that if the restrictions imposed on the liberty of those against whom these supposedly civil measures are imposed in fact amount to a form of punishment, then these should be regarded as a form of *indirect criminalisation*. Hence, one of the most important challenges posed by these middle ground interventions relates to their classification.

## 1.2. IMPORTANT TERMINOLOGY

Before I engage further with some of the normative and practical challenges posed by civil preventive measures, it is imperative to explain what I mean by indirect criminalisation and civil preventive measures. By indirect criminalisation,

[44] McCulloh and Wilson (n 17) 43.

[45] Zedner, *Security* (n 41) 84; McCulloh and Wilson (n 17) 3.

[46] Zedner, *Security* (n 41) 1–2; Ramsay, *The Insecurity State* (n 8) 6.

[47] K Mann, 'Punitive Civil Sanctions: The Middleground Between Criminal and Civil Law' (1991–92) 101 *Yale Law Journal* 1795, 1799; Ashworth and Zedner, *Preventive Justice* (n 8) 14; L Campbell et al, *The Criminal Process*, 5th edn (Oxford, Oxford University Press, 2019) 436.

[48] S Shute, 'Rationalising Civil Preventive Orders: Opportunities for Reform' in J Child and A Duff (eds), *Criminal Law Reform Now: Proposal & Critique* (Oxford, Hart Publishing, 2019) 64.

I mean the process of criminalising certain kinds of behaviour through legal interventions which are classified by the legislature as non-criminal. As I will explain below, to criminalise is to punish. Of course, this poses a really important question for criminal law theorists: what is to punish? To address this question, in chapter three I formulate and defend a working definition of criminalisation. This will enable me to look beyond the official classification of civil preventive measures allowing me to examine their implementation and whether this amounts to a form of indirect criminalisation. The purpose of my analysis is not to examine whether civil preventive measures can be justified. To do so, it is imperative first to determine their true nature. Rather, the main purpose of this study is to apply the working definition of criminalisation formulated in chapter three in practice and examine whether the implementation of the injunction introduced under Part 1 of the Anti-social Behaviour, Crime and Policing Act 2014 led to the indirect criminalisation of certain kinds of anti-social behaviour (ASB).

Civil preventive measures can broadly be divided into two categories: post-conviction and non-conviction civil preventive measures. The first category includes measures/orders that can be imposed only on those who have already been convicted of a criminal offence. Some of these measures are discretionary, that is for the sentencing court to decide whether *additional* restrictions should be imposed on the offender's liberty,[49] whereas others are imposed automatically on individuals who have been convicted of certain offences. Under section 80 of the Sexual Offences Act 2003, for instance, those who are found guilty of any of the offences listed under Schedule 3 of the 2003 Act, such as rape, are automatically subjected to Notification Requirements. These require offenders to provide periodic information, such as their current home address, to the police immediately after their conviction. The duration of these requirements is dependent on the punishment received.[50] Breach of these requirements 'without any reasonable excuse' or due to the offender providing false information constitutes an offence which carries a maximum sentence of five years' imprisonment.[51] Similarly, in the United States many of those convicted of a criminal offence face a series of restrictions in terms of their ability to access 'public housing, certain types of

[49] One example of a discretionary post-conviction measure which will be discussed in more detail throughout this study is the Criminal Behaviour Order. Other examples include the Serious Crime Prevention Order (Serious Crime Act 2007, s 19); the Sexual Harm Prevention Order (Sexual Offences Act 2003, s 103A(2)); the Slavery and Trafficking Prevention Order (Criminal Justice and Police Act 2001, s 33); the Restraining Order (Sentencing Act 2020, s 360); the Violent Offender Order (Criminal Justice and Immigration Act 2008, s 98); the Football Banning Order (Football Spectators Act 1989, s 14A); and the Knife Crime Prevention Order (Offensive Weapons Act 2019, s 19).

[50] For instance, those who receive a custodial sentence of more than 30 months are subjected to these Notification Requirements for an indefinite period (Sexual Offences Act 2003, s 82).

[51] Sexual Offences Act 2003, s 91.

employment, welfare, driver's licenses, adoption, public office, and numerous other goods and opportunities'.[52] Although these measures can only be imposed following a criminal conviction, they do not form part of the sentence given for the offence committed since they are not 'designed to punish'.[53] Rather, as Shute explains, they are regarded as ancillary measures which 'serve the public by disrupting, restricting, preventing, or inhibiting the opportunities some convicted offenders' have through an early intervention that would otherwise have not been possible.[54] Notwithstanding the preventive orientation of these post-conviction measures, it is argued that if the imposition of these *additional* restrictions amounts to criminal punishment, then they should be treated as part of the sentence imposed for the triggering offence.[55]

The second category includes measures/orders that can be imposed even in the absence of a criminal conviction.[56] Similar to the post-conviction measures, the primary aim of these interventions is the prevention of certain types of criminality rather than to punish people for their past behaviour. Although non-conviction measures do not require the commission of an offence, this does not necessarily mean that they are less restrictive than post-conviction measures. In fact, as the close analysis of the Part 1 injunction will reveal,[57] these interventions can be equally restrictive, albeit based on a *significantly less reliable* risk assessment.[58]

## 1.3. CIVIL PREVENTIVE MEASURES AND THE LIBERAL STATE

As their name suggests, civil preventive measures are civil interventions (at least this is the official label attached to them by the legislature) and their primary

[52] These restrictions are often referred to as the collateral legal consequences of criminal convictions. The potential severity of these additional burdens imposed on those convicted of certain criminal offences clearly demonstrates that the concept of indirect criminalisation goes well beyond discretionary civil preventive orders imposed by courts. For a comprehensive analysis of the collateral legal consequences of criminal convictions, see Z Hoskins, *Beyond Punishment: A Normative Account of the Collateral Legal Consequences of Conviction* (New York, Oxford University Press, 2019).

[53] *R v Hancox and Duffy* [2010] EWCA Crim 102 [12].

[54] Shute (n 48) 64.

[55] As mentioned above, the main focus of this study will be the Part 1 injunction of the 2014 Act which is a non-conviction measure. Inevitably, therefore, post-conviction measures will not be discussed in a lot of detail. Some of the arguments made about non-conviction measures though will have important implications for post-conviction orders as well.

[56] Other non-conviction civil preventive measures include the Terrorism Preventive and Investigation Measures (Terrorism Prevention and Investigation Measures Act 2011, s 2); the Football Banning Order (Football Spectators Act 1989, s 14B); and the Restraining Order (Protection from Harassment Act 1997, s 5A).

[57] Anti-social Behaviour, Crime and Policing Act 2014, Part 1.

[58] As Hoskins rightly points out, although many offenders do not reoffend, a criminal conviction is the best predictor of future criminal conduct. Hence, the imposition of post-conviction measures appears to be less contentious and problematic since those subjected to these additional restrictions have already gone into the realm of criminality. It has already been proven that they pose a risk to the

objective is to prevent certain types of criminality ranging from everyday ASB to terrorism-related activities. To this end, they allow for the imposition of certain restrictions on the liberty of those who allegedly pose a risk to others in order to prevent them from engaging in certain activities in the future and/or causing future harm.[59] The fact that these measures formally lie outside the ambit of the criminal law means that they offer more flexibility to law enforcement agents and the courts since they are not restrained by the same procedural and evidential rules, such as the higher standard of proof, that are so important to restrict criminal rules. Although these measures have been labelled as not criminal, they appear to allow for the imposition of restrictions akin to criminal punishment and are therefore susceptible to indirect criminalisation. This prospect becomes even more worrying in light of the fact that these measures are imposed in the absence of the enhanced procedural protections afforded to those facing criminal prosecution.[60] In fact, it seems that these measures were deliberately designed to extend the net of social control while prioritising expediency over due process values which are increasingly seen as an obstacle to the prevention of crime and should therefore be circumvented.[61]

The above analysis of civil preventive measures is not to question the need for the liberal state to prevent crime and/or other (serious) undesirable events that might jeopardise the security of its citizens. In fact, as seen above, the liberal state has a duty to do so. My analysis therefore does not really focus on whether the prevention of certain types of criminality should be the proper concern of the liberal state. They should be. Instead, the main focus of this study is *how* this is to be achieved. The fact that the liberal state has a duty to protect its citizens does not necessarily warrant the imposition of sanctions akin to criminal punishment in the absence of the enhanced procedural protections. As Loader rightly points out, as members of a contemporary liberal society, we should not only focus on what kinds of behaviour should be controlled and prevented, but we should also be mindful of 'how we do so'.[62] If these measures result in the

security of others and therefore these additional restrictions imposed on their liberty can be justified on the offender's failure to reassure other members of the polity about their security. This, of course, is not necessarily the case with non-conviction measures. Non-convictions measures do not require a criminal conviction and therefore the risk assessment conducted is less reliable, something that raises serious questions as to whether the imposition of restrictions on the liberty of those subjected to these measures can be justified. See Hoskins (n 52) 180; Ramsay, *The Insecurity State* (n 8) 61.

[59] A Ashworth and L Zedner, 'Preventive Orders: A Problem of Undercriminalization?' in A Duff et al (eds), *The Boundaries of the Criminal Law* (Oxford, Oxford University Press, 2010) 61.

[60] The term 'enhanced procedural protections' is used by Henry and King to describe all of those extra procedural and evidential safeguards afforded under both domestic legislation and the European Convention on Human Rights to those facing criminal prosecution. See J Henry and C King, 'Expediency, Legitimacy, and the Rule of Law: A Systems Perspective on Civil/Criminal Procedural Hybrids' (2017) 11 *Criminal Law and Philosophy* 733, 733. For more on the importance of the enhanced procedural protections see ch 2.

[61] L Zedner, 'Penal Subversions: When is a Punishment not Punishment, Who Decides and on What Grounds?' (2016) 20 *Theoretical Criminology* 3, 8; Henry and King (n 60) 734.

[62] I Loader, 'Review Symposium: The Anti-politics of Crime' (2008) 12 *Theoretical Criminology* 399, 405.

imposition of criminal punishment, then it is essential to subject them to the same constraints and level of theoretical critique as criminal rules.[63] Failure to restrain the preventive powers of the state will inevitably lead to the significant expansion of the net of social control while severely restricting individual liberty.[64]

The first challenge faced by legal theorists, therefore, with regard to civil preventive measures, relates to the label attached to them by the legislature and whether these are indeed civil in nature. This requires a close analysis of these measures, moving beyond the label attached to a particular legal rule by the legislature examining whether their implementation results in the indirect criminalisation of certain kinds of behaviour. To this end, a working definition of criminalisation must be formulated through which instances of indirect criminalisation can be identified.

The above are some of the broader philosophical issues posed by the rise of the preventive state and the proliferation of civil preventive measures in particular. This study engages with the above-mentioned challenges using the law relating to ASB in England and Wales, in particular the Part 1 injunction of the 2014 Act, as its primary case study. It is important at this stage to explain why the main focus of this study will be the injunction rather than any other civil preventive measure introduced in England and Wales since the late twentieth century. The reason for choosing the injunction over other civil preventive measures is threefold.

The first reason relates to the range of conduct that can be regarded as anti-social and therefore the wider application (and use) of the relevant tools and powers. In contrast to other civil preventive measures, such as the Terrorism Prevention and Investigation Measures and the Serious Crime Prevention Order which focus on the prevention of serious kinds of criminality, ASB can be more far-reaching since it can range from conduct which is unregulated and/or falls within the realm of everyday human interaction, such as unruly neighbours, to behaviour that already constitutes a criminal offence, such as criminal damage.[65] Hence, the injunction can be used to deal with a wide range of behaviour and therefore have an impact on the liberty of any individual. This is evident from both the number and the diversity of ASB incidents reported and/or witnessed each year by members of the public in England and Wales.[66]

[63] C Steiker, 'The Limits of the Preventive State' (1998) 88 *Journal of Criminal Law and Criminology* 771, 777–78.

[64] Carvalho (n 8) 11–13.

[65] L Koffman, 'The Use of Anti-social Behaviour Orders: An Empirical Study of a New Deal for Communities Area' (2006) 7 *Criminal Law Review* 593, 611–12. See also ch 5.

[66] Despite the downward trend after 2008, evidence suggests that more than 1.7 million incidents of ASB have been recorded by the police alone in England and Wales in the year ending in September 2021. See Office for National Statistics, *Crime in England and Wales: Year ending September 2021* (Office for National Statistics, 2022), available at: www.ons.

Second, as we shall see later, the relevant statutory provisions provide (at least as they appear on the statute book) courts and those tasked with the implementation of the injunction with a significant magnitude of discretion both as to the scope of the law in this area and the kinds of restrictions that can be imposed on those against whom the injunction is used.[67] The importance of this is heightened by the fact that local enforcement agents use an array of informal interventions to deal with ASB before resorting to formal legal action.[68] It appears possible therefore for the implementation of the injunction to vary considerably across the country. What this means is that despite the legislature's intention for this to be a civil instrument, legal commentators still need to be mindful of how this is implemented in practice since it can still operate as a de facto criminal measure.

Finally, another cause for concern that prompted me to focus on the injunction rather than on other civil preventive measures is the 2014 amendments in the law. As we will see below, the injunction's predecessor, that is the Anti-social Behaviour Order (ASBO), was a hybrid method of social regulation. Although the ASBO was a civil order, its breach constituted a criminal offence, something that essentially meant that the issue of an ASBO resulted in the creation of a bespoke criminal offence that only applied to the person against whom the order was issued. The ASBO was therefore a hybrid order. In contrast to the ASBO, the injunction is a purely civil measure since its breach constitutes a civil contempt of court rather than a criminal offence. Consequently, following the repeal and replacement of the ASBO in 2014, the proximity of the injunction to the criminal law has been officially distanced. As a result, the implementation of the injunction might attract less attention and external scrutiny.[69] The importance of this lack of scrutiny lies in the potential punitive nature of the restrictions imposed on those against whom an injunction is issued. It is for these reasons that this study will focus primarily on the implementation of the injunction examining whether this resulted in the indirect criminalisation of certain kinds of ASB.

## 1.4. ANTI-SOCIAL BEHAVIOUR IN ENGLAND AND WALES

Having contextualised civil preventive measures by analysing the constant tension between liberty and security faced by the liberal state and by highlighting some

gov.uk/peoplepopulationandcommunity/crimeandjustice/bulletins/crimeinenglandandwales/yearendingseptember2021#anti-social-behaviour.

[67] The same of course applies to some of the other ASB tools and powers introduced under the 2014 Act, such as the Community Protection Notices.

[68] S Lewis et al, 'Nipping Crime in the Bud? The use of Anti-social Behaviour Interventions with Young People in England and Wales' (2017) 57 *British Journal of Criminology* 1230, 1236–43.

[69] This is evidenced by the government's decision not to collect data about the implementation of the injunction.

of the broader normative and practical challenges posed by them, it is important to proceed by providing an overview of the law relating to ASB in England and Wales. The brief analysis of the law in this area will not only lay the foundations for our discussion in the rest of this book, but it will also illustrate further why it is imperative to engage with the concept of indirect criminalisation in the first place.[70]

### 1.4.1. The Pre-2014 Approach to Anti-Social Behaviour

The first major legislative attempt to address ASB as a specific legal concept came through the introduction of the ASBO under section 1 of the Crime and Disorder Act 1998.[71] In 2002, the post-conviction ASBO (CrASBO) was introduced under section 64 of the Police Reform Act 2002. The ASBO constituted a 'two-step criminalisation process' where a 'civil prohibitory order' was issued.[72] Breach of the order without reasonable excuse constituted a criminal offence carrying a maximum sentence of five years' imprisonment and a fine.[73] If someone's behaviour 'caused or was likely to cause harassment, alarm or distress to one or more persons not of the same household as himself', then one of the relevant authorities listed under section 1 of the 1998 Act, such as the police, could submit an application to court for the issue of an ASBO against that individual. If the court examining the application was satisfied that the perpetrator behaved in an anti-social manner, it could then approve the imposition of any restrictions

[70] A more in-depth analysis of the law on ASB, including the impact of the 2014 amendments, is offered in ch 4.

[71] Before the introduction of the ASBO, the police and local authorities could use a range of tools and powers to deal with various types of behaviour ranging from housing-related 'nuisance and annoyance' to serious forms of public disorder. Under s 5 of the Public Order Act 1986, for instance, the police can arrest anyone who uses, either in a public or a private space, 'threatening or abusive words or behaviour, or disorderly behaviour … within the hearing or sight of a person likely to be caused harassment, alarm or distress thereby'. Similarly, local authorities could, under s 152 of the Housing Act 1996, apply to the High Court or the county court for the issue of an ASB injunction against anyone whose conduct was causing or was likely to cause 'nuisance and annoyance' in residential premises. Although the Part 1 injunction is often presented as the consolidation of different powers into a single multi-purpose instrument (see House of Commons, *Anti-social Behaviour, Crime and Policing Act 2014: Explanatory Notes* [HL Bill 52] (2013) para 173), it is evident from the similarities between the two that the s 152 injunction provided the inspiration for this new instrument. Notwithstanding the existence of the aforementioned instruments, none of these tools and powers was explicitly designed to deal with what later became known as ASB. For a more detailed analysis of the differences between the ASBO and the above-mentioned powers see S Bright and C Bakalis, 'Anti-social Behaviour: Local Authority Responsibility and the Voice of the Victim' (2003) 62 *Cambridge Law Journal* 305, 310.

[72] A Simester and A von Hirsch, 'Regulating Offensive Conduct through Two-Step Prohibitions' in A von Hirsch and A Simester (eds), *Incivilities: Regulating Offensive Behaviour* (Oxford, Hart Publishing, 2006) 213.

[73] Crime and Disorder Act 1998, s 1(10) and 1(10)(b) respectively.

deemed necessary on the perpetrator in order to prevent him from engaging in further ASB, as long as there was a 'practical way of policing the order'.[74] Some of the most common types of restriction imposed on those against whom an ASBO was issued included home curfews, geographical exclusions and 'prohibitions on certain kinds of conduct'.[75] It is also worth noting that an ASBO could be imposed on anyone over the age of 10 and that the minimum duration of an order was two years.[76]

Although the imposition of an ASBO could have a significant and longstanding effect upon the perpetrator's liberty, the order was deemed by the House of Lords in *McCann* to be civil rather than criminal in nature.[77] The importance of this classification lies in the enhanced procedural protections guaranteed to those charged with a criminal offence, such as those under Article 6 of the European Convention on Human Rights (ECHR).[78] Nonetheless, the House of Lords held that given the potential impact that the order could have on someone, in examining an application for the issue of an ASBO, the court at hand should have been satisfied to the criminal standard of proof that the perpetrator's behaviour 'caused or [was] likely to cause harassment, alarm or distress'.[79]

In determining the nature of the ASBO's first limb, the House of Lords did not simply focus on the official classification of the order, but it also paid particular attention to the underlying rationale for the introduction of this hybrid form of regulation.[80] For the Labour Party, which was the main driving force behind the introduction of the ASBO when it came to power in 1997, the link between ASB and criminality was undeniable. Nonetheless, it was argued by the Labour Party that local enforcement agents[81] should be able to 'nip [crime] in the

[74] *R v Boness and others* [2005] EWCA Crim 2395 [48].

[75] C Bakalis, 'ASBOs, "Preventative Orders" and the European Court of Human Rights' (2007) 6 *European Human Rights Law Review* 427, 427.

[76] Crime and Disorder Act 1998, s 1.

[77] *R (on the application of McCann) v Manchester Crown Court* [2002] UKHL 39 [77].

[78] The purpose of Article 6 of the ECHR is to guarantee that those facing criminal prosecution are given a fair trial. To achieve this, under Article 6(3), those charged with the commission of a criminal offence are entitled to a set of minimum rights, such as the right to remain silent. For more on Article 6 see: R Goss, *Criminal Fair Trial Rights: Article 6 of the European Convention on Human Rights* (Oxford, Hart Publishing, 2014).

[79] *R (on the application of McCann)* (n 77) [83].

[80] In determining the nature of the ASBO's first limb, the House of Lords applied the anti-subversion doctrine formulated by the European Court of Human Rights in *Engel v Netherlands* (1979–1980) 1 EHRR 647 [81]–[82]. As explained in more detail in ch 3, the anti-subversion doctrine constitutes a three-part test based on which courts can determine whether a particular legal rule should be regarded as criminal in nature (and therefore subject to the enhanced procedural protections) regardless of the label attached to it by the legislature. As we will see later on, however, reservations can be raised about both the anti-subversion doctrine, the way this was applied in practice (especially by the House of Lords in *McCann*), and whether indeed this can be a useful tool in identifying instances of indirect criminalisation.

[81] Local enforcement agents include police officers (and Police Community Support Officers) and local practitioners, ie, ASB officers working for local authorities and housing associations.

bud, and so prevent future criminality'.[82] This rhetoric is closely associated with the 'broken windows' theory formulated by Kelling and Wilson.[83] According to them, 'disorder and crime are usually inextricably linked, in a kind of developmental sequence'.[84] Consequently, if the authorities fail to adequately deal with a seemingly minor incident of disorder, then this is likely to be perceived by the perpetrator and others as 'a signal that no one cares' leading to more crime and disorder.[85] For this reason, the New Labour government did not believe that more criminal offences were needed in order to deal swiftly and effectively with such conduct.[86] Instead, it was argued that a new method of social regulation was needed to enable the state to intervene at an early stage and prevent ASB from escalating to serious criminality.[87]

In line with the Labour Party's rhetoric, the House of Lords held that the primary intention of the legislature was to introduce a civil order which aimed to prevent certain kinds of behaviour rather than their criminalisation.[88] It was crucial to the Lords decision that the legislature intended for this to be a civil order.[89] The preventive nature of the ASBO was therefore sufficient to warrant the imposition of any restrictions deemed necessary on the perpetrator, despite the absence of many enhanced procedural protections and the potential severity of the restrictions that could be imposed on the liberty of those against whom such an order was imposed.

This perceived need for an early intervention was also reflected in the drafting of the ASB legal framework which could operate pre-emptively. In particular, there was no need within the 1998 Act to prove that someone's behaviour had actually caused 'harassment, alarm, or distress'.[90] Instead, the relevant authority applying for the issue of an ASBO needed only to prove that the defendant's behaviour was *likely* to cause any of the above-mentioned negative experiences to others. In effect, this meant that: (i) severe restrictions could be imposed on someone's liberty even if his behaviour had not actually caused 'harassment,

[82] Labour Party, *A Quiet Life: Tough Action on Criminal Neighbours* (London, Labour Party, 1995) 7.

[83] George Kelling and James Wilson, 'Broken Windows: The Police and Neighbourhood Safety' *The Atlantic* (1 March 1982), available at: www.theatlantic.com/magazine/archive/1982/03/broken-windows/304465/.

[84] ibid.

[85] ibid. For a critique of the 'broken windows' theory see R Taylor, *Breaking Away from Broken Windows* (Abingdon, Routledge, 2018).

[86] Labour Party (n 82) 6–7.

[87] A Crawford, 'Governing Through Anti-Social Behaviour' (2009) 49 *British Journal of Criminology* 810; P. Squires, 'New Labour and the Politics of Antisocial Behaviour' (2006) 26 *Critical Social Policy* 144; J Jacobson et al, 'Why Tackle Anti-Social Behaviour?' in P Squires (ed), *ASBO Nation: The Criminalisation of Nuisance* (Bristol, Policy Press, 2008) 44.

[88] *R (on the application of McCann)* (n 77) [72].

[89] ibid [27].

[90] This is still the case under the current law. See section 1.4.2.

alarm, or distress' to any other person; and (ii) one could face a lengthy custodial sentence simply for breaching a civil order.[91]

For the proponents of this hybrid form of regulation, alongside prevention and the need to reassure others about their safety,[92] another important reason for the introduction of the ASBO was the supposed inability of the criminal law to deal swiftly and effectively with ASB. As Prime Minister Tony Blair put it, victims of ASB were often left unprotected from low-level criminality and their only hope was the criminal law which was, however, not sufficiently adequate for this purpose.[93] The reason for this was twofold. First, the fact that the criminal law focuses paradigmatically[94] on isolated events rather than on the cumulative impact of a series of incidents meant that no permanent relief could be provided to those experiencing prolonged ASB and low-level criminality.[95] Second, the criminal justice system was deemed to be particularly costly and time-consuming for dealing with this type of criminality.[96] This can be partly attributed to the enhanced procedural protections afforded to those facing criminal prosecution. The exclusion of hearsay evidence,[97] for instance, could be a significant disincentive for people to report incidents of ASB to the authorities since on many occasions these involve disputes between neighbours.[98] Moreover, as Sanders and Jones contend, giving evidence in court can be a very daunting prospect for victims who might regard this as a form of secondary victimisation.[99]

[91] G Pearson, 'Hybrid Law and Human Rights – Banning and Behaviour Orders in the Appeal Courts' (2006) 27 *Liverpool Law Review* 125, 127.

[92] Ramsay, *The Insecurity State* (n 8) 11.

[93] Tony Blair, 'Britain's Liberties: The Great Debate' *Guardian* (23 April 2016), available at: www.theguardian.com/commentisfree/2006/apr/23/humanrights.constitution. This view was also echoed by the House of Lords in *McCann* with Lord Hope pointing out 'the apparent inability of the criminal law to restrain [the perpetrators'] activities'. See *R (on the application of McCann)* (n 77) [42].

[94] A notable exception of course is the offence of harassment and stalking under ss 2, 2A, 4 and 4A of the Protection from Harassment Act 1997.

[95] Blair (n 93); Koffman (n 65) 603–04.

[96] S Chakrabarti and J Russell, 'ASBOmania' in P Squires (ed), *ASBO Nation: The Criminalisation of Nuisance* (Bristol, Policy Press, 2008) 308.

[97] s 114(1) of the Criminal Justice Act 2003 provides that 'in criminal proceedings a statement not made in oral evidence in the proceedings can be admissible as evidence of any matter stated' only under certain circumstances, such as where 'all parties to the proceedings agree to it being admissible'. In principle, therefore, hearsay evidence is inadmissible in criminal proceedings unless one of the conditions specified under s 114(1) is met. Bakalis argues that following the enactment of the 2003 Act and the changes brought to the law in this area, the question as to whether the ASBO was in fact civil or criminal in nature became less important since the rules governing the admissibility of hearsay evidence were relaxed. Although Bakalis is right to hold that the 2003 amendments resulted in the adoption of a more relaxed (and potentially over-inclusive) legal framework regarding the admissibility of hearsay evidence, as we will see in ch 2, the question as to whether the ASBO and its successor should be treated as civil or criminal instruments goes well beyond the admissibility of hearsay evidence. See Bakalis (n 75) 438.

[98] Home Office, *More Effective Responses to Anti-Social Behaviour* (London, Home Office, 2011) 7.

[99] A Sanders and I Jones, 'The Victim in Court' in S Walklate (ed), *Handbook of Victims and Victimology* (Cullompton, Willan Publishing, 2007) 282.

The above considerations provided the basis for an alternative (and hybrid) method of social regulation which would combine the flexibility of the civil law with the deterrent effect of the criminal law.[100]

Although providing relief to victims and the prevention of crime and ASB are objectives worth pursuing by the liberal state, the adoption of this hybrid form of regulation in conjunction with the extensive magnitude of discretion granted to courts and local enforcement agents were heavily criticised for being open to misuse. One of the main criticisms levied against the ASBO was its ability to effectively criminalise what courts and local communities regarded as intolerable behaviour, albeit not conduct proscribed by criminal law.[101] Focusing on the second, that is the criminal, limb of the ASBO, Alvaro Gil-Robles, the then Human Rights Commissioner for the Council of Europe, noted in 2005 that the ASBOs were essentially 'personalised penal codes, [through which] non-criminal behaviour becomes criminal for individuals who have incurred the wrath of the community'.[102] This, of course, appears to be in stark contrast to the very foundations of a liberal society where respect for individual autonomy is of paramount significance.[103] As Mill rightly pointed out, individuals should not only be protected from the will of the state, but they must also be protected from the will of the majority.[104] As mentioned earlier, what lies at the heart of the liberal state's promise to its citizens is not just to guarantee their safety, but to maintain those conditions in society that are necessary for them to realise their full potential.

Notwithstanding the general focus on the second limb of the ASBO, the first limb also attracted criticism by legal commentators. For Duff and Marshall, for instance, the restrictions imposed when the order was issued, could be so severe that they could constitute a form of punishment in their own right, despite the ASBO's civil nature.[105] On this view, it was possible for the first limb of this two-part process to result in the *indirect* criminalisation of certain kinds of behaviour.

[100] P Squires, 'Introduction: Why "Anti-Social Behaviour"? Debating ASBOs' in P Squires (ed), *ASBO Nation: The Criminalisation of Nuisance* (Bristol, Policy Press, 2008) 17–18.

[101] Ramsay contends that the actual focus of the ASBO was 'behaviour that causes or risks causing insecurity rather than offence as such'. This, however, does not change the fact that any kind of behaviour could potentially fall within the scope of the ASBO as long as it was capable of causing a (subjective) feeling of insecurity to others. See Ramsay, *The Insecurity State* (n 8) 11.

[102] A Gil-Robles, Commissioner for Human Rights, on his Visit to the United Kingdom 4th–12th November 2004 for the Attention of the Committee of Ministers and the Parliamentary Assembly (CommDH (2005)6) (Office for the Commissioner of Human Rights, 2005) 37, available at: wcd.coe.int/ViewDoc.jsp?id=865235.

[103] J Locke, *The Second Treatise of Government* (Indianapolis, IND, Hackett Publishing Company, 1980) 17.

[104] Mill (n 2) 4.

[105] A Duff and S Marshall, 'How Offensive Can You Get?' in A von Hirsch and A Simester (eds), *Incivilities: Regulating Offensive Behaviour* (Oxford, Hart Publishing, 2006) 80.

Allowing the state to criminalise behaviour indirectly through non-criminal interventions is morally problematic since it seems possible for courts and law enforcement agents to expand (even unwittingly) the reach of the criminal law into areas that had been concluded by the legislature as not appropriate for criminalisation.[106] This becomes more problematic in light of the fact that those subjected to indirect criminalisation are denied, at least to some extent, all of those enhanced procedural and evidential protections afforded to those subjected to direct criminalisation.[107] It is essential, therefore, for criminal law theorists to find ways through which instances of indirect criminalisation can be identified and addressed.

Apart from the criminalisation of unregulated conduct and/or conduct that falls within the ambit of everyday human interaction, concerns were also expressed about the possibility of using the ASBO against behaviour which was already proscribed by the criminal law. Duff, for instance, characterised the ASBO as a 'pseudo-non-criminal' measure, since it could be used as an alternative to criminal prosecution in order to address behaviour which should have been dealt with by the criminal law.[108] Similarly, Ashworth and Zedner contend that if non-criminal interventions, such as the ASBO, are utilised to address behaviour that 'appears to meet the criteria for criminalisation', then the legislature should consider the possibility of introducing a new criminal offence in order to deal with the issue identified rather than resorting to alternative forms of social control.[109] For them, failure to do so constitutes a form of *under-criminalisation* since it denies those subjected to these measures the enhanced procedural protections of the criminal law.[110]

Evidence from a 2006 study conducted by Koffman suggests that on a number of occasions the ASBO was indeed used as a means of addressing 'relatively serious forms of misconduct and offending'.[111] For Koffman, this was attributed to the fact that drawing a precise distinction between behaviour which is purely anti-social and behaviour which is criminal in nature is not always possible.[112] This was also acknowledged by the Home Office which notes that ASB includes, inter alia, behaviour which is already proscribed by the criminal law, such as criminal damage.[113]

The use of the ASBO against certain kinds of behaviour which were already proscribed by the criminal law is also evident through a line of cases, such as

[106] I elaborate further on the main normative and practical challenges posed by indirect criminalisation in ch 2.

[107] Direct criminalisation refers to the criminalisation of certain kinds of behaviour through legislation which is formally labelled by the legislature as criminal in nature.

[108] A Duff, *Answering for Crime: Responsibility and Liability in the Criminal Law* (Oxford, Hart Publishing, 2007) 13.

[109] Ashworth and Zedner, 'Preventive Orders' (n 59) 60.

[110] ibid.

[111] Koffman (n 65) 601.

[112] ibid.

[113] Home Office, *More Effective Responses to Anti-Social Behaviour* (n 98) 7.

*R v Curtis Braxton*[114] and *R v Tripp*,[115] through which it was acknowledged that it was possible for the court to impose restrictions on the perpetrator which, in effect, would duplicate certain pre-existing criminal offences. In *Curtis Braxton*, for instance, an ASBO was issued against an individual prohibiting him from 'using threatening, abusive or similar behaviour towards any person or property in a city centre'.[116] In *Tripp*, the perpetrator was prohibited from 'using threatening, abusive or insulting words or behaviour or disorderly behaviour within the hearing or sight of a person'.[117] The prohibitions imposed in these cases resemble the wording of section 4 of the Public Order Act 1984 which already makes it a criminal offence to use 'threatening, abusive or insulting words or behaviour' towards other people. What is important about this overlap between the two is that on many occasions the maximum sentence for breach of an ASBO was significantly higher than then maximum sentence for the criminal offence at hand. Although those found guilty of the section 4 offence face a maximum custodial sentence of six months, those found in breach of their ASBOs faced a maximum five-year custodial sentence and a fine. In theory, therefore, the ASBO could be used as a means of increasing the maximum sentence available for certain offences. As held by the Court of Appeal in *Boness* though, courts 'should be reluctant to impose an order which prohibits an offender from … committing a specific criminal offence' since the purpose of the ASBO was to prevent ASB rather than to deal with criminal offences.[118]

The second major statutory instrument introduced to address ASB as a specific legal concept was the CrASBO. In contrast to the ASBO, the CrASBO was a post-conviction order.[119] Notwithstanding the sentence imposed for the offence committed, if the criminal court in question was convinced that some *additional* restrictions were necessary to prevent the perpetrator from engaging in further ASB in the future, then a CrASBO could be issued.[120] Consequently, the issue of a CrASBO was an *addition* to the sentence received for the commission of the triggering offence.[121] Similar to the ASBO, breach of a CrASBO without reasonable excuse constituted a criminal offence.[122]

At first sight, the CrASBO appeared to be less contentious than the ASBO since it could only be issued against those who had already been convicted of an offence and therefore have already gone into the realm of criminality. Similar to the ASBO though, a number of concerns could be raised about the CrASBO.

[114] *R v Curtis Braxton* [2005] 1 Cr App R (S) 36.
[115] *R v Tripp* [2005] EWCA Crim 2253.
[116] *R v Curtis Braxton* (n 114) [167].
[117] *R v Tripp* (n 115) [2].
[118] *R v Boness and others* (n 74) [35].
[119] Crime and Disorder Act 1998, s 1C(1).
[120] ibid s 1C(2)(b).
[121] ibid s 1C(4).
[122] ibid s 1C(9).

Although the CrASBO could only be imposed by a criminal court after the perpetrator was found guilty of an offence, it was evident that not all enhanced procedural protections were afforded to those against whom such an order was issued. Section 1C(3B) of the 1998 Act explicitly stated that it was possible for the prosecution and/or the defence to submit evidence that might not 'have been admissible in the proceedings in which the offender was convicted', such as hearsay evidence. What was also morally problematic about the CrASBO was the fact that there was no need for the offence that triggered the issue of the order to be associated with the ASB at hand. It was, therefore, possible for the triggering offence to be completely unrelated to the offender's ASB.

### 1.4.2. The Current Law on Anti-Social Behaviour

In March 2015, the ASBO was repealed and replaced by a new civil injunction under Part 1 of the 2014 Act.[123] Part 1 of the 2014 Act consolidated a number of orders and injunctions, such as the ASBO and the Anti-social Behaviour Injunction, into a single multi-purpose injunction.[124]

Although the two-step regulation model adopted by the ASBO was retained, the injunction is a purely civil mechanism.[125] Similar to the ASBO, proceedings for the issue of an injunction are civil in nature and therefore civil procedural and evidential rules apply. In contrast to the ASBO though, breach of the injunction does not constitute a criminal offence. Instead, it constitutes a civil contempt of court which carries a maximum sentence of two years' imprisonment and an unlimited fine.[126] That said, it is worth noting that the applicable standard of proof for breach proceedings is the criminal, rather than the civil, standard.[127] This is attributed to 'the potential severity of the penalties which the court can impose on respondents'.[128]

The CrASBO was repealed and replaced by the Criminal Behaviour Order (CBO) under Part 2 of the 2014 Act. Following the consolidation of all

[123] A transitional period of five years was put in place for ASBOs issued before Part 1 came into force. Those ASBOs which were issued prior to the 2014 Act and which last for more than five years, would automatically transform into Part 1 injunctions at the end of this transitional period, ie, in March 2020 (see s 21(5) of the 2014 Act). For an overview of the main differences between the ASBO and the Part 1 injunction see Figure 1.

[124] House of Commons (n 71) para 107.

[125] The impact of the 2014 amendments of the law on ASB is discussed in more depth in ch 4, section 4.1.2.

[126] Home Office, *Anti-social Behaviour, Crime and Policing Act 2014: Reform of Anti-social Behaviour Powers – Statutory Guidance for Frontline Professionals* (London, Home Office, 2021) 33.

[127] ibid.

[128] ibid.

sentencing provisions into a single statutory instrument, all provisions relating to the CBO can now be found under Part II (Chapter 4) of the Sentencing Act 2020. Although the CBO retains most of the CrASBO's key features, it seems that the threshold that must be met in order for this new order to be issued is significantly lower than the one required under the 1998 Act. In particular, a CrASBO could only be issued if the court examining the application was satisfied that this was *necessary* to protect members of the public from further ASB. What this meant, according to Ramsay, was that in order for a CrASBO to be imposed on someone, the court had to be convinced that 'if obeyed the order would have the effect of protecting others'.[129] In contrast, in order for a CBO to be issued, the sentencing court must be satisfied that this 'order will help in preventing the offender from engaging' in further ASB.[130] What this revised legal test appears to suggest is that sentencing courts can still issue a CBO even if they are not satisfied that the imposition of such order, if obeyed, will surely prevent the perpetrator from behaving in an anti-social manner in the future.

### 1.4.3. Conceptualising Anti-Social Behaviour under the Current Law

According to the Home Office, ASB 'cover[s] a broad range of crime, disorder and nuisance'.[131] ASB can range from mere incivilities, such as noisy neighbours, which can be regarded as part of everyday human interaction to behaviour which is already proscribed by criminal law, such as begging and criminal damage.[132] At first sight, certain kinds of ASB, especially those situated at the lower end of the spectrum, can be dismissed as too trivial to warrant any kind of formal legal intervention.[133] What is really problematic about ASB, though, is often the cumulative impact of someone's behaviour on others rather than the seriousness of each isolated incident. It was this need to protect the public from persistent (and often low-level) criminality that provided the impetus for the introduction of the initial ASB legal framework back in the late 1990s.[134] As the tragic case of Fiona Pilkington and her two children revealed, the cumulative impact of ASB can indeed be devastating. Following prolonged ASB directed at her and her family, Fiona Pilkington set fire to her car killing herself as well as one of her children.[135]

[129] This was also the case for the ASBO. See, Ramsay, *The Insecurity State* (n 8) 23.

[130] Sentencing Act 2020, s 331(2)(b).

[131] Home Office, *More Effective Responses to Anti-Social Behaviour* (n 98) 8.

[132] Home Office, *Putting Victims First: More Effective Responses to Anti-Social Behaviour* (London, Home Office, 2012) 3.

[133] A Cornford, 'Criminalising Anti-social Behaviour' (2012) 6 *Criminal Law and Philosophy* 1, 3.

[134] S Macdonald, 'The Principle of Composite Sentencing: Its Centrality to, and Implications for, the ASBO' (2006) 9 *Criminal Law Review* 791, 792.

[135] Although Fiona Pilkington and her mother complained on numerous occasions to the police about the prolonged harassment experienced between 1997 and 2007, the relevant police force failed to classify them as a vulnerable family. Moreover, despite the numerous complaints received, the

Another important characteristic of ASB is that it cannot only vary in terms of its severity, but it can also vary in terms of its nature. As noted in 2012, by the then Home Secretary Theresa May, ASB is 'a fundamentally local issue, one that looks and feels different in every area, in every neighbourhood and to every victim'.[136] Consequently, what can be perceived as anti-social in one part of the country, might go unnoticed in another. For this reason, according to Theresa May, local enforcement agents should be given the necessary flexibility needed to deal with each incident of ASB 'in the way they see fit'.[137] To this end, a promise was made in 2012 by the then Conservative–Lib Dem coalition government to replace the ASBO and the CrASBO with a new and more flexible legal framework that would enable local enforcement agents to address those kinds of behaviour that really have a negative impact on their communities.[138]

This need for a flexible legal framework was reflected by both the range and scope of the tools and powers introduced under the 2014 Act. Apart from the repeal and replacement of the ASBO and the CrASBO, a number of new tools and powers were introduced, such as the Public Spaces Protection Orders (PSPO)[139] and the Community Protection Notices (CPN),[140] which enable local enforcement agents to deal with various types of behaviour swiftly and effectively without the need to apply to the court for the issue of an injunction against the perpetrator. As far as the scope of these measures is concerned, it is worth noting that the legislature did not opt for a universally applicable definition of ASB. Instead, each measure focuses on specific types of ASB extending the net of social control well beyond the contours of the 1998 Act. The ASBO's successor, for instance, focuses on behaviour which 'caused, or is likely to cause, harassment, alarm or distress to any person' and behaviour which is 'capable of causing nuisance and annoyance' in a housing-related context.[141] The CBO's scope on the other hand is narrower since it focuses only on behaviour which 'caused or was likely to cause harassment, alarm or distress to any person'.[142] The CPN targets any kind of behaviour which 'is [unreasonably] having a

Leicestershire Police failed to consider Pilkington's neighbourhood as an 'anti-social behaviour "hot spot" and … it was never targeted for a more proactive police response'. See Independent Police Complaints Commission, *IPCC Report into the contact between Fiona Pilkington and Leicester Constabulary 2004–2007* (IPCC, 2009) para 1212.

[136] Home Office, *Putting Victims First* (n 132) 3.

[137] ibid 4.

[138] ibid 3.

[139] For a more comprehensive analysis of the PSPOs, see K Brown, 'The Hyper-regulation of Public Space: The Use and Abuse of Public Spaces Protection Orders in England and Wales' (2017) 37 *Legal Studies* 543.

[140] For more on the CPN see: N Parpworth, 'Challenging a Community Protection Notice: A Defence in Criminal Proceedings for Its Breach?' (2019) 83 *Journal of Criminal Law* 307; V Heap et al, 'Preventive Justice: Exploring the Coercive Power of Community Protection Notices to Tackle Anti-social Behaviour' (2022) 24 *Punishment & Society* 305.

[141] Anti-social Behaviour, Crime and Policing Act 2014, s 2.

[142] Sentencing Act 2020, s 331(2)(a).

detrimental effect, of a persistent or continuing nature, on the quality of life of those in the locality'.[143]

Despite the absence of a universally applicable definition of ASB, it is evident that each of the aforementioned measures can be utilised against a range of behaviour which has or is *likely* to have an adverse impact on other people's quality of life. This is primarily due to the fact that particular attention is paid by each measure to the impact that someone's behaviour has or can have on others rather than on its nature. In effect, this means that any kind of behaviour can potentially be regarded as anti-social if it is *likely* to cause any of the above negative experiences to other people. This is a purely subjective test which on many occasions, such as when applying for the issue of an injunction, does not even take into consideration whether the alleged perpetrator has a reasonable excuse for their conduct.[144]

From a victim's perspective, the broad and ambiguous boundaries of the ASB tools and powers provide local enforcement agents with the necessary flexibility needed to deal swiftly and effectively with a number of long-standing issues which could not have been adequately addressed otherwise.[145] The ambiguous nature and the seemingly unrestrained ambit of the ASB tools and powers, which was extended even further following the 2014 amendments, have been severely criticised by a number of legal commentators. Cornford, for example, contends that 'caused or was likely to cause harassment, alarm or distress' can potentially include behaviour which is well beyond what society would commonly regard as anti-social.[146] Indeed, numerous cases emerged where the ambit of the ASBO was extended to rather bizarre situations raising concerns regarding the implementation of the relevant statutory provisions.[147] One of the most illustrative examples is the case of Alexander Muat whose tendency to make sarcastic comments to his neighbours was deemed as anti-social.[148]

The subjective definition of ASB means that victims, local enforcement agents and the courts play a crucial role in terms of shaping the limits of the ASB tools and powers at a local level. As Ashworth et al put it, the ASBO provided courts and local enforcement agents with a 'vast power to create a new breed

[143] Anti-social Behaviour, Crime and Policing Act 2014, s 43(1).

[144] As explained above though, this is not the case with the CPN. Moreover, s 1(5) of the 1998 Act explicitly noted that in examining an application for the issue of an ASBO, the court had to 'disregard any act of the defendant which he shows was reasonable in the circumstances'.

[145] In a number of Home Office reports and in the Statutory Guidance for the 2014 Act, those affected by these kinds of behaviour are referred to as 'victims' of ASB. See Home Office, *Putting Victims First* (n 132); Home Office, *Anti-social Behaviour, Crime and Policing Act 2014* (n 126).

[146] Cornford (n 133) 3.

[147] Statewatch, 'Extreme Cases' (2010), available at: www.statewatch.org/observatories/2004-2010-asbowatch-monitoring-the-use-of-anti-social-behaviour-orders/case-studies/extreme-cases/.

[148] BBC News, 'Anti-social OAP Faces Jail' (22 July 2003), available at: news.bbc.co.uk/1/hi/england/merseyside/3087007.stm.

of outcasts and outlaws'.[149] This might be particularly the case with certain social groups, such as rough sleepers, whose voices are not often heard and whose interests are often neglected by the majority. It is for this reason that ASB must be interpreted with caution, since if left unrestrained it can lead to situations where personal eccentricities, such as making sarcastic remarks, can be regarded as anti-social simply because someone's behaviour diverges from what is perceived as normal or goes beyond what is tolerated by others within any given neighbourhood or community.[150]

## 1.5. SCOPE OF THE BOOK

Thus far, I have engaged with some of the broader philosophical debates underpinning the criminal law of the liberal state highlighting the constant tension between liberty and security that has become more obvious in many Western jurisdictions since the late twentieth century. This was done to demonstrate that while the prevention of crime and other undesirable types of conduct, such as ASB, are a legitimate objective for the state to pursue, as legal commentators we need to be mindful of *how* (and at what cost in terms of individual liberty and autonomy) this is to be achieved. If we, as members of a liberal polity, allow the state to use security as a trump card, then we will soon reach the point where liberty is no more one of the cornerstones of the liberal society. Although the jurisdictional focus of this book will be England and Wales, the proliferation of preventive-led interventions (both within and outside the criminal law) in many Western jurisdictions, such as the United States[151] and Australia,[152] means that

[149] A Ashworth et al, 'Neighbouring on the Oppressive: The Government's "Anti-Social Behaviour Order" Proposals' (1998) 16 *Criminal Justice* 7, 9.

[150] P Ramsay, 'What is Anti-social Behaviour?' [2004] *Criminal Law Review* 908, 915.

[151] A very illustrative example of a civil preventive measure from the United States is the gang injunction. Similar to the ASBO, gang injunctions are civil measures that draw inspiration from the 'broken windows' theory. In particular, on several occasions, in an attempt to disturb the activities of gangs, city prosecutors and the police applied to court for the issue of a civil injunction through which suspected gang members were prohibited from engaging in certain activities, such as socialising with other individuals listed on the injunction. Breach of the injunction constitutes a criminal offence carrying a lengthy custodial sentence.

[152] In Western Australia, for example, the Prohibited Behaviour Orders (PBOs) were introduced in 2010. The PBO is essentially a variant of the CrASBO/CBO that can be utilised to target certain kinds of ASB (as this is defined under s 3 of the Prohibited Behaviour Orders Act 2010 (Western Australia)). More precisely, if someone has been convicted of a relevant offence, ie, an offence that has an anti-social element, and in the past three years he has been convicted of another relevant offence (s 8(2)), then the sentencing court can issue a PBO against that person. Through the issue of a PBO, the sentencing court can prohibit the offender from behaving in a particular manner in the future, such as to associate with certain individuals (s 10(3)). Similar to the CrASBO/CBO, the PBO is a civil measure and therefore the civil procedural and evidential rules apply (s 27). What is of particular concern with the PBOs is that s 34 of the 2010 Act requires (unless the issuing court has decided otherwise) the Attorney-General to publish on their Department's website the details, such as their name and where they live, along with the photograph of those against whom such an order

this study will be relevant to legal commentators, lawmakers, law enforcement agents and courts across the world who work in the areas of criminal law theory, preventive justice, punishment, ASB and community safety.[153] Legal commentators, for instance, might wish to utilise the working definition of criminalisation formulated for the purposes of this study in order to examine the true nature of a supposedly civil measure in another jurisdiction. In the remainder of this introductory chapter, I will elaborate further on what exactly this study does.

In *The Insecurity State*, which is one of the most important studies on the ASBO, Ramsay sought through an 'immanent critique' of the law on ASB to explore its justification.[154] Ramsay's main objective was to examine recent developments in penal policy (including the introduction of the ASBO) in order to identify the 'law's justification', that is the justification the legislature offers for these recent developments.[155] Ramsay's conclusion is that for the legislature the introduction of those measures, such as the ASBO and many pre-inchoate offences, can be justified on the need for members of the polity to reassure others about their security.[156] On this view, someone who was found in breach of the ASBO imposed on him was not punished for defying a court order, but for the failure to reassure other members of the polity that he does not pose a threat to their security. Ramsay's work not only lays bare the foundations and structure of many preventive-led interventions introduced in England and Wales since the end of the twentieth century, but it has broader implications about the relationship between the liberal state and its citizens. It clearly demonstrates that in order for someone to acquire the rights/privileges that come with full citizenship, he needs to fulfil his prior obligation to others' security.[157]

The present study is different from the one conducted by Ramsay since it does not focus on the law's justification, but on its actual nature. My main objective is to examine whether the restrictions imposed during the first stage of this two-step process of regulation, that is through the imposition of an injunction, amount to criminal punishment and therefore constitute a form of indirect criminalisation. Despite the 2014 amendments and the shift towards a purely civil injunction, these criticisms about the first limb of the ASBO remain largely unaddressed. The unrestrained ambit of ASB's statutory definition, for instance, still enables local enforcement agents to deal with behaviour which

was issued. The importance of the publication of the offender's details lies in the potential adverse consequences that this publicity might have on them in the future especially in terms of employment and accommodation. For a more comprehensive analysis of the PBOs, see T Crofts, 'The Law and ASBO Campaign in Western Australia' (2011) 22 *Current Issues in Criminal Justice* 399.

[153] It should be noted from the outset that a different scheme operates in Scotland. Hence, some of the comments made about the ASB legal framework of England and Wales will not be applicable to that of Scotland. See Antisocial Behaviour etc (Scotland) Act 2004.

[154] Ramsay, *The Insecurity State* (n 8) 6–10.

[155] ibid.

[156] ibid ch 1.

[157] ibid 54.

appears to be part of everyday social interaction and therefore extend the net of social control to 'potentially "all spheres of life"'.[158] Most importantly, the restrictions imposed during the first stage of this process of regulation can be so severe that they can constitute a form of punishment in their own right,[159] albeit 'not subject to the kind of constraint that could legitimate them as punishments'.[160] In theory, therefore, the issue of an injunction, that is the first limb of the process, can still result in the indirect criminalisation of certain kinds of behaviour.[161]

The potential indirect criminalisation of certain kinds of behaviour through the injunction's first limb raises a number of normative and practical questions for criminal law theorists and criminologists. For instance, it could be argued that given ASB's 'sweeping and vague' statutory definition,[162] the implementation of the injunction can result in the creation of localised criminal codes with courts and local enforcement agents deciding what kinds of behaviour (and in what context) are acceptable or not. The foregoing hypothesis, which provided the impetus for this study, becomes more concerning in light of the fact that through the 2014 amendments the proximity of the injunction to the criminal law has been officially distanced. This means that the implementation of the injunction is likely to attract less attention and scrutiny, enabling courts and local enforcement agents to use this tool (along with other ASB measures) as a means of criminalising indirectly what *they* consider to be ASB.

The potential creation of localised criminal codes is not an entirely novel concept[163] especially for American legal scholars who have been engaging with the issue of criminal law localism, that is the ability of local governments to enact criminal offences, since the late twentieth century.[164] Criminal law localism is a particularly contested topic. As we shall see, many of the arguments and counter-arguments raised about criminal law localism are directly applicable to the potential creation of localised criminal codes through the implementation of the ASB tools and powers. On the one hand, advocates of criminal law

[158] D Stephen, 'The Responsibility of Respecting Justice: An Open Challenge to Tony Blair's Successors' in P Squires (ed), *ASBO Nation: The Criminalisation of Nuisance* (Bristol, Policy Press, 2008) 321–22.

[159] As discussed in more detail in ch 4, section 4.1.2, the first limb of the injunction and of the CBO are potentially even more restrictive than the first limb of the ASBO and of the CrASBO since under the 2014 Act positive obligations can be imposed as well, such as to attend alcohol-rehabilitation treatment.

[160] Duff and Marshall (n 105) 80.

[161] This, of course, is also true for all other civil preventive measures which allow for the imposition of similar restrictions on the liberty of those against whom they are issued.

[162] Ashworth et al (n 149) 9.

[163] Logan (n 35) 1414; N Davidson, 'The Dilemma of Localism in an Era of Polarization' (2019) 128 *Yale Law Journal* 954, 963.

[164] It should be noted that 'localism' is not restricted only to the area of criminal law since local governments in the United States have enacted laws covering a wide range of topics, such as minimum wage. See, further, Davidson (n 163) 957.

localism are pointing out that this devolution of power from the state towards local governments can 'maximize an array of values including liberty, equality and efficient experimentation … [allowing the] criminal justice to better reflect societal viewpoints'.[165] Simply put, local politicians are in a better position to determine which (and how) social phenomena should be addressed due to their close proximity to the communities affected. On the other hand, critics of criminal law localism highlight the potential dangers that accompany this devolution of power. For Fissell, criminal law localism posses a threat to individual liberty and autonomy since local governments can only introduce new criminal offences rather than repeal (or at least restrict the ambit of) existing state laws.[166] This limited ability of local governments inevitably results in the further expansion of the net of social control.[167] Localism can also be regarded as a 'double-edged sword' since local lawmakers can use the powers granted to them for 'desirable as well as pernicious ends', such as to introduce laws that will advance the interests of the ruling majority while neglecting those of other social groups whose voices are not often heard.[168]

This book examines whether localised criminal codes have been created through the implementation of the injunction's first limb at a local level. To this end, the book engages with a number of normative debates, such as the difference between criminal punishment and other forms of sanctions imposed by the state, while formulating a working definition of criminalisation which will enable me to look beyond the official label attached to the injunction by the legislature and to examine its true nature. This will be followed by an empirical evaluation of the ASBO's successor through which I will examine whether the implementation of the injunction has indeed led to the indirect criminalisation of certain kinds of ASB.

The importance of the subsequent analysis is twofold. First, we cannot really assess the legitimacy and justifiability of a particular intervention if we first do not ascertain its true nature. What justifies a criminal intervention might not be sufficient to justify a non-punitive measure and vice versa. Also, even if the restrictions imposed through the issue of an injunction do not amount to criminal punishment, we still need a proper discussion about how indirect criminalisation can be prevented and the proper limits of the preventive state.[169] Second, regardless of the justification offered by the legislature for the

[165] B Fissell, 'Against Criminal Law Localism' (2022) 81 *Maryland Law Review* 1188, 1188 and 1190; R Schragger, 'The Limits of Localism' (2001) 100 *Michigan Law Review*) 371, 381–82; S Smith, 'Localism and Capital Punishment' (2011) 64 *Vanderbilt Law Review En Banc* 105, 110.

[166] Fissell (n 165) 1188 and 1218.

[167] ibid 1190.

[168] Davidson (n 163) 958. See also, Logan (n 35) 1448–49.

[169] Steiker (n 63) 784. For a notable attempt to set limits to the scope of the preventive state see Ashworth and Zedner, *Preventive Justice* (n 8) ch 11.

introduction of a particular measure, such as the prevention of crime, if we are serious about the preservation of individual liberty, then we should look beyond the stated objective of liberty intrusive interventions. As Dripps put it, if 'we start down the road of calling time spent in jail by sane people suspected of unproved crimes anything other than punishment, I fear to see the end of the road'.[170] The formulation of a working definition of criminalisation that enables legal commentators, law enforcement agents and courts to look beyond the official label attached to a particular intervention can certainly contribute to the identification of instances of indirect criminalisation. One of this book's key objectives therefore is to question the legal methods through which the prevention of crime and other undesirable kinds of behaviour are to be achieved.

## 1.6. METHODOLOGY

The hybrid nature of the ASBO along with its ambiguous scope has generated a rich academic literature both at an empirical and theoretical level. At a theoretical level, the initial decision to tackle ASB through a hybrid method of social control, for instance, was criticised by a number of academics, such as Duff, and Ashworth and Zedner, who argued that the ASBO was guilty of blurring the normative distinction between the criminal and the civil law.[171] Other critics of the ASBO, such as Cornford and Lewis et al, focused on the alleged over-inclusiveness of ASB's statutory definition and the possibility of extending the reach of social control to behaviour which is 'merely offensive'[172] and/or to 'minor infractions commonly associated with young people'.[173] At an empirical level, a number of studies have already been conducted focusing on specific aspects of the ASBO and related measures.[174] However, thus far, there have been no empirical studies on the implementation of the ASBO's successor. Moreover, none of the empirical studies conducted prior to the 2014 amendments were

[170] D Dripps, 'The Exclusivity of the Criminal Law: Toward a Regulatory Model of, or Pathological Perspective on, the Civil–Criminal Distinction' (1996) 7 *Journal of Contemporary Legal Issues* 199, 220.

[171] A Duff, 'Perversions and Subversions of Criminal Law' in A Duff et al (eds), *The Boundaries of the Criminal Law* (Oxford, Oxford University Press, 2010) 99; Ashworth and Zedner, 'Preventive Orders' (n 59) 66.

[172] Cornford (n 133) 3.

[173] Lewis et al (n 68) 1231.

[174] For small-scale studies on different aspects of the ASBO, see: K Bullock and B Jones, *Acceptable Behaviour Contracts Addressing Antisocial Behaviour in the London Borough of Islington* (London, Home Office, 2004); Koffman (n 65); R Matthews et al, *Assessing the Use and Impact of Anti-Social Behaviour Orders* (Bristol, Policy Press, 2007); J Donoghue, *Anti-social Behaviour Orders: A Culture of Control?* (Basingstoke, Palgrave Macmillan, 2010). For a large-scale study on the ASBO see: Lewis et al (n 68); A Crawford et al, '"It ain't (just) what you do, it's (also) the way that you do it": The Role of Procedural Justice in the Implementation of Anti-social Behaviour Interventions with Young People' (2017) 23 *European Journal on Criminal Policy and Research* 9.

designed to investigate the implementation of the ASBO through the lens of indirect criminalisation and in light of a working definition of criminalisation and this is precisely what this book does.

Before I elaborate further on the empirical study conducted as part of this research project, it is imperative first to explain why this was necessary. As explained earlier, one of the main concerns raised about the first limb of the ASBO (and therefore of the injunction) is that it could result in the imposition of restrictions akin to criminal punishment. Hence, the first question to be addressed is: what is it to punish? The working definition of criminalisation formulated in chapter three allows me to address this question. It does not, though, answer the main question put forward by this study: has the implementation of the injunction's first limb led to the indirect criminalisation of certain kinds of ASB? Although a purely theoretical analysis of the relevant legislation could expose the potential for indirect criminalisation, it was only through an empirical study that I could examine whether based on my working definition of criminalisation the injunction operated as a de facto criminal measure.

For the purposes of this research, an empirical study, using semi-structured interviews, was conducted, between May 2015 and April 2016, which focused on the implementation of the injunction by local enforcement agents in two areas in England. It is worth noting that this study did not examine the implementation of the injunction from the perspective of those against whom this measure was used or from the perspective of victims.[175] This was due to the working definition of criminalisation formulated for the purposes of this study which focuses on the intentions of local enforcement agents, that is whether the perpetrators were *publicly* and *purposefully* condemned for their behaviour.[176]

The selection of possible locations was based on the 'maximum variation (heterogeneity) sampling' technique.[177] For Patton, the underlying objective of this method of purposive sampling is to 'capture and describe the central themes that cut across a great deal of variation'.[178] This, according to him, can result in the identification of 'common patterns that emerge from great variation [which] are of particular interest and value in capturing the core experiences and central, shared dimensions of a setting or phenomenon'.[179] The importance of these common patterns lies with the fact that they 'emerge out of great variation'.[180] To achieve variegation, it was necessary to study one site which experienced

[175] At least some of those against whom an injunction is issued might feel that the restrictions imposed on them amount to punishment, albeit this not being consistent with my working definition of criminalisation (eg, see Heap et al (n 140)).

[176] See ch 3, section 3.3.

[177] M Patton, *Qualitative Research and Evaluation Methods*, 3rd edn (Thousand Oaks, CA, Sage Publications, 2002) 234–35.

[178] ibid.

[179] ibid 235.

[180] ibid.

high levels of ASB when compared with other sites, that is Site A, and one which experienced moderate to low levels of ASB, that is Site B.

The process of identifying potential locations was based on the findings from the Crime Survey for England and Wales with regard to 'the percentage of adults aged 16 and over who have witnessed/experienced anti-social behaviour by police force area, in the year ending December 2013'.[181] Although, the figures provided were estimates, they were indicative of the level of ASB experienced/ witnessed in these areas. The reason why this selection process was not based on the actual number of injunctions issued was twofold. First, the government decided not to collect data on the number of applications made to court under Part 1 of the 2014 Act. Second, there is strong evidence to suggest that it is common practice, for local enforcement agents to use a number of informal interventions through which they try to address the perpetrator's behaviour before applying to court for an injunction or a CBO.[182] It was possible, therefore, for an area to have a relatively low ratio of orders to population, but in reality, having individuals punished through the use of informal interventions. This might have been particularly prevalent in areas with high levels of ASB, where local enforcement agents might have found it more convenient and efficient (maybe due to lack of resources) to deal with perpetrators through informal interventions.

As part of this empirical study, 29 semi-structured interviews were conducted across both sites. In Site A, 19 interviews were conducted: (i) nine with police officers; and (ii) 10 with local practitioners. In Site B, 10 interviews were conducted: (i) four with police officers; and (ii) six with local practitioners. In total, 13 police officers and 16 local practitioners were interviewed from both sites. The interview recordings were fully transcribed and then analysed thematically using NVivo.[183] Through this process, a number of themes which could assist in examining whether the implementation of the injunction led to the indirect criminalisation of certain kinds of ASB were identified.[184] That said, the findings of this study should be approached with caution for two reasons. First, as mentioned above, this study examined the implementation of the injunction only from the perspective of local enforcement agents whose perceptions

[181] Office for National Statistics, *Experiences of Anti-social Behaviour by Police Force Area, English Regions and Wales, year ending December 2013 CSEW* (London, The Stationery Office, 2014).

[182] Home Office, *How Many ABCs/ABAs Issued?* (London, The Stationery Office, 2009), available at: webarchive.nationalarchives.gov.uk/20100303141407/http://asb.homeoffice.gov.uk/uploadedFiles/Members_site/Documents_and_images/Resources/ABCs_ABAs_Issued.pdf; P. Squires and D Stephen, *Rough Justice: Anti-social Behaviour and Young People* (Cullompton, Willan Publishing, 2005) 132–33.

[183] NVivo is a software designed to facilitate the analysis of research data. It allows researchers to upload their data, such as interview transcripts, and organise them based on their research objectives. Researchers are also able to create their own codes and sub-codes through which common themes can be identified.

[184] A Bryman, *Social Research Methods*, 5th edn (Oxford, Oxford University Press, 2016) 584–88.

might vary considerably from those of perpetrators (and their legal advisers) and victims of ASB. Second, it is worth reiterating that the 2014 Act provides local enforcement agents and courts with a significant magnitude of discretion regarding the implementation of all ASB tools and powers including the injunction. In effect, this means that the implementation of these measures can vary considerably across England and Wales. Consequently, the findings of this study do not necessarily present how the injunction and the other ASB tools and powers are implemented in other parts of the country, but they do provide an indication about the use of these measures.

## 1.7. STRUCTURE OF THE BOOK

Chapter two of the book identifies and engages with what is problematic about indirect criminalisation. It is argued, for instance, that one of the main functions of the criminal law is to declare which values underpin society. By criminalising a particular kind of behaviour, the legislature declares that the wrong proscribed undermines a core value, such as the principle of equality, of society and it should therefore be *condemned*. Through this process the legislature seeks to educate members of the public about the values that underpin society. In order for this to be achieved though, a clear distinction between criminalisation and other forms of social regulation must be maintained. Instances of indirect criminalisation undermine this clear distinction and are likely to dilute the moral message conveyed through direct criminalisation. In order to prevent this from happening, we need to be in a position to identify and address instances of indirect criminalisation.

The main objective of chapter three is to formulate a working definition of criminalisation which will enable me to examine whether indeed the implementation of the injunction's first limb led to the indirect criminalisation of certain kinds of ASB. As mentioned earlier, in *Engel v Netherlands* the European Court of Human Rights (ECtHR) formulated the anti-subversion doctrine as a means of identifying potential instances of indirect criminalisation.[185] The formulation of the anti-subversion doctrine was an unequivocal acknowledgment by the ECtHR that the implementation of certain legal rules classified under domestic legislation as non-criminal can potentially result in the indirect imposition of criminal punishment. Although the formulation of the anti-subversion doctrine was a step in the right direction, it is argued that the narrow interpretation of liberty adopted along with the attention paid to the lawmaker's intentions render this doctrine too rigid in its application. For this reason, chapter three proceeds to formulate a new working definition of criminalisation which identifies and elaborates on the circumstances under which the implementation of

[185] *Engel v Netherlands* (n 80).

a legal rule will constitute a form of criminalisation. Central to this working definition is the need to look beyond the official classification of legal rules and investigate if they operate as de facto criminal measures.

Chapter four moves on to examine in more detail the current legal framework on ASB and what impact the 2014 amendments had on the law in this area. The purpose of this analysis is twofold. First, it provides a more detailed account of the relevant statutory provisions and lays the foundations for the empirical and theoretical evaluation of the ASB legal framework in chapters five, six and seven. Second, this analysis aims to illustrate that, despite the 2014 amendments through which the ASBO was repealed and replaced by a civil injunction, it is still necessary to investigate how this measure has been used in practice. This is due to the potential impact that the issue of an injunction can have on those against whom it is used. The chapter then examines more closely the injunction with reference to the working definition of criminalisation formulated in chapter three. The purpose of this assessment is to demonstrate how the implementation of the injunction could lead to the indirect criminalisation of certain kinds of behaviour.

Chapter five presents the first set of findings of the empirical study conducted with local practitioners and police officers in the two sites under investigation. The findings presented in this chapter relate to: (i) how ASB is being conceptualised at a local level by the research participants; and (ii) what impacts the 2014 amendments in legislation are having on the daily administration of ASB. The chapter highlights that despite the overly broad definition of ASB under section 2 of the 2014 Act, the decision of local enforcement agents to classify someone's behaviour as anti-social is informed by a number of factors, such as the availability of resources, which tend to narrow significantly the scope of the law.

Chapter six proceeds to present the second set of findings from this empirical study focusing on the procedure followed by local enforcement agents after they were notified about a potential incident of ASB. Based on the data collected, it was evident that in both sites a pyramidal system of regulation, which resembles Ayres and Braithwaite's model of responsive regulation, was in place enabling local enforcement agents to escalate their response if the perpetrator did not alter his behaviour.[186] Another common theme that emerged was local enforcement agents' endeavours to strike a fair balance between the need to address the underlying causes of the perpetrators' behaviour and the need to prevent crime and ASB in their localities. This highlights a really important tension at the heart of enforcement between welfarism and crime prevention which was caused mainly by the proliferation of civil preventive measures. Although it is concluded that the implementation of the injunction's first limb rarely amounted to a form of indirect criminalisation, it is argued that it is the implementation and the

[186] I Ayres and J Braithwaite, *Responsive Regulation: Transcending the Deregulation Debate* (New York, Oxford University Press, 1992).

procedures in place at a local level that manage to constrain what is an otherwise far-reaching legal instrument.

The conclusion reflects further on the study and its main findings while highlighting the need to be mindful of instances of indirect criminalisation. It also draws on the most important findings of the empirical study, their broader philosophical implications and the contribution of this book to the academic literature on criminalisation, punishment and ASB. The final part of the book concludes by highlighting the need for additional measures to be put in place in order to prevent the indirect criminalisation of certain kinds of behaviour through the implementation of the ASB tools and powers.

# 2

# *The Problem with Indirect Criminalisation*

## 2.1. INTRODUCTION

In chapter one, I argued that although the prevention of crime and other undesirable outcomes that can undermine the security of its citizens is a legitimate objective for the liberal state to pursue, I emphasised the need to be mindful of *how* and *at what cost*, in terms of individual autonomy, this is to be achieved. Of particular concern for the purposes of this book are legal instruments that formally lie outside the scope of the criminal law and are susceptible to what I call indirect criminalisation, primarily the Part 1 injunction of the Anti-social Behaviour, Crime and Policing Act 2014. My main objective in chapter two is to explain why indirect criminalisation matters and further problematise the proliferation of civil preventive measures in recent years. In particular, I contend that indirect criminalisation is morally problematic because: (i) it poses a threat to liberty and individual autonomy by allowing the net of social control to be extended to the private sphere; (ii) it allows for the imposition of criminal punishment in the absence of (at least some of) the enhanced procedural protections; (iii) it undermines the normative distinction between the criminal law and other forms of social regulation used by the state; and (iv) it is not subjected to certain rules and principles that are so important to restrict the punitive state. For these reasons, instances of indirect criminalisation *cannot be warranted* regardless of the stated objective of civil preventive measures. This is not to suggest that the implementation of civil preventive measures always results in the indirect criminalisation of certain kinds of behaviour. Instead, what I am arguing is that when the implementation of a civil preventive measure constitutes a form of indirect criminalisation, then the restrictions imposed on the perpetrator's liberty cannot be justified despite the supposedly civil/preventive nature of the instrument at hand.

In section 2 of this chapter, I engage with Hobbes's political theory which has been instrumental in the development of the contemporary liberal state. I do so in order to demonstrate that even from a Hobbesian perspective, which grants absolute power to the state to introduce those measures that it deems necessary for the protection of its citizens, respect for liberty and individual autonomy still lies at the heart of the liberal state. I argue that indirect criminalisation matters because it is capable of circumventing many of the constraints imposed on the state's ability to regulate our behaviour through the use of the criminal law, such as the need to criminalise only conduct that falls within the public realm. In section 3, I highlight the coercive nature of criminalisation arguing that what is problematic about indirect criminalisation is that it allows for the imposition of punishment in the absence of the enhanced procedural protections afforded to those facing criminal prosecution. Clearly, the enhanced procedural protections afforded to those facing criminal prosecution are an important safeguard against state abuse of power. However, as we shall see later, these additional protections represent a double-edged sword since they encourage the introduction of supposedly non-punitive interventions which aim, inter alia, to the circumvention of these safety valves. Moreover, indirect criminalisation erodes the normative distinction between the criminal and the civil law, something that can significantly undermine the former's ability to educate members of the public about society's core values. Finally, I contend that indirect criminalisation is capable of circumventing a number of rules and principles, such as the prohibition of retroactive criminalisation, that are so important to restrict the scope of the punitive state. The subsequent analysis demonstrates further why it is so important to investigate empirically whether the implementation of the injunction resulted in the indirect criminalisation of certain kinds of anti-social behaviour (ASB).

## 2.2. THE LIMITS OF THE LIBERAL STATE

Before I explain why indirect criminalisation poses a threat to individual liberty, it is important to explain why I am focusing on Hobbes's political theory here. As explained in chapter one, the introduction of the Anti-social Behaviour Order (ASBO) along with a series of pre-inchoate offences enacted since the late stages of the twentieth century in England and Wales,[1] in order to target potentially dangerous individuals, can be justified by the need to reassure the rest of the polity about their security, that is to address others' subjective feelings of insecurity.[2] On this view, someone who was found in breach of the ASBO imposed on them was not punished for his defiance of a court order, but for his failure to reassure others that he did not pose a threat to their security. This need to reassure others about their security, according to Ramsay, is based on the idea that full membership of a liberal society does not just grant citizens certain

[1] See, eg, Hodgson and Tadros's analysis of the offence created by s 58(1)(b) of the Terrorism Act 2000. See J Hodgson and V Tadros, 'How to Make a Terrorist Out of Nothing' (2009) 72 *Modern Law Review* 984.

[2] P Ramsay, *The Insecurity State: Vulnerable Autonomy and the Right to Security in the Criminal Law* (Oxford, Oxford University Press, 2012) ch 1.

rights, but it also imposes various obligations on them.[3] This idea of citizens bearing certain rights and obligations is, as mentioned in chapter one, consistent with Hobbes's political theory which is based on a trade-off between individual autonomy and security.[4] What is problematic about this 'need' to reassure others about their security is that it imposes no constraints on the state's ability to interfere with people's liberty. In fact, security can be used as a trump card for the introduction of far-reaching interventions, such as civil preventive measures and pre-inchoate offences, that can *severely* curtail individual liberty and autonomy.

Although a trade-off between liberty and security is a necessary prerequisite for the formulation of a liberal society, a fair balance between the two should still be maintained. Failure to strike a fair balance between the two will be *antithetical* to the liberal state's promise to its citizens. What sets the liberal state apart from other political orders is not its ability to protect its citizens, but its promise to do so while respecting liberty and individual autonomy as much as possible. A close analysis of Hobbes's theory will demonstrate that indirect criminalisation is morally problematic because it allows state interference with behaviour that falls within the private sphere and therefore conduct that should not be the state's business at all.

Hobbes's political theory is based on the assumption that in the absence of a commonwealth, men 'are in that condition which is called war; and such a war as is of every man against every man'.[5] In this state of war men enjoy absolute freedom since there is no 'right and wrong, justice and injustice'.[6] What this means though is that men rely only on their own strengths for their survival and that they are vulnerable to others' ability to exercise their right of nature, that is to do whatever they deem appropriate to protect themselves.[7] This causes continual fear and uncertainty to them about their future, something which undermines their ability to realise their full potential.[8] This constant sense of

[3] ibid 54.

[4] See ch 1, section 1.1.

[5] T Hobbes, *Leviathan* (Hertfordshire, Wordsworth Editions, 2014) 97.

[6] In contrast to Hobbes, Locke's account is based on the idea that although in the state of nature there is no superior authority (and therefore there is what he calls 'perfect equality'), men are guided by reason and common equity even when punishing those who commit wrongs against them. Reason and common equity, according to Locke, are principles set by God and ensure the mutual security of all men. Hence, for Locke, men do not seek the formulation of a commonwealth simply to enhance their security. Rather, based on his account, men formulate commonwealths in order to address some of the shortcomings of the state of nature. For example, part of the reasoning behind the formulation of commonwealths is the need to 'restrain the partiality and violence of men'. If, according to Locke, men are allowed to judge their own cases, then it is likely for their judgement to be negatively affected by their 'passion and [desire for] revenge' leading to the imposition of excessive punishment. Hence, an independent authority is needed that can judge each case impartially reaching a fair outcome. It is for this reason that Locke also argued for the separation of power between the different branches of the state. See Hobbes (n 5) 98–99; J Locke, *The Second Treatise of Government* (London, 1689) chs II and XII.

[7] Hobbes (n 5) 97.

[8] ibid. See also Locke (n 6) ch IX.

insecurity prompts men, who are regarded as rational agents, to seek peace.[9] To achieve this, men agree to enter into a social covenant with others. As part of this covenant, every man agrees with every man to abandon their right of nature allowing for the formulating of the commonwealth which is an artificial entity.[10] As part of this social covenant, men who agree to abandon their right of nature are promised security and the ability to enjoy (what is left of) their liberty without any unjustifiable interference by others including the state itself. To this end, according to Hobbes, the sovereign, acting on behalf of the entire community, is given the absolute authority to create those laws that are necessary for the preservation of the commonwealth.[11] Inevitably, some of those who entered this social covenant might not be able to restrain themselves from interfering with the liberty of others.[12] It is for this reason that the sovereign is also given the exclusive power to punish, as it deems fit, those who are found in breach of the covenant.[13] The importance of having a centralised institution of punishment not only lies in the need to prevent members of the public from taking matters into their own hands, but it also ensures that the law applies equally and proportionately to everyone.[14]

Hobbes's theory is based on the idea that people seek the formulation of a commonwealth primarily as a 'means to peace and security'.[15] They accept the imposition of some limits to their liberty and in return they expect to be able to live freely without any *unjustifiable* interference by others. Although members of the polity consent to this trade-off, liberty still lies at the heart of the liberal state's promise to its citizens. Parties to this social covenant do not agree to give up their liberty entirely. They only agree to sacrifice what is absolutely necessary for the formulation of a commonwealth. Consequently, if the liberal state is to uphold its promise to its citizens, then constraints must be imposed on its ability to interfere with their liberty. It is for this reason that I argue that what really distinguishes the liberal state from other social orders is its promise to restrict state interference with people's liberty to what is necessary for the preservation of the polity. The legislature must therefore determine what kinds of behaviour should potentially be the proper concern of the state and which should not. To this end, a distinction must be drawn between conduct that falls within the public realm (and therefore the proper concern of the state) and those kinds of behaviour that are private in nature and thus not the state's business.[16] On what basis though should such a distinction be drawn? What makes a particular kind

[9] Hobbes (n 5) 98–99.
[10] ibid 103 and 136.
[11] ibid 138–40 and 236–37.
[12] ibid 131.
[13] ibid 236–37.
[14] Z Hoskins, *Beyond Punishment: A Normative Account of the Collateral Legal Consequences of Conviction* (New York, Oxford University Press, 2019) 138.
[15] Hobbes (n 5) x.
[16] A Duff, *The Realm of Criminal Law* (Oxford, Oxford University Press, 2018) 78–79.

of behaviour a public matter and therefore the proper concern of the state and what does not?[17] According to Duff, in order to 'develop such a conception of the public realm … we must [first] articulate a conception of the polity whose public realm it is'.[18] Duff is right to hold this view since the public realm of a monolithic society which seeks to maintain the status quo will (and should) certainly be different from the public realm of a contemporary liberal and diverse society which values not only the security of its citizens, but their liberty and autonomy as well. In order to answer the above-mentioned questions, one will need to formulate a normative political theory. It is not my intention to do so here. Instead, what I want to do is to highlight the need for the legislature of a liberal state to strike a fair balance between liberty and security when determining the contours of the public realm. In doing so, the legislature must not lose sight of the principles and values underpinning society (in the case of a liberal polity, the protection of the public *and* respect for liberty and autonomy) and the need for state interference with people's lives to be justified.

The importance of setting clear limits to the state's ability to interfere with individual autonomy is heightened even further when the legislature decides to utilise the criminal law to deal with behaviour that falls within the public realm. Even if it is concluded that a particular kind of behaviour falls within the public realm this does not necessarily mean that the legislature should resort to its criminalisation. Similarly, even if the criminal law is to be utilised, the legislature might decide to restrict its ambit to cover only those kinds of behaviour that are particularly blameworthy and problematic.[19] The reason for this is that criminalisation is the most coercive means of social regulation available at the state's disposal and therefore sufficient justification must be provided by the legislature for its use.[20] How is the above analysis of Hobbes's political theory then relevant to indirect criminalisation?

The above analysis reiterates that both security and liberty lie at the heart of the liberal state's promise to its citizens. In contrast to other political orders that can also offer security, the liberal state promises to do so while respecting individual liberty and autonomy as much as possible. Consequently, even if the introduction of a particular measure, such as the injunction, can be justified on the need to prevent certain threats and/or reassure members of the public about their security, it is important to be mindful of what impact this instrument will

[17] According to Marshall and Duff, what makes a particular kind of behaviour a public wrong (as opposed to a private wrong), is that wrongs of this nature concern society as a whole and thus necessitate a collective response by the entire polity. Hence, criminal wrongs should not be seen as wrongs done to a particular victim, but they should be seen as wrongs done to the 'common good'. S Marshall and A Duff, 'Criminalisation and Sharing Wrongs' (1998) 11 *Canadian Journal of Law and Jurisprudence* 7, 7–8 and 11–12.

[18] Duff, *The Realm of Criminal Law* (n 16) 88.

[19] S Demetriou and N Partington, 'Criminalising Hate: The Need for Rationalisation and Reform' (2022) 6 *Criminal Law Review* 448, 461–64.

[20] In section 2.3, I explain further why criminalisation is the most coercive means of social control.

have on people's liberty regardless of its stated objective. Liberty and autonomy should not be seen by the legislature and those responsible for the implementation of the law as a barrier to security, but as one of the cornerstones of any liberal society. Indirect criminalisation is morally problematic because it allows the state to use security as a justification for potentially far-reaching interventions that can have a significant and long-lasting impact on the liberty of those subjected to these measures. By far-reaching interventions, I mean measures the ambit of which can be extended to cover behaviour that is otherwise lawful and therefore not the proper concern of the state.[21] The same of course can be said about pre-inchoate offences. Indirect criminalisation is different though from pre-inchoate offences since the former lies outside the ambit of the criminal law. The importance of this is twofold. First, measures susceptible to indirect criminalisation are not subject to the enhanced procedural protections afforded to those facing criminal prosecution. As we shall see below, the absence of these protections matters because criminalisation (either direct or indirect) is the most coercive means of social regulation and therefore those subjected to it must be offered additional protections, such as the higher standard of proof, to ensure that only those who are truly blameworthy are punished for their conduct.

Second, measures susceptible to indirect criminalisation are likely to attract less attention and outside scrutiny precisely because they lie outside the ambit of the criminal law.[22] What this means is that even if the use of these supposedly non-punitive interventions leads to the significant expansion of the net of social control, their implementation and the impact that these have on individual liberty is less likely to be questioned due to their allegedly preventive nature. A good illustration of the potential far-reaching implications that civil preventive measures can have on individual liberty is of course the ASBO's successor, that is the injunction introduced under Part 1 of the 2014 Act.[23] This is primarily due to the breadth of ASB's statutory definition along with the significant and long-lasting restrictions that can be imposed on the liberty of those against whom an injunction is issued. Based on how the law appears on the statute book, any kind of behaviour can be regarded as anti-social as long as it is likely to cause 'harassment, alarm or distress' or 'nuisance and annoyance' to others.[24] Consequently, very few (if any) constraints are imposed on the state's ability to interfere with the liberty of its citizens, which as mentioned above contradicts with the promise made by the liberal state to those who agree to abandon their right of nature.

[21] According to Hobbes, if the sovereign did not proscribe a particular kind of conduct, then members of the polity should be able to decide for themselves if they wish to behave in such a way. See Hobbes (n 5) 170.

[22] See ch 4, section 4.2.2.

[23] As mentioned in ch 1, to some extent similar concerns can be raised about the gang injunctions that have been operating in the United States since the late 1980s and the Prohibited Behaviour Orders of Western Australia.

[24] See ch 1, section 1.4.3.

## 2.3. THE COERCIVE AND EDUCATIVE NATURE OF CRIMINALISATION

Thus far, it has been argued that although the liberal state has a duty to prevent crime and other undesirable kinds of behaviour, it still has an obligation to respect its citizens' liberty and autonomy. To this end, state interference with individual autonomy should be limited to behaviour that falls within the public realm. Indirect criminalisation poses a threat to individual liberty and autonomy not only because it allows for the criminalisation of behaviour that falls within the private sphere, but also due to the fact that it operates in a legal lacuna where very little protection is offered to those subjected to these measures. In what follows, my main objective is to illustrate what makes criminalisation the most coercive means of social regulation and why it is so important for additional protections to be offered to those facing the prospect of punishment.

Since the age of Plato, legal and political philosophers have introduced and defended principles and theories through which a fair balance between individual autonomy and state control is to be maintained.[25] This is done primarily by identifying and defending constraints on the conditions under which state interference with our liberty and freedoms can be warranted.[26] Some of these theories, such as legal moralism, were formulated explicitly to set limits to the legitimate use of the criminal law by the state.[27] Other theories, such as Mill's harm principle,[28] were introduced as broader political theories, but they were later adopted and modified by criminal law theorists, such as Feinberg, in order to determine criminal law's proper boundaries.[29] Similarly, many criminal law philosophers sought to determine what purpose(s) criminal punishment should serve. For some, such as Bentham, punishment is an inherently evil practice due to its adverse consequences.[30] Nonetheless, it can still be warranted if it promotes 'the happiness of the party whose interest is in question … [or if it] prevent[s] the happening of mischief, pain, evil, or unhappiness to the party whose interest is considered'.[31] That is a consequentialist approach to punishment. For some non-consequentialist theorists, through the imposition of punishment the wrongdoer must get what he *deserves* for his past behaviour regardless of whether this results in less crime.[32] To achieve this, the punishment imposed must be *proportionate* to the wrong committed by the offender.[33] That

[25] M Mackenzie, *Plato on Punishment* (California: University of California Press, 1981).
[26] J Mill, *On Liberty* (New York, Dover Publications, 2002) 8.
[27] D Husak, *Overcriminalization: The Limits of the Criminal Law* (New York, Oxford University Press, 2008) 196.
[28] Mill (n 26) 4.
[29] J Feinberg, *Harm to Others* (Oxford, Oxford University Press, 1984).
[30] J Bentham, *Introduction to the Principles of Morals and Legislation* (New York, Dover Press, 2007).
[31] ibid 2.
[32] M Moore, *Placing Blame: A Theory of the Criminal Law* (New York, Oxford University Press, 2010) 153.
[33] Husak, *Overcriminalization* (n 27) 83.

is, the sentence imposed should be commensurate with the blameworthiness of the wrong committed.[34]

Although there is currently a lack of common consensus amongst criminal law theorists as to the kinds of behaviour that should fall within the ambit of the criminal law and what purposes punishment should serve, the formulation of these normative theories of criminalisation and punishment plainly highlights the need for criminalisation and the imposition of punishment to be justified and based on clear moral foundations.[35] Simply put, criminal law 'theorists disagree about how punishment is justified, but not about whether a justification is needed'.[36] This is mainly because of criminalisation's coercive nature. The criminal law is the most coercive means of social control due to the nature of the sanctions imposed on those who violate its commands.[37] The criminal law does not impose mere penalties, but it punishes those who offend.[38] As we shall see below, in addition to the significant restrictions that can be imposed on someone's liberty, to be convicted of a criminal offence is to be labelled as a serious moral wrongdoer. That is, as someone whose conduct undermines some of the core values that hold our society together. It is for this reason that conviction for a criminal offence can lead to stigmatisation and social isolation.[39] And it is precisely because of the impact that criminal punishment can have on individual liberty that it must be warranted.

Notwithstanding criminalisation's coercive nature, the proliferation of pre-inchoate offences and civil preventive measures that are susceptible to indirect criminalisation during the last two decades in many Western jurisdictions suggests that indeed lawmakers have 'become far too cavalier about punishment'.[40] Far-reaching preventive-led interventions (both within and outside the

[34] A von Hirsch, *Censure and Sanctions* (New York, Oxford University Press, 1993) 15–18.

[35] A very illustrative example of this lack of common consensus regarding the proper limits of the criminal law is the debate in the 1960s between Lord Devlin, who was a legal moralist, and HLA Hart, who was advocating for a more liberal approach. The impetus for this debate was provided by the publication of the Wolfenden Committee's report which recommended, inter alia, the decriminalisation of homosexuality. See Home Office, *Report of the Committee on Homosexual Offences and Prostitution* Cmnd 247 (London, Her Majesty's Stationery Office, 1957); Lord Devlin, *The Enforcement of Morals* (London, Oxford University Press, 1965); HLA Hart, *Law, Liberty, and Morality* (Stanford, CA, Stanford University Press, 1963).

[36] D Husak, 'Limitations on Criminalisation and the General Part of Criminal Law' in S Shute and A Simester (eds), *Criminal Law Theory: Doctrines of the General Part* (Oxford, Oxford University Press, 2002) 31–32.

[37] D Husak, 'Reservations about Overcriminalisation' (2011) 14 *New Criminal Law Review* 97, 102.

[38] D Husak, 'The Criminal Law as Last Resort' (2004) 24 *Oxford Journal of Legal Studies* 207, 211.

[39] Figures released by the Ministry of Justice, for example, suggest that only 17 per cent of 'ex-offenders manage to get a job within a year of release' suggesting that employers are extremely reluctant to hire those convicted of serious offences. See Ministry of Justice, *Employing Prisoners and Ex-offenders* (2020), available at: www.gov.uk/government/publications/unlock-opportunity-employer-information-pack-and-case-studies/employing-prisoners-and-ex-offenders.

[40] Although Husak is critical of criminal offences the scope of which cover conduct that it is not 'worthy of condemnation', his argument is readily applicable to civil preventive measures as well

criminal law) are increasingly seen as a panacea for newly identified threats to the polity's security. Individual liberty and due process values are no longer regarded as the cornerstone of the liberal society, but rather as obstacles to the pursuit of security.

What renders criminalisation the most coercive means of social regulation is the combination of 'hard treatment' and censure.[41] For Feinberg, 'hard treatment' refers to the financial and/or physical deprivations imposed on those who violate a given legal rule.[42] As he has pointed out, however, not every deprivation imposed on the perpetrator amounts to 'hard treatment'. Based on his conception of 'hard treatment', a custodial sentence is a paradigmatic example of punishment.[43] This is not the case though with parking fines which, according to him, constitute mere penalties.[44] The difference between penalties and punishments lies, according to Feinberg, in the second prerequisite of punishment, that is that the physical/financial deprivation must *intentionally* communicate censure.[45] Based on his account, both penalties and punishment aim to prevent certain kinds of 'undesirable behaviour', such as unauthorised parking.[46] But punishment has an additional element. Punishment, according to him, 'is a conventional device for the expression of attitudes of resentment and indignation, and of judgments of disapproval and reprobation, either on the part of the punishing authority … or of those "in whose name" the punishment is inflicted'.[47] As Husak succinctly puts it, 'a state response to conduct does not qualify as punitive unless it is designed to censure and to stigmatise'.[48]

Although Husak and Feinberg are right to hold that what really distinguishes criminal punishment (and therefore criminalisation from other forms of social regulation) is the *public* and *purposeful* expression of censure, the importance of hard treatment should not be underestimated. In fact, from a retributivist perspective, the imposition of hard treatment is inextricably linked with the censuring function of the criminal law since the level of hard treatment imposed should be a further testament of the blameworthiness of the wrong committed by the offender. Suppose, for instance, that Jonathan has been convicted

since their implementation cannot only result in the indirect criminalisation of otherwise lawful behaviour, but they do so in the absence of most of the enhanced procedural protections afforded to those facing criminal prosecution. See Husak, 'Limitations on Criminalisation and the General Part of Criminal Law' (n 36) 23–24 and 27.

[41] J Feinberg, 'The Expressive Function of Punishment' (1965) 49 *The Monist* 397, 400; Husak, *Overcriminalisation* (n 27) 57; H Packer, *The Limits of the Criminal Sanction* (Stanford, CA, Stanford University Press, 1968) 262.

[42] Feinberg, 'The Expressive Function of Punishment' (n 41) 400.

[43] ibid 398.

[44] ibid.

[45] ibid 402–03.

[46] ibid 399.

[47] ibid 400.

[48] D Husak, 'Why Criminal Law: A Question of Content?' (2008) 2 *Criminal Law and Philosophy* 99, 104.

of burglary, which carries a maximum sentence of 14 years' imprisonment, whereas Lucy has been convicted of aggravated burglary, which carries a life sentence, because she was carrying a firearm with her when she committed the offence.[49] Based on the label attached to each offence, it is evident that the legislature regards aggravated burglary a more serious offence than burglary. In order to make sure that this message is conveyed to members of the public, though, the legislature decided to set a higher maximum sentence for aggravated burglary. Regardless of the label attached to each offence, if (all things being equal) Jonathan and Lucy receive the exact same sentence for their conduct, then members of the public might not be able to fully comprehend the message conveyed by the legislature, that is that those who commit aggravated burglary are more blameworthy than those who commit burglary.

Criminal punishment therefore does not only interfere with the perpetrator's liberty, but it also labels him as a serious wrongdoer. It conveys a message to both the offender and the rest of the community that the behaviour in question constitutes a serious moral wrong which is worthy of society's reprobation. Seen in this way, criminalisation symbolises society's 'formal and solemn pronouncement of the moral condemnation' against the kinds of behaviour proscribed.[50] Through criminalisation, a dialogue is generated between the community and individual citizens where the former does not only seek to deter the latter from offending, but also aims to inform them about the principles by which they should abide.[51] Through this dialogue, as members of the community we are not only provided with 'prudential reasons for desistence', but we are also provided with a moral one.[52] The criminal law assumes the role of an educator who seeks to communicate to its subjects the core principles that underpin our society.[53] Through criminalisation, members of the public are not simply told that they need to refrain from behaving in a certain manner because they will face certain unpleasant consequences, such as imprisonment, but they are *reminded* and asked to embrace the values that hold the polity together. They are asked to see this as their law.[54] They are treated as rationale agents who have the required capacity to understand the moral rather than just the prudential reasons, that is the infliction of hard treatment, for not committing an offence. Criminalisation therefore symbolises the moral denunciation of society towards both the offender and the wrong committed.[55]

[49] Theft Act 1968, ss 9 and 10 respectively.

[50] H Hart, 'The Aims of the Criminal Law' (1958) 23 *Law & Contemporary Problems* 401, 405.

[51] A Duff, *Punishment, Communication, and Community* (Oxford, Oxford University Press, 2001) ch 3.

[52] von Hirsch (n 34) 12.

[53] J Coffee, 'Does "Unlawful" Mean "Criminal"? Reflections on the Disappearing Tort/Crime Distinction in American Law' (1991) 71 *Boston University Law Review* 193, 194.

[54] Duff, *The Realm of Criminal Law* (n 16) 72.

[55] von Hirsch (n 34) 9.

It would be instructive here to examine in more detail how this communicative and educational function of the criminal law operates in practice. One of the most illustrative examples of this, is the various hate crime laws introduced in many Western jurisdictions since the second half of the twentieth century[56] to deal with the prevalence and the unique damage caused to society's social fabric by identity-based criminality.[57] As far as England and Wales is concerned, for example, 11 racially or religiously aggravated offences (RRAOs) were created under sections 29–32 of the Crime and Disorder Act 1998 Act.[58] In order to establish liability for an RRAO, the prosecution must prove to the criminal standard of proof that: (i) the defendant has committed one of the base offences included in sections 29–32, such as the infliction of grievous bodily harm contrary to section 20 of the Offences Against the Person Act 1861, and; (ii) that the offence was either motivated (wholly or partly) by racial or religious hostility[59] or that the defendant demonstrated 'at the time of committing the offence, or immediately before or after doing so … towards the victim of the offence hostility based on the victim's membership or presumed membership of a racial or religious group'.[60] The creation of these bespoke offences by the legislature sends an unequivocal message to society that identity-based criminality is not only *qualitatively* different from parallel crimes,[61] but it is behaviour that undermines some of the core values that hold our society together.[62] Compare, for example, an assault which is aggravated by religious hostility under section 29 of the 1998 Act and common assault. The criminal law draws a distinction between the two offences as a means of emphasising society's reprobation towards crimes motivated by religious hatred or prejudice. This is a direct message to the public that our society will not tolerate certain forms of hostility against a group of

[56] For a detailed analysis of the hate crime legal framework adopted in many Western jurisdictions, such as Canada, Scotland and New Zealand, see J Chalmers and F Leverick, *A Comparative Analysis of Hate Crime Legislation: A Report to the Hate Crime Legislation Review* (University of Glasgow, 2017), available at: consult.gov.scot/hate-crime/independent-review-of-hate-crime-legislation/supporting_documents/495517_APPENDIX%20%20ACADEMIC%20REPORT.pdf.

[57] Commission for Countering Extremism, *COVID-19: How Hateful Extremists are Exploiting the Pandemic* (2020) 3, available at: assets.publishing.service.gov.uk/government/uploads/system/uploads/attachment_data/file/898925/CCE_Briefing_Note_001.pdf; College of Policing, *Hate Crime Operational Guidance: Consultation* (2019) para 11.3; Lord Bracadale, *Independent Review of Hate Crime Legislation in Scotland: Final Report* (Justice Directorate, 2018) para 5.26.

[58] The English and Welsh criminal law also includes a number of offences which cover the stirring up of hatred (Public Order Act 1986, Parts 3 and 3A) as well as a football-specific offence relating to 'racialist chanting' (Football (Offences) Act 1991, s 3). Moreover, under s 66 of the Sentencing Act 2020 the sentencing court is able to impose a sentence uplift if the offence was motivated by hostility or the offender demonstrated 'at the time of committing the offence, or immediately before or after doing so' hostility based on the victim's actual or presumed race, religion, sexual orientation, disability, or transgender identity. See further, Demetriou and Partington (n 19).

[59] Crime and Disorder Act 1998, s 28(1)(b).

[60] ibid s 28(1)(a).

[61] By parallel crimes I mean offences that lie outside the scope of the hate crime laws.

[62] Demetriou and Partington (n 19).

individuals due to their religious and/or ethnic background since conduct of this nature 'undermine[s] fundamental values of tolerance, acceptance and equality'.[63] One of the primary objectives of the criminal law, therefore, is to educate members of the public about society's core values and principles. To this end, the criminal law is used as a means of maintaining certain positive norms while diluting existing (negative) attitudes, such as certain forms of identity-based prejudice.[64] As Robinson points out, the criminal law is the only set of legal rules in a diverse contemporary liberal society which 'transcends cultural and ethnic differences' because it focuses on society's core values.[65]

In order for society to fully comprehend the moral messages conveyed through criminalisation, however, it is essential for the criminal law to remain distinct from other forms of regulation. As Husak puts it, 'the criminal law is and ought to be *different* – importantly dissimilar from other kinds of law'.[66] To hold otherwise is to blur the normative distinction between the criminal law and other forms of social control.[67] If this normative distinction is blurred, those to whom 'the criminal law is directed' might not be able to comprehend the moral wrongfulness of certain kinds of behaviour.[68] Members of the public will not be able to understand that there are both moral and prudential reasons for not violating criminal law's commands.[69] To take the example of hate crime laws, if the normative distinction between the criminal law and other forms of social regulation collapses, members of the public might not be able to fully understand that identity-based criminality is qualitatively different from parallel crimes because the defendant's behaviour undermines the victim's status as an equal member of the polity.[70] As explained above, the criminal law should not be seen as a mere set of prohibitions, but as an interconnected corpus of laws that aims to prevent certain undesirable events while educating/reminding members of the public about the values that underpin society. Why is it though so important for members of the public to understand and embrace the

[63] M Walters, 'Conceptualizing "Hostility" for Hate Crime Law: Minding "the Minuatiae" when Interpreting Section 28(1)(a) of the Crime and Disorder Act 1998' (2014) 34 *Oxford Journal of Legal Studies* 47, 53.

[64] P Robinson, 'The Criminal–Civil Distinction and the Utility of Desert' (1996) 76 *Boston University Law Review* 201, 212.

[65] ibid 212.

[66] Husak, 'The Criminal Law as Last Resort' (n 38) 211.

[67] J Coffee, 'Paradigms Lost: The Blurring of the Criminal and Civil Law Models. And what Can be Done about It' (1992) 101 *Yale Law Journal* 1875, 1875–76.

[68] Based on the current state of the criminal law though, not every criminal prohibition addresses the entire population. In fact, according to Chalmers and Leverick, many offences, especially regulatory ones, are directed only at specific groups of people, such as those responsible for the manufacturing of certain goods. See J Chalmers and F Leverick, 'Quantifying Criminalisation' in A Duff et al (eds), *Criminalization: The Political Morality of the Criminal Law* (Oxford, Oxford University Press, 2014) 74–75.

[69] von Hirsch (n 34) 12.

[70] Demetriou and Partington (n 19).

underlying rationale for the criminalisation of the behaviour at hand? Arguably, the prospect of criminal punishment alone should be a sufficient deterrent for would-be offenders. Although this sounds plausible, evidence suggests that what really deters individuals from committing a crime is not the gravity of the sanction available for that particular offence, but the likelihood of detection and prosecution.[71] Consequently, the prospect of punishment has little if any impact on potential offenders.[72] Thus, regardless of how severe the maximum sanction for a particular offence is, if a potential offender believes that the possibility of detection and prosecution is minimal, then he is unlikely to refrain from offending simply because the wrong he is about to commit constitutes a criminal offence.[73] If, however, members of the public understand and embrace the moral foundations of the offence at hand, then it is more likely for them to 'voluntarily assume the obligation to follow' the law regardless of how likely it is for them to be apprehended and punished for their conduct.[74] It is due to this educative function of criminalisation that this normative distinction between the criminal law and other forms of social regulation must be maintained. As I will argue below, one of the reasons why indirect criminalisation matters is because it undermines this normative distinction.

Criminalisation of course does not only communicate society's censure towards particular kinds of behaviour, but it also expresses the community's reprobation towards those who offend. Society's condemnation towards the perpetrator is articulated through criminal conviction. To be convicted for an offence is to be *publicly condemned* for violating society's core values. It is for this reason that a criminal conviction can stigmatise offenders and can have a devastating effect on their future lives.[75] If, for example, the perpetrator is found guilty of an offence which can lead to the imposition of a custodial sentence, then this offence will be registered on the perpetrator's record.[76] This can have a detrimental impact on the perpetrator's future prospects for employment since he can be automatically disqualified from certain professional bodies and from holding public office.[77] Even after the perpetrator has served any direct criminal

[71] See J Halliday et al, *Making Punishments Work: Report of a Review of the Sentencing Framework for England and Wales* (London, Home Office, 2001) 9; W Chambliss, 'The Deterrent Influence of Punishment' in S Grupp (ed), *Theories of Punishment* (Bloomington, IND, Indiana University Press, 1971) 202.

[72] A Doob and C Webster, 'Sentence Severity and Crime: Accepting the Null Hypothesis' (2003) 36 *Crime and Justice* 143, 144.

[73] ibid 144.

[74] T Tyler, *Why People Obey the Law* (Princeton, NJ, Princeton University Press, 2006) 3.

[75] A Ashworth, 'Four Threats to the Presumption of Innocence' (2006) 123 *South African Law Journal* 63, 72.

[76] National Police Records (Recordable Offences) Regulations 2000/1139, reg 3(1)(a).

[77] eg, under s 66(3)(c) of the Police Reform and Social Responsibility Act 2011 someone will automatically be disqualified from running as a candidate to become a Police and Crime Commissioner if they have been convicted of a recordable offence. See, eg, Owen Bennett, 'UKIP's Steven Woolfe Admits he Broke Electoral Rules by Failing to Reveal Drink-Drive Conviction' (*Huffington Post*,

sentence imposed on him as a result of his past wrongdoings, the label of 'offender' may continue to have an adverse impact on his future. This is particularly the case when the offender has committed a very serious offence and/or an offence that carries with it negative connotations. A particularly apposite and illustrative example is conviction for an RRAO, which essentially labels the offender as a hater, something that can have a very stigmatising effect on him.[78] It is for this reason that criminalisation (and therefore the imposition of criminal punishment) should be reserved for serious wrongs that undermine society's core values and for those who are truly blameworthy.[79]

The main purpose of the above analysis was to highlight the unique and at the same time coercive nature of criminalisation. In particular, it was argued that what distinguishes criminalisation from other methods of social regulation is the imposition of punishment. In contrast to penalties, punishment has a dual aspect, that is it imposes hard treatment and *purposefully* communicates censure. It is because of criminal punishment's coercive nature that enhanced procedural protections are afforded to those facing criminal prosecution.[80] Under Article 6 the European Convention on Human Rights (ECHR), for example, a number of procedural and evidential protections/rights are provided to those who are prosecuted for the commission of a criminal offence as a means of ensuring that they receive a fair trial.[81] The most important of these include: Article 6(1) ECHR, which provides that 'in the determination of [someone's] civil rights and obligations or of any criminal charge against him, everyone is entitled to a fair and public hearing'; Article 6(2) ECHR, which provides that every individual 'charged with a criminal offence shall be presumed innocent

1 August, 2016), available at: www.huffingtonpost.co.uk/entry/ukip-steven-woolfe-drink-driving_uk_579f5db3e4b07cb01dd020b3.

78 This is further evidenced by a rich body of empirical evidence which suggests that judges and jurors are extremely reluctant to convict a defendant of an RRAO if his conduct was not 'deeply racial and set out to upset' the victim(s). This clearly suggests that the trier of fact acknowledges the potential ramifications that a conviction for an RRAO will have on the accused. See E Burney and G Rose, *Racist Offences – How is the Law Working? The Implementation of the Legislation on Racially Aggravated Offences in the Crime and Disorder Act 1998* (Home Office, 2002) 21; K Goodall, 'Incitement to Religious Hatred: All Talk and No Substance?' (2007) 70 *Modern Law Review* 89, 104; M Walters et al, 'Hate Crime and the "Justice Gap": The Case for Law Reform' (2018) 12 *Criminal Law Review* 961, 968 and 976.

79 The Law Commission, for instance, has been very critical of the increased use of the criminal law for regulatory objectives noting that given the stigma attached to a criminal conviction, criminalisation should only focus on 'seriously reprehensible conduct'. See Law Commission, *Criminal Liability in Regulatory Contexts: A Consultation Paper* (Consultation Paper No 195, 2010) para 1.28–1.29.

80 J Henry and C King, 'Expediency, Legitimacy, and the Rule of Law: A Systems Perspective on Civil/Criminal Procedural Hybrids' (2017) 11 *Criminal Law and Philosophy* 733, 733.

81 As a line of cases that reached the ECtHR suggests, such as *Murray v UK* [1996] 22 EHRR 29, in determining whether the defendant has received a fair trial, courts will 'evaluate the overall fairness of the criminal proceedings'. Hence, even if the defendant was denied one of the minimum rights provided by under Art 6(3) ECHR, the court might still conclude that he has received a fair trial. See *Ibrahim and others v UK* (2016) (Applications nos 50541/08, 50571/08, 50573/08 and 40351/09) [210].

until proven guilty according to law'; and Article 6(3) ECHR, which provides, inter alia, that a defendant should be allowed to examine all evidence against him including any witnesses who wish to testify.[82] The importance of these enhanced procedural protections is threefold.

First, the fact that a number of additional protections are provided for those facing the prospect of criminal punishment is an unequivocal acknowledgement by the Council of Europe (and the British Parliament which ratified most of the Convention's provisions into domestic legislation through the enactment of the Human Rights Act 1998) of what is at stake for the accused.[83] Second, these additional protections can act as a safety net against the arbitrary use of the criminal law by the state. As Sidhu explains,

> '[t]he Article 6 catalogue of rights was not devised in a vacuum, but was informed by the past … [they] emerged and endured through different stages of procedural history because of their contribution to juridical activity perceived at the time as well-founded and fair'.[84]

For example, the defendant's ability to examine and challenge all evidence against him can act as a safety valve for the prevention of wrongful convictions since an obligation is imposed on the state to make full disclosure of any material that might assist the defence preparing their case.[85] This also includes material that can undermine the prosecution's case.

Third (and most importantly for our purposes), these enhanced procedural protections can represent a double-edged sword since they can encourage what Duff calls subversions to the criminal law.[86] That is, when supposedly non-criminal measures, such as the injunction, are used to deal with behaviour that falls within the ambit of the criminal law, such as criminal damage. Suppose, for example, that a number of bus stops have been vandalised in the city centre during the last couple of weeks. Andrew notified the police that the person who vandalised the bus stops is Stacey, but he is unwilling to give a statement. Instead of charging Stacey with criminal damage, the police decide

[82] It is worth noting that while Art 6(1) ECHR applies both to criminal and civil proceedings, Articles 6(2) and 6(3) apply only to criminal proceedings. See, further, B Rainey et al, *The European Convention on Human Rights*, 7th edn (Oxford, Oxford University Press, 2017) ch 12.

[83] In fact, various regional and international treaties, such as the United Nations Universal Declaration of Human Rights and the Charter of Fundamental Rights of the European Union, as well as the constitution of many jurisdictions (see, eg, the Fifth, Sixth and Eighth Amendments of the US Constitution) explicitly afford a number of enhanced procedural protections to those facing criminal prosecution. For a more detailed analysis of the enhanced procedural protections afforded by the US Constitution see C Steiker, 'Punishment and Procedure: Punishment Theory and the Criminal–Civil Procedural Divide' (1997) 26 *Annual Review of Criminal Procedure* 775.

[84] O Sidhu, *The Concept of Equality of Arms in Criminal Proceedings under Article 6 of the European Convention on Human Rights* (Cambridge, Intersentia, 2017) ch 1.

[85] Criminal Procedure and Investigations Act 1996, s 3.

[86] A Duff, 'Perversions and Subversions of Criminal Law' in A Duff et al (eds), *The Boundaries of the Criminal Law* (Oxford, Oxford University Press, 2010) 92.

that it would be more expedient to apply to court for the issue of an injunction against her under Part 1 of the 2014 Act. As mentioned above, the enhanced procedural protections provided under Article 6(2) and (3) are only available to those facing criminal prosecution and therefore Stacey will not be afforded these additional protections. The label attached to each legal rule is therefore of paramount significance since it will determine the level of protection that should be afforded to the alleged perpetrator. Simply put, those charged with a criminal offence will be afforded these additional protections in acknowledgement of what is at stake for them, but this is not the case for those, such as Stacey, who face civil proceedings. The fact that civil preventive measures are not subjected to these enhanced procedural protections means that they often provide law enforcement agents with a more expedient response to criminality. Hence, although the enhanced procedural protections afforded to those facing criminal prosecution can balance the scales of justice between the state with its unlimited resources and the accused acting as a safety net for the prevention of wrongful convictions, they can at the same time encourage subversions to the criminal law.[87] What is of particular concern for the purposes of this study is the possibility that these subversions to the criminal law also result in the indirect criminalisation of the behaviour at hand.[88]

## 2.4. FURTHER REFLECTIONS ON INDIRECT CRIMINALISATION AND PUNISHMENT

The main objective of the above analysis was to highlight the unique, albeit coercive nature of criminalisation. This was done to point out some of the main normative challenges posed by indirect criminalisation. In particular, it was argued that one of the key functions of the criminal law is to educate members of the polity about the core values that hold society together. In order for this to be achieved though, it is imperative for the criminal law to remain distinct from other types of social regulation. Failure to do so, can dilute the communicative/educative function of the criminal law. Indirect criminalisation poses a threat to the criminal law's distinctiveness because it allows for the imposition of criminal punishment through the implementation of supposedly non-criminal interventions. If punishment is imposed through non-criminal rules, then members of the public might not be able to fully comprehend the moral blameworthiness of

[87] L Zedner, 'Penal Subversions: When is a Punishment not Punishment, Who Decides and on What Grounds?' (2016) 20 *Theoretical Criminology* 3, 8; D Dripps, 'The Exclusivity of the Criminal Law: Toward a Regulatory Model of, or Pathological Perspective on, the Civil–Criminal Distinction' (1996) 7 *Journal of Contemporary Legal Issues* 199, 207.

[88] I will discuss further the use of non-criminal interventions, such as the injunction, to deal with behaviour that already falls within the scope of the criminal law in ch 7 where I engage in more detail with the findings of the empirical study.

those found guilty of an offence.[89] The importance of this lies in the fact that members of the public will only be provided with prudential reasons not to commit crimes and it is therefore less likely for them to 'voluntarily assume the obligation to follow' the criminal law.[90]

Another important normative challenge posed by indirect criminalisation relates to punishment's coercive nature. In particular, due to the fact that criminalisation is the most coercive means of social regulation, a number of enhanced procedural protections are afforded to those facing criminal prosecution. Indirect criminalisation matters because it allows for the imposition of criminal punishment in the absence of (or at least some of) those additional protections.[91] These are two of the main reasons why I argue that indirect criminalisation *cannot* be warranted notwithstanding the need to prevent certain kinds of undesirable conduct. And it is for these reasons that it is essential to investigate further whether certain (supposedly) non-criminal interventions that are susceptible to indirect criminalisation, such as the injunction, operate as de facto criminal rules. If this is indeed the case, I argue that those subjected to these measures should be afforded the same level of protection as those facing criminal prosecution.[92] Moreover, I contend that these non-criminal measures should be subjected to the same theoretical critique and principles that are so important to restrict criminal rules and punishment.

These principles include, but are not limited to, the enhanced procedural protections afforded to those facing criminal prosecution. One of the basic principles underpinning the criminal law, for instance, is that no one should be punished if his behaviour was not at the time a criminal offence. That is the principle against retroactive criminalisation. This principle is enshrined in Article 7(1) ECHR and its aim is not simply to prevent the introduction of criminal rules which will have a retrospective effect, but also to ensure that the application of existing rules by courts does not result in the imposition of punishment for conduct which at the time was not proscribed by the criminal

[89] As Logan rightly points out, criminal law's educative function can also be undermined through the criminalisation of 'behaviors that otherwise might be deemed innocuous, or worthy of less forceful condemnation, threaten[ing] trivialization of the "stigma" associated with the criminal law and its sanctions'. See, W Logan, 'The Shadow Criminal Law of Municipal Governance' (2001) 62 *Ohio State Law Journal* 1409, 1448.

[90] Tyler (n 74) 3.

[91] In fact, as seen earlier, the presence of these enhanced procedural protections was one of the main reasons for the introduction of the ASBO. See ch 1, section 1.4.1.

[92] This is not to suggest that if it is concluded that a non-criminal intervention is in fact merely preventive that it should not be subjected to any limiting principles at all. As Ashworth and Zedner rightly point out, even if civil preventive measures do not reach the threshold required to be regarded as punitive interventions, they can still result in the imposition of severe restrictions on the liberty of those against whom they are issued. Hence, if individual liberty and autonomy are to remain the cornerstones of our society (along with security), it is imperative for limits to be imposed on the reach of the preventive state. See A Ashworth and L Zedner, *Preventive Justice* (Oxford, Oxford University Press, 2014) 11.

law.[93] The importance of this principle lies in the need to ensure that 'a person ought not to be punished in the name of a political community unless it can confidently be said that the community officially regards his conduct as warranting the criminal punishment at issue'.[94] If members of the polity are to embrace the moral message conveyed through criminalisation, they should be provided with a clear warning about the kinds of behaviour that are likely to fall within the scope of the criminal law. Moreover, given the potential ramifications of a criminal conviction, the criminal law should allow people to decide for themselves whether they want to undermine society's core values and be labelled as a serious moral wrongdoer. As Robinson puts it, providing a 'fair notice, [is] a quality of special importance in criminal law, where a defendant's life and liberty are often at stake'.[95] The law should let people know in advance that certain wrongs are criminal and those who are convicted of these wrongs will be publicly condemned. This will provide people with an opportunity to plan their future behaviour accordingly without being unsure as to whether they might be in breach of a criminal rule.[96] This requires criminal rules to be easily accessible by the public, with clear and identifiable limits ensuring that a 'fair warning' is given to people about the kinds of behaviour criminalised.[97] That said, a certain degree of flexibility is necessary in order to ensure that the criminal law 'keep[s] pace with changing circumstances'.[98]

Based on the above analysis of the principle against retroactive criminalisation, what can be problematic about the injunction's first limb is that its implementation can result in the criminalisation of behaviour which at the time was not proscribed under the criminal law. Apart from the fact that punishment can be imposed in the absence of the enhanced procedural protections, what is also problematic about this is that certain kinds of behaviour have been criminalised without informing the rest of the polity that the perpetrators' conduct was in fact treated as a crime.[99] Thus, no 'fair warning' is given to the rest of the

[93] *Achour v France* (2007) 45 EHRR 9.

[94] P Westen, 'Two Rules of Legality in Criminal Law' (2007) 26 *Law and Philosophy* 229, 230.

[95] P Robinson, 'Fair Notice and Fair Adjudication: Two Kinds of Legality' (2005) 154 *University of Pennsylvania Law Review* 335, 340.

[96] J Gardner, 'Introduction' in HLA Hart, *Punishment and Responsibility*, 2nd edn (Oxford, Oxford University Press, 2008) xxxvi.

[97] Robinson, 'Fair Notice and Fair Adjudication (n 95) 340.

[98] *Kokkinakis v Greece* (1994) 17 EHRR 397, para 40.

[99] Apart from the 'fair labelling' concerns that can be raised here, attention should also be paid to the fact that the law does not apply equally to all members of the polity. Simply put, what might constitute a breach of an injunction by one person, such as visiting a particular shopping centre, can be totally permissible for others. According to Hendry, what is problematic about this discrepancy is that a 'core element of the rule of law is that it does not permit fundamental differentiations in status amongst members of the relevant polity. Indeed, the rule of law can be understood as "equality before the law"'. Although Hendry is critical here of the potential implementation of the Knife Crime Prevention Orders, her argument is readily applicable in the context of the Part 1 injunction (and other civil preventive measures, such as the gang injunctions) as well since both instruments allow for the formulation of bespoke prohibitions that apply only to the person against whom these measures are used. See J Hendry, '"The Usual Suspects": Knife Crime Prevention Orders and the "Difficult" Regulatory Subject' (2022) 62 *British Journal of Criminology* 378, 386.

polity as to which kinds of conduct can be regarded as behaviour that is likely to cause 'harassment, alarm or distress' or that it is capable of causing 'nuisance and annoyance' and as to the possibility that these might result in the indirect imposition of criminal punishment.[100] Moreover, concerns can be raised about the delegation of law-making powers to courts, local enforcement agents, non-governmental organisations[101] and other unelected officials that are tasked with the implementation of the injunction at a local level and how this undermines the separation of power between the legislative and the judicial branch of the state. If there is evidence to suggest, for instance, that indeed the injunction has been operating as a de facto criminal rule, then this delegation of law-making powers will have 'profound implications, not least for [the] democratic values' upon which our society is founded.[102] Given criminalisation's coercive nature, it should be for the legislature (following public deliberation about the proper limits of the punitive state) to decide which kinds of behaviour (and under what circumstances) warrant the imposition of punishment. As seen earlier, the 2014 Act provides a significant magnitude of discretion to courts and local enforcement agents not only to determine the scope of the law in this area, but also to decide what restrictions should be imposed on the liberty of those who behave in an anti-social manner.[103] It was the combination of this significant magnitude of discretion afforded to courts and local enforcement agents, and the potential punitive nature of the restrictions imposed on the liberty of those subjected to these measures, that provided the impetus for this study.[104]

The purpose of the above discussion was to re-emphasise the need for a holistic examination and analysis of the implementation of the injunction at a local level by engaging with some of the main normative challenges posed by indirect criminalisation. In particular, it was argued that if there is empirical evidence to suggest that the injunction has been operating as a de facto criminal rule, it must then be subjected to the same scrutiny as criminal rules. As part of our theoretical evaluation, for instance, we need to investigate the clarity of the relevant legislation and whether a 'fair warning' has been given to the community about the behaviour criminalised. Based on our earlier theoretical analysis of the law relating to ASB, it seems extremely difficult for the relevant statutory provisions to survive close scrutiny primarily due to their ambiguous scope.[105] This reinforces the need to examine empirically the implementation of the injunction's first limb and investigate whether this has in fact resulted in the *indirect* criminalisation of certain kinds of behaviour.

[100] The force of this argument can be less powerful though when someone breaches the injunction imposed on them since they are already aware of the kinds of behaviour that can be regarded as anti-social.

[101] Non-governmental organisations, such as private housing providers, can apply for the issue of an injunction under s 5(1) of the 2014 Act.

[102] L Zedner, *Security* (Abingdon, Routledge, 2009) 30; Ramsay (n 2) 223–24.

[103] See ch 1, section 1.5.

[104] ibid.

[105] See ch 1, section 1.4.3.

## 2.5. CONCLUSION

As with every political decision, criminalisation is a complex process which involves many conflicting interests and considerations.[106] One of the most important factors is the influence exerted by various pressure groups and strong public opinion regarding criminalisation.[107] This is due to the fact that members of the Parliament are 'ultimately accountable to the populace and are therefore liable to be influenced by what they think are prevailing opinions'.[108] Public deliberation regarding criminalisation and any other important decision that can influence society as a whole is an inherent characteristic of a democratic society.[109] The impact of this public deliberation, however, must be approached with caution. As Garland contends, politicians tend to calculate the potential appeal of their actions before planning their strategies.[110] As far as penal policy is concerned, such a tendency can be particularly problematic since in an attempt to avoid any 'signs of weaknesses' politicians tend to adopt more punitive measures, such as harsher sentences, which can sometimes contradict penal expertise.[111] Similarly, politicians' tendency of 'tapping into and using for their own purposes, what they believe to be the public's generally punitive stance' often leads to the adoption of a more punitive approach towards criminality.[112] It is due to the effects of penal populism that the state is unable 'to create and maintain rational criminal law policy'.[113]

What is of particular concern, though, for the purposes of this study is the proliferation in the last two decades of supposedly non-punitive interventions in the name of public protection.[114] What is problematic about these supposedly civil interventions is that they are susceptible to indirect criminalisation. The importance of this lies primarily in the coercive nature of criminalisation and

[106] W Stuntz, 'The Pathological Politics of Criminal Law' (2001–02) 100 *Michigan Law Review* 505, 523; G Stoker, *Why Politics Matters: Making Democracy Work* (London, Palgrave, 2006) 2.

[107] N Lacey, 'Criminalization as Regulation: The Role of Criminal Law' in C Parker et al (eds), *Regulating Law* (Oxford, Oxford University Press, 2004) 147.

[108] C Wells and O Quick, *Reconstructing Criminal Law*, 4th edn (Cambridge, Cambridge University Press, 2010) 28.

[109] Stoker (n 106) 2.

[110] D Garland, *The Culture of Control: Crime and Social Order in Contemporary Society* (Chicago, IL, University of Chicago Press 2001) 111–12.

[111] ibid 111; D Brown, 'Democracy and Decriminalization' (2007–08) 86 *Texas Law Review* 223, 224. For more in-depth analysis of this phenomenon, see J Pratt, *Penal Populism* (Abingdon, Routledge 2007).

[112] A Bottoms, 'The Philosophy and Politics of Punishment and Sentencing' in C Clarkson and R Morgan (eds), *The Politics of Sentencing Reform* (Oxford, Oxford University Press, 1995) 40.

[113] Brown (n 111) 223.

[114] According to Duggan and Heap, this is particularly the case with ASB policy. Based on their account, the need to offer greater protection to victims was used by the government as a Trojan Horse for the adoption of a more punitive stance towards ASB. See M Duggan and V Heap, *Administrating Victimisation: The Politics of Anti-Social Behaviour and Hate Crime Policy* (Basingstoke, Palgrave Macmillan, 2014) 110.

the need for the state to offer additional protections to those facing the prospect of criminal punishment akin to those afforded to those facing criminal prosecution. To this end, a mechanism is needed through which instances of indirect criminalisation can be identified and addressed. Thus, in chapter three I propose a working definition of criminalisation that will enable courts and those tasked with the implementation of measures susceptible to indirect criminalisation to determine whether the legal instrument at hand should be regarded as criminal regardless of the label attached to it by the legislature.[115]

[115] See ch 3, section 3.2.

# 3

# *Conceptualising Criminalisation*

## 3.1. INTRODUCTION

EXAMINING WHETHER THE implementation of a given rule constitutes a form of criminalisation presupposes a clear understanding of what it is to criminalise. This could be reduced to a simple examination of how the rule in question was classified by the legislature, that is as either criminal or non-criminal. On this view, to criminalise a particular kind of conduct is to label it as a criminal wrong, that is direct criminalisation. Although this rationale appears to be theoretically plausible, it fails to take into consideration the possibility of *indirect* criminalisation. It fails to acknowledge that the implementation of certain supposedly non-punitive interventions, such as the successor of the Anti-social Behaviour Order (ASBO), can result in the imposition of sanctions that constitute a form of criminal punishment. Failure to do so matters because, as we saw in chapter two, criminalisation is the most coercive means of social regulation. And it is for this reason that additional protections are offered to those facing the prospect of criminal punishment. Indirect criminalisation is morally problematic because it *circumvents* many of these enhanced procedural protections.

Having analysed in chapter two the main normative challenges posed by indirect criminalisation, this chapter proceeds by formulating a single viable test through which instances of indirect criminalisation can be identified. Before doing so, I engage with the way criminalisation has been conceptualised in academic discourse and how courts dealt with measures susceptible to indirect criminalisation. In particular, I scrutinise the anti-subversion doctrine formulated by the European Court of Human Rights (ECtHR) in *Engel v Netherlands*[1] and examine whether this can be utilised to determine whether the Part 1 injunction of the Anti-social Behaviour, Crime and Policing Act 2014 has been operating as a de facto criminal measure. As I argue later, although the way criminalisation has been conceptualised in academic discourse and by courts provides us with a good starting point, a more flexible definition of criminalisation is needed that will truly enable us to really look beyond the label attached by the legislature,

[1] *Engel v Netherlands* (1979–80) 1 EHRR 647.

examining the true nature of the measure at hand. The chapter then proceeds by formulating a working definition of criminalisation which can assist us in identifying instances of indirect criminalisation. The working definition formulated below does not constitute a complete departure from the accounts of criminalisation that will be examined earlier in this chapter. Rather, it utilises these accounts and seeks to overcome some of the concerns and problems encountered by them. The chapter concludes by offering an evaluation of the working definition of criminalisation formulated by scrutinising its main limitations and advantages. It is worth reiterating that it is not my intention to examine on what basis the introduction of the injunction or other civil preventive measures can be justified. This task is beyond the scope of this study. Instead, my main objective is to examine empirically whether the implementation of the injunction resulted in the indirect criminalisation of certain kinds of anti-social behaviour (ASB). To do this though, I first need to engage with a central question within criminal law theory: what is to criminalise? This is precisely what this chapter does.

## 3.2. CONCEPTUALISING CRIMINALISATION: THE EXISTING APPROACHES

In order to identify (and then possibly address) instances of indirect criminalisation, it is essential to first determine under what circumstances a legal rule should be regarded as criminal. The importance of this task lies in the very nature of indirect criminalisation. In contrast to direct criminalisation, indirect criminalisation formally lies outside the contours of the criminal law. Our examination, therefore, should also be extended to rules that are labelled as non-criminal but are susceptible to indirect criminalisation. To achieve this, a working definition of criminalisation is needed through which we will be able to look beyond the official classification of legal rules and examine whether (based on their implementation) they should be regarded as criminal or non-criminal.

At first sight, the need to formulate a new working definition of criminalisation can be questioned for two reasons. First, there is already a well-established understanding of criminalisation in academic discourse.[2] Many prominent criminal law theorists agree that what really distinguishes criminalisation from other forms of regulation is the imposition of criminal punishment. These theorists have also provided a very compelling account of criminal punishment. Second, as mentioned before, courts have already dealt with legal rules which were labelled as non-criminal and were susceptible to indirect criminalisation. In *McCann*,[3] for instance, the House of Lords scrutinised the ASBO's first limb and concluded that it should be regarded as a civil rather than a punitive order.[4]

[2] See ch 2, section 2.3.
[3] *R (on the application of McCann) v Manchester Crown Court* [2002] UKHL 39.
[4] See ch 1, section 1.4.1.

Thus, courts have already acknowledged the possibility that the implementation of some non-criminal measures might result in the indirect imposition of punishment and have already formulated their own mechanisms through which instances of indirect criminalisation can be identified.

It is therefore important before elaborating further on the working definition of criminalisation formulated for the purposes of this study, to explain why a new test is needed bearing in mind the presence of these pre-existing accounts both in academic discourse and in case law. To this end, it is imperative to engage further with these pre-existing accounts and to explain why a new working definition of criminalisation is needed. It is worth reiterating that the working definition of criminalisation formulated below is not a completely new account. Instead, it builds upon some of the most important challenges/problems faced by these pre-existing approaches. The main objective of this endeavour is to formulate and articulate a single viable test that can be applied to all non-criminal rules enabling courts, law enforcement agents and legal commentators to identify potential instances of indirect criminalisation.

### 3.2.1. The Current Academic Literature on the Criminal–Civil Divide

For many leading criminal law theorists, such as Feinberg,[5] Husak,[6] and Ashworth and Zedner,[7] criminalisation must be associated with punishment.[8] According to them, what distinguishes a criminal rule from other forms of regulation is that the former punishes those who offend whereas the latter imposes mere penalties. Based on their formulation of punishment, sanctions imposed by the criminal law comprise of two main features both of which must be present in order for them to amount to criminal punishment: (i) they must intentionally impose 'hard treatment'; and (ii) they must intentionally convey censure.

The pressing question for the purposes of this study is whether the above formulation of criminal punishment can assist us to examine the true nature of the injunction. Simply put, can the above-mentioned formulation of punishment assist us to identify when conduct has been criminalised indirectly? Although the working definition of criminalisation provided below is based on the view that the imposition of hard treatment and the purposeful communication of censure

[5] J Feinberg, 'The Expressive Function of Punishment' (1965) 49 *The Monist* 397, 400.

[6] D Husak, *Overcriminalization: The Limits of the Criminal Law* (New York, Oxford University Press, 2008) 57.

[7] A Ashworth and L Zedner, *Preventive Justice* (Oxford, Oxford University Press, 2014) 14.

[8] For an alternative approach see Tadro's account based on which the main objective of criminalisation should be deterrence rather than censuring. See V Tadros, 'Criminalization and Regulation' in A Duff et al (eds), *The Boundaries of the Criminal Law* (Oxford, Oxford University Press, 2010) 169.

are *necessary* conditions for a particular sanction to be regarded as a form of punishment, it should be acknowledged at the outset that it was not Feinberg and Husak's intention for their accounts to be used as a mechanism through which instances of indirect criminalisation can be identified. Instead, what Feinberg and Husak intended through the above-mentioned conceptualisation of criminalisation was to provide a normative account of punishment. Simply put, to explain what the difference is between criminal punishment and mere penalties. As we will see later though, it is possible that state censure can also be communicated without resorting to direct criminalisation. It is for this reason that I argue that a more fine-grained account of punishment is needed which will enable us to look beyond the label attached to each legal rule and examine whether its implementation constitutes a form of (indirect) criminalisation.

This need for a more fine-grained account of punishment is particularly evident by the introduction and rise of civil preventive measures, such as the injunction and the Terrorism Prevention and Investigation Measures (TPIMs), which undermine the normative distinction between the criminal law and other forms of social regulation. As Coffee explains, 'the line between civil and criminal penalties is rapidly collapsing' rendering the separation between the two almost impossible.[9] In a similar fashion, Mann contends that based on the current state of the criminal law there is no real difference between the nature of the sanctions imposed by it and the sanctions imposed through the civil law.[10] For him, this can be attributed to the introduction of 'punitive civil sanctions' which form the middle ground between the criminal and the civil law.[11] Punitive civil sanctions are, according to Mann, those penalties that are able to punish the perpetrator through the civil procedure.[12] As he explains, legal rules which allow for the imposition of punitive civil sanctions form a 'hybrid jurisprudence' which is very similar to the ASBO. What is of particular concern for our purposes about these measures that form the middle ground between the criminal and the civil law is that they fall in a legal lacuna with limited legal protection available to those subjected to these measures.

In order to illustrate further why a more fine-grained account of punishment specifically designed to identify instances of indirect criminalisation is needed, let us consider in more detail how the TPIMs operate. The close analysis of TPIMs will further highlight the need for an account of punishment that will enable us to look beyond the label attached to civil preventive measures by the legislature and examine their true nature. Section 3 of the Terrorism Prevention and Investigation Measures Act 2011 allows for the imposition of severe

[9] J Coffee, 'Paradigms Lost: The Blurring of the Criminal and Civil Law Models. And what Can be Done about It' (1992) 101 *Yale Law Journal* 1875, 1875.

[10] K Mann, 'Punitive Civil Sanctions: The Middleground between Criminal and Civil Law' (1991–92) 101 *Yale Law Journal* 1795, 1798.

[11] ibid 1797–98.

[12] ibid 1799.

restrictions on an individual's liberty if: (i) 'the Secretary of State is satisfied on the balance of probabilities [that is the civil standard of proof] that the individual is, or has been, involved in a terrorism-related activity'; (ii) this is a new terrorism-related activity that has not been the subject matter of a TPIMs notice before; and (iii) the Secretary of State 'reasonably considers that it is necessary' to impose certain restrictions on the individual's liberty in order to prevent or restrict his ability to engage in a terrorism-related activity. These restrictions can include, amongst others, overnight curfews, travel bans and restrictions on movement.[13] It should also be noted that breach of the restrictions imposed without reasonable excuse constitutes a criminal offence which carries a maximum penalty of five years' imprisonment and a fine.[14] If, however, the suspected terrorist was found in breach of a travel restriction imposed on him (in this case providing a reasonable excuse is not a defence),[15] then the maximum penalty is 10 years' imprisonment and a fine.[16] Moreover, it is worth mentioning that there is no need for the suspected terrorist to have been convicted of a criminal offence in order for such a notice to be issued against him. The Secretary of State need only be satisfied to the civil standard of proof that the individual at hand has been involved in a new terrorism-related activity. Although, therefore, the stated objective of these measures is the prevention of terrorism, it is evident from the above analysis of the law that a TPIMs notice allows for the imposition of severe restrictions on an individual's liberty (akin to those imposed following the conviction for a criminal offence) despite the supposedly civil nature of these measures. This is not to question the need for the state to prevent terrorism-related activities. As mentioned before, the liberal state has a duty to do so.[17] Rather, it is to highlight the need to look beyond the official label attached to TPIMs and examine whether they operate as de facto criminal rules. The importance of this is heightened by the fact that the potential restrictions that can be imposed through the issue of a TPIMs notice are imposed in the absence of many of the enhanced procedural protections afforded to those facing criminal prosecution.

In cases, for instance, where the threat of a terrorist attack is imminent, there is no need for the Secretary of State to apply to the High Court to receive permission to issue such a notice to someone.[18] Little if any safeguards are in place in this case to prevent the misuse of these measures. Even in cases where the court's permission is needed, it is evident from the wording of section 6(3) and 6(4) of the 2011 Act that the enhanced criminal procedural protections do not apply.

[13] The full list of restrictions that can be imposed on someone against whom a TPIM has been issued is provided in Schedule 1 of the 2011 Act.

[14] Terrorism Prevention and Investigation Measures Act 2011, s 23(3).

[15] ibid s 23(1A).

[16] ibid s 23(3A).

[17] See ch 1, section 1.1.

[18] Terrorism Prevention and Investigation Measures Act 2011, s 3(5)(a).

The court examining the issue of a TPIMs notice, for example, need only be satisfied that the Secretary of State's decision to use this measure is not 'obviously flawed' in order to grant permission for the imposition of these restrictions on a suspected terrorist.[19]

To illustrate further the need to look beyond the stated objective and the label attached to civil preventive measures, consider the following hypothetical scenario. Suppose that Sam, a suspected terrorist, has recently downloaded a document on his laptop titled 'How to make a bomb yourself'. Sam has been convicted under section 57(1) of the Terrorism Act 2000 for being in possession of 'an article in circumstances which give rise to a reasonable suspicion that his possession is for a purpose connected with the commission, preparation or instigation of an act of terrorism'. Sam received a custodial sentence of one year for this offence.[20] In contrast to Sam, Mary has not committed any offences yet, but there is intelligence to suggest that she has close ties with a number of suspected terrorists who are planning an imminent terrorist attack. The Secretary of State 'is satisfied, on the balance of probabilities' that Mary is also involved in this terrorist attack and decides that a TPIMs notice should be imposed on her in order to prevent the attack. Using the power provided to them under section 3(5)(b) of the 2011 Act, the Secretary of State issues a TPIMs notice against Mary without obtaining the High Court's permission due to the urgency of the matter. Through the TPIMs notice issued, an overnight home curfew is imposed on Mary.[21] Also, restrictions are imposed on Mary's ability to use electronic devices and she is not allowed to make any contact with a number of other people.[22] Although the TPIMs notice served on Mary lasts for one year, the Secretary of State may extend this for another year if they reasonably consider that this is necessary for the protection of the public from terrorism.[23]

The pressing question for our purposes is whether the sanctions imposed on Sam and Mary amount to criminal punishment. Based upon Feinberg and Husak's formulation of criminal punishment, clearly the custodial sentence imposed on Sam satisfies both prerequisites of punishment. That is the imposition of hard treatment (one year's imprisonment) and censure since Sam is labelled as a serious wrongdoer (in this case a terrorist) whose conduct is worthy of society's reprobation. As far as the sanctions imposed on Mary are concerned, although the imposition of the above-mentioned restrictions can be regarded as a form of 'hard treatment', these cannot amount to criminal punishment because

[19] ibid s 6(3).

[20] According to the relevant sentencing guidelines published by the Sentencing Council, the minimum sentence that can be imposed for the s 57 offence is one year's imprisonment. See Sentencing Council, *Terrorism Offences: Definitive Guideline* (2018) 45, available at: www.sentencingcouncil.org.uk/wp-content/uploads/Terrorism-offences-definitive-guideline-Web.pdf.

[21] Terrorism Prevention and Investigation Measures Act 2011, Sch 1, para 1.

[22] ibid Sch 1, paras 7 and 8 respectively.

[23] ibid s 5.

based on the above-mentioned conceptualisation of punishment, censure is tied exclusively to the criminal label. The TPIMs were labelled by the legislature as civil measures the purpose of which is to protect 'members of the public from a risk of terrorism' and to assist the investigation of terrorism-related incidents.[24] Seen in this way, the legislature's intention was not for TPIMs to intentionally and publicly condemn suspected terrorists. Consequently, the restrictions imposed on Mary cannot amount to criminal punishment despite their severity simply because of the label attached to these notices. It should also be borne in mind that although Sam was entitled to all the enhanced procedural protections afforded to those facing criminal prosecution, this was certainly not the case with Mary since TPIMs are regarded as civil interventions. This is neither to suggest that every restriction imposed through the issue of a TPIMs notice amounts to punishment nor that the restrictions imposed on Mary cannot be warranted. As mentioned before, it is not my intention to examine the justifiability of civil preventive measures. Rather, my aim is to point out that we should not tie censure exclusively to the criminal label. Instead, we should look beyond the official classification of each rule and explore whether its implementation resulted in the indirect criminalisation of the behaviour at hand.

Therefore, although Feinberg and Husak's account of punishment can be regarded as an accurate reflection of the normative difference between the penalties imposed by the criminal law and those imposed through other means of social regulation, it does not take into consideration the possibility of indirect criminalisation. What if, for example, the implementation of the TPIMs notice leads to the imposition of severe restrictions on Mary's liberty and her public and purposeful condemnation? This is not to undermine the validity of the arguments raised by criminal law theorists regarding the normative distinction between punishment and penalties. Rather, it is to point out the need for an alternative account of punishment that will enable us to determine under what circumstances the implementation of supposedly non-criminal sanctions amounts to criminal punishment.

The importance of being able to identify instances of indirect criminalisation lies beyond the need of ensuring that the right label is attached to each legal rule. It has broader and much more important implications for the rule of law and the way the state chooses to regulate our behaviour. The law should not just be predictable, but it has to be unequivocal and stable as well.[25] The law must develop in a clear, coherent and principled manner allowing the public to safely predict whether their future behaviour is likely to result in the imposition of punishment. And it should be up to individual members of the public to decide if they wish to run the risk of committing a criminal offence. This is a fundamental value of liberal societies since it clearly sets out the limits of the state's

[24] ibid s 3(3).
[25] J Raz, *The Authority of the Law*, 2nd edn (New York, Oxford University Press, 2009) 213–14.

ability to interfere with individual liberty while treating its members as rational agents capable of deciding themselves whether they wish to be subjected to hard treatment and state censure. Laws, such as the injunction and the TPIMs, that are very broadly drafted and that are susceptible to indirect criminalisation clearly undermine the rule of law since they impose very few (if any) constraints on the state's ability to interfere with individual liberty.

The above criticisms of the way some of the most prominent legal theorists have conceptualised criminalisation should not be regarded as an invitation to disregard the official classification of legal rules. Rather, what I am suggesting is that the legislature's intention should not distract us from examining whether the implementation of a given legal rule constitutes a form of criminalisation regardless of the label attached to it. As Ashworth and Zedner rightly point out, 'the key question [to be addressed here] is whether the measure is punitive: it may also be preventive in its purpose, but the classification depends on whether it is punitive in substance'.[26] If there is evidence to suggest that the legal rule under scrutiny has resulted in the indirect criminalisation of certain kinds of behaviour, we can then refer back to the legislature's original intentions to assess the legitimacy of this rule and/or of its implementation. The fact that the legal rule at hand aims to prevent certain kinds of undesirable conduct, does not necessarily mean that this cannot be punitive in nature. It is for this reason that I argue for the formulation of a more fine-grained account of punishment that will enable us to look beyond the official label attached to its legal rule and examine its true nature.

### 3.2.2. Moving Beyond Direct Criminalisation: The Anti-Subversion Doctrine

Thus far, I argued that the way we conceptualise criminalisation should take into consideration both instances of *direct* and *indirect* criminalisation. This will enable us to look beyond the official classification of legal rules susceptible to indirect criminalisation and investigate if their implementation resulted in the imposition of punishment on those against whom these measures were used. In an attempt to do so, the ECtHR in *Engel* formulated a mechanism for distinguishing criminal from non-criminal rules based on the nature of the sanctions imposed rather than on the label attached to each measure by the legislature. That is the anti-subversion doctrine. Although the formulation of the anti-subversion doctrine was a step in the right direction and an explicit acknowledgement by the ECtHR that it is possible for punishment to be imposed indirectly, as we shall see below, its focus on the legislature's intentions along with the high threshold that needs to be met in order for the sanction imposed to amount to a form of punishment facilitate rather than prevent the introduction of measures that are susceptible to indirect criminalisation.

[26] Ashworth and Zedner (n 7) 15.

In *Engel*, the ECtHR had to determine whether sanctions imposed on members of the Dutch armed forces through disciplinary proceedings should have been regarded as criminal in nature and thus trigger the Article 6 enhanced procedural protections.[27] The applicants argued that they were entitled to the same procedural safeguards as those charged with a criminal offence, because 'the disciplinary penalty or penalties, measure or measures pronounced against them contravened Article 5(1)', that is the right to liberty and security.[28] The ECtHR acknowledged that 'the Convention without any doubt allows the States, in the performance of their function as guardians of the public interest, to maintain or establish a distinction between criminal law and disciplinary law'.[29] It was held, however, that Article 6(3) of the European Convention on Human Rights (ECHR) can still be applicable regardless of the label attached by domestic legislation to a legal rule if it 'counts as "criminal" within the meaning of Article 6'.[30]

In order to determine whether these disciplinary proceedings against the applicants were criminal in nature, the ECtHR devised a three-stage test known as the anti-subversion doctrine.[31] The test is as follows:

> (i) It is first necessary to know whether the provision(s) defining the offence charged belong, according to the legal system of the respondent State to criminal law, disciplinary law or both concurrently …
> (ii) The very nature of the offence … [and]
> (iii) The seriousness of what is at stake.[32]

The introduction of this test was deemed necessary in order to prevent states from classifying legal rules as non-criminal simply as a means of circumventing the extra layers of protection guaranteed by the Convention to those facing a criminal trial.[33] To illustrate how the anti-subversion doctrine operates in practice, let us consider the following hypothetical scenario. Suppose that one of the contracting states to the ECHR decided to re-label many of the offences included in its penal code as a civil set of wrongs without changing the substance of any of the rules in question as a means of circumventing the time-consuming criminal process. In such a situation, although these offences are now labelled as civil rules, the anti-subversion doctrine enables courts to determine whether each legal rule should be regarded as criminal regardless of its new label.[34]

[27] *Engel v Netherlands* (n 1) [79].
[28] ibid [56].
[29] ibid [81].
[30] ibid [82]–[83].
[31] ibid [72].
[32] ibid [81]–[82].
[33] ibid [81].
[34] In *Öztürk v Germany* (1984) 6 EHRR 409, for example, the ECtHR had to determine whether certain minor motoring offences should still be treated as punitive in nature despite their re-labelling by the legislature as regulatory offences.

Based on the anti-subversion doctrine, our starting point should be the classification made by domestic legislation, that is whether the legislature classified this as a criminal or a non-criminal wrong.[35] The domestic classification should provide us with an initial indication of the legislature's intentions, though that is not definitive. The second step is to examine the nature of the offence committed by that individual.[36] In *Engel*, the fact that the applicants were members of the armed forces and the offences committed were inextricably linked with their occupation meant that the classification of the offence as disciplinary rather than as criminal could be justified.[37] Third, according to this test, one should assess 'the degree of severity of the penalty that the person concerned risks incurring'.[38] The ECtHR held that if the sanction imposed is so severe that it amounts to a deprivation of someone's liberty under Article 5 of the Convention, then it should be regarded as a form of criminal punishment.[39] According to the ECtHR, 'in a society subscribing to the rule of law, [sanctions of this severity] belong to the "criminal" sphere'.[40] It is worth mentioning that post-*Engel*, the ECtHR treated the second and the third stages of the anti-subversion doctrine as alternative criteria. Simply put, if either of them is clearly satisfied, then there is no need for the other criterion to be satisfied as well in order for the penalty at hand to amount to a form of punishment. In *Öztürk v Germany*, for example, the ECtHR concluded that the regulatory offences in question should be regarded as criminal in nature notwithstanding the fact that the maximum sentence for each contravention was a fine.[41]

Before analysing in more depth this three-part test, it is imperative to examine how terms like 'liberty' and 'deprivation' have been conceptualised by the ECtHR. Based on *Engel*, liberty in this context should be given its classic meaning and interpreted as 'the physical liberty of the person' excluding any 'mere restrictions upon liberty of movement'.[42] This approach is in harmony with the interpretation given to liberty by both Article 5 and Article 2 of Protocol No. 4 of the Convention which make reference to individuals' right to move freely within the contracting states' jurisdiction.

In determining whether the sanction imposed amounts to a deprivation of someone's liberty, the ECtHR held that 'account should be taken of a whole range of factors such as the nature, duration, effects and manner of execution of the penalty or measure in question'.[43] In *Engel*, the court focused on the severity of the sanctions imposed on the applicants, that is the number of days they had

[35] *Engel v Netherlands* (n 1) [81]–[82].
[36] ibid [82].
[37] ibid.
[38] ibid.
[39] ibid.
[40] ibid.
[41] (1984) 6 EHRR 409 [52].
[42] *Engel v Netherlands* (n 1) [58].
[43] ibid [59].

to spend under arrest.[44] For the ECtHR, only in those cases where individuals were actually locked in a cell and were completely deprived of their freedom of movement would that amount to a deprivation of their liberty under Article 5, that is they must have been 'kept under lock and key'.[45]

At first sight, the three-part test introduced by the ECtHR in *Engel* seems a positive development, especially in cases where severe restrictions on an individual's liberty have been imposed in the absence of the enhanced procedural protections guaranteed under Article 6. Although the anti-subversion doctrine provides a good starting point for a more holistic approach to criminalisation, two key reservations can be expressed about the test formulated by the ECtHR.

First, according to *Engel*, it is essential to pay attention to the legislature's original intentions with regard to the legal rule under scrutiny, that is the first limb of the test.[46] If the expressed intention of the legislature was not to punish those who violate this legal rule, then this should be an initial indication against criminalisation.[47] This is an explicit acknowledgement by the ECtHR that the national legislature is in a better position to determine how domestic legislation should be labelled.

In effect, however, reliance on the lawmaker's original intentions can be problematic since it provides national legislatures with a significant leeway through which they can manage to circumvent the anti-subversion doctrine. To elucidate how this can work in practice, let us re-examine the TPIMs in light of the *Engel* test. As noted above, through the issue of a TPIMs notice significant restrictions can be imposed on suspected terrorists, even though they have committed no offence.[48] As the wording of the 2011 Act suggests, the main objective of these measures is to prevent terrorism-related activities. If we were to strictly apply the first limb of the *Engel* test, then our analysis would depart from the premise that the TPIMs are civil in nature because the legislature's intention was to introduce a preventive instrument rather than to punish suspected terrorists. Consequently, the first limb of the test can encourage states to label legislation as non-criminal in the name of prevention, even though, in theory, it seems possible for the rule in question to be implemented in a manner that results in the indirect criminalisation of certain kinds of behaviour. As King explains, however, labelling a specific legal rule either as civil or preventive 'does not [necessarily] relieve proceedings of their criminal nature'.[49] In order to examine the true nature of

[44] ibid [61]–[64].

[45] ibid.

[46] ibid [81]–[82].

[47] ibid.

[48] See section 3.2.1.

[49] King is critical here of the approach adopted by the ECtHR in *Air Canada v United Kingdom* (1995) 20 EHRR 150 which in effect mirrored the first limb of the anti-subversion doctrine. In this case, the ECtHR had to determine, inter alia, whether s 141(1) of the Customs and Excise Management Act 1979 (by virtue of which the applicant's property was seized) constituted a criminal offence and thus triggered the Art 6 protections, such as the presumption of innocence (para 164). In determining the nature of s 141, the ECtHR placed particular emphasis upon the legislature's intention,

the legal rule in question, we need to look beyond the label attached by the legislature and 'concentrate on the realities of the situation'.[50] In other words, as the ECtHR rightly pointed out in *Ezeh*, the official classification made by the legislature has 'only a formal and relative value'.[51]

Although in both *Engel* and *Ezeh* the need 'to look beyond appearances and the language used' was highlighted,[52] it is evident through a line of cases that the ECtHR on many occasions was in fact reluctant to do so.[53] This reluctance of the ECtHR to actually look beyond the official label attached by domestic legislation is particularly evident in cases involving civil forfeiture.[54] One of the most illustrative examples of this is the case of *M*. In *M*, the applicant had a number of previous convictions including 'membership of an organisation of the mafia type …, lending money at an extortionate rate, obtaining money with menaces and demanding money with menaces'.[55] The Italian authorities managed to obtain a compulsory residence order as well as a confiscation order

which according to the Strasbourg court, was not the imposition of a penalty (paras 164–65). Rather, according to the majority, the £50 000 payment made by the applicant for the return of its property should 'be seen as a measure limiting the harm caused' to them (paras 164–65). As Judge Trechsel (dissenting) rightly pointed out, however, when determining the nature of a particular provision we should look 'behind appearances … [and investigate] what [has] actually happened in the present case' (para 166). See C King, 'Civil Forfeiture and Article 6 of the ECHR: Due Process Implications for England & Wales and Ireland' (2014) 34 *Legal Studies* 371, 382.

[50] *Ezeh and Connors v United Kingdom* (2004) 39 EHRR 1 [16]. This case involved disciplinary proceedings against the applicants who were already serving a custodial sentence. As a result of these disciplinary proceedings, additional days of custody were imposed on both applicants. The applicants claimed that these proceedings were criminal in nature and thus denial of legal representation constituted a violation of their rights under Art 6(3)(c) of the Convention. In determining the true nature of these disciplinary proceedings, the Grand Chamber of the ECtHR held that in order for the Art 6 protections to be triggered, the 'offence [in question must make] the person liable to a sanction which, by its nature and degree of severity, belongs in general to the "criminal" sphere' (para 86). In this case, the Grand Chamber of the ECtHR, indeed, looked beyond the stated objectives of these disciplinary proceedings noting that prevention and punishment 'are not mutually exclusive' (para 105). On this view, since one the purposes of the sanctions imposed was to punish the applicants, then the disciplinary proceedings against them should be regarded as criminal for the purposes of the Convention.

[51] *Ezeh and Connors v United Kingdom* (n 50) [9]. This was reaffirmed in a number of cases by the ECtHR, such as in *Öztürk v Germany* (n 34) [52] where it was held that of the three-part test formulated in *Engel* 'the second and third factors are of greater weight'.

[52] *Ezeh and Connors v United Kingdom* (n 50) [123].

[53] In effect, this created certain anomalies (see, for instance, my analysis of *M v Italy* (12386/86) and *Ezeh* below) and ambiguities which enabled domestic courts to turn a blind eye (at least in certain cases) to the realities of the situation. This was particularly evident in *McCann* where the House of Lords paid particular attention to the legislature's intentions with regard to the ASBO. As Bakalis maintains, 'the House of Lords [in this case] … was rather selective in the parts of the Strasbourg judgments it chose to apply' choosing to neglect or dismiss cases, such as *Lauko v Slovakia* (1998) 33 EHRR 9, where the ECtHR in fact focused on the actual impact of the sanctions/restrictions imposed on those subjected to legal rules which were susceptible of indirect criminalisation. See C Bakalis, 'Anti-Social Behaviour Orders: Criminal Penalties or Civil Injunctions?' (2003) 62 *Cambridge Law Journal* 583, 584.

[54] For a more comprehensive analysis of these cases see King (n 49).

[55] *M v Italy* (n 53) [82]–[83].

against him on the basis that his vast fortune 'could only have been accumulated from the proceeds of [his] unlawful activities'.[56] According to the domestic legislation in question, it was sufficient for the Italian authorities to establish a prima facie case regarding the unlawful origins of the applicant's assets. Simply put, there was no need for the authority applying for the issue of a confiscation order to prove beyond reasonable doubt that M's assets were in fact the product of his criminal activities.[57] This was due to the nature of the relevant legislation which, according to the Italian government, was to prevent dangerous individuals from committing crimes, rather than to punish them for their past behaviour. If a prima facie case was established against an individual's assets, then he had to provide an explanation for his assets.

For the applicant, the confiscation of his property constituted a form of criminal punishment and thus violated his rights under both Article 6(2), that is the presumption of innocence, and Article 7(1), that is the prohibition against retrospective punishment. For the respondent, there was no violation of the Convention since these rights only apply to criminal offences and do not extend to preventive interventions. Similar to the approach taken in *Engel*, in determining the true nature of the legal rule at stake, the ECtHR focused on what the legislature aimed at through the introduction of this legal provision and how domestic courts had dealt with measures of this kind before. Since, according to the Strasbourg court, 'proceedings on an application for a preventive measure are autonomous in relation to criminal proceedings and do not involve a finding of guilt', then a confiscation order against the applicant 'does not imply a finding that he was guilty of a specific offence'.[58]

Depriving criminals of their unlawfully obtained assets is a defensible objective for the state to pursue since this not only prevents future criminality, it also communicates a message to society that crime does not pay. Nonetheless, as members of a liberal society which values liberty we should not only be concerned with what kinds of behaviour are regulated by the state, but we should also be mindful of how this is done and at what cost in terms of individual autonomy.[59] Although the primary objective of the confiscation order issued against M might have indeed been the prevention of future crime, we cannot simply overlook the realities of the situation. In this case, the appellant was not only deprived of most of his property, but he was also labelled (at least indirectly) by the Italian authorities as a criminal whose behaviour is worthy of reprobation. It follows that regardless of the legislature's objectives, preventive measures such as the confiscation order imposed on M, might result in the imposition of sanctions

[56] ibid [84].

[57] As far as M is concerned, there was 'a substantial body of circumstantial evidence' against the unlawful origins of his assets. See *M v Italy* (n 53) [83].

[58] *M v Italy* (n 53) [97]–[98].

[59] I Loader, 'Review Symposium: The Anti-politics of Crime' (2008) 12 *Theoretical Criminology* 399, 405.

akin to criminal punishment. This was also acknowledged by Lord Bingham in the case of *Secretary of State for the Home Department v MB* where he stated that preventive interventions can be equally restrictive as criminal offences.[60] In his words, 'this distinction [between preventive and criminal interventions] is not watertight, since prevention is one of the recognised aims and consequences of punishment and the effect of a preventative measure may be so adverse as to be penal in its effects if not in its intention'.[61] Hence, if we are truly determined to investigate the actual nature of the law in question, it is imperative to look beyond its stated objectives and focus on its impact on those subjected to it.

The foregoing criticisms illustrate further why it is necessary for legal theorists to look beyond the official classification of legal rules and investigate if their implementation has resulted in the imposition of criminal punishment. Clearly, the official classification of a legal rule provides a good starting point in terms of determining whether it should be regarded as criminal or non-criminal, but we should take care not to place too much weight on it. This should only be a starting point, not a criterion. Unfortunately, despite repeated calls by the ECtHR to look beyond the official classification of legal rules and examine their true nature, both the House of Lords in *McCann* and the Strasbourg court itself failed on many occasions to do so. This is primarily due to the emphasis paid on the legislature's original intentions with regard to the legal rule at hand. This is one of the main reasons why a new working definition of criminalisation is needed.

The second cause for concern relates to the severity of the sanction that must be imposed on the perpetrator in order for this to satisfy the third limb of the anti-subversion doctrine. Based on *Engel*, if the sanction imposed on the perpetrator constitutes a severe deprivation of his liberty under Article 5, then it should be regarded as a form of criminal punishment.[62] It is important to note

[60] In this case the House of Lords had to determine, inter alia, whether a non-derogating control order issued under s 2 and s 3(1)(a) of the Prevention of Terrorism Act 2005, 'constituted a criminal charge for the purposes of Article 6' (para 3). Similar to the approach adopted in *McCann*, the House of Lords (relying on the *Engel* test) held that these non-derogating control orders were civil in nature since they 'do not involve the determination of a criminal charge … only a foundation of suspicion' (para 24). Nonetheless, it was acknowledged that 'in any case in which a person is at risk of an order containing obligations of the stringency found in this case', that person should be entitled to the Art 6 protections (para 24).

[61] *Secretary of State for the Home Department v MB* [2007] UKHL 46 [23]. As Stahlberg and Lahmann explain, this distinction is particularly problematic in the context of terrorism-related preventive measures which might include 'retributive and punitive element(s)'. According to them, the *Engel* test affords national courts with a significant degree of discretion regarding the classification of these measures since it allows them to place particular emphasis on their preventive objectives. This is further evident through the House of Lords decision in *MB* (discussed above) where a balancing act was conducted in order to determine whether the non-derogating control orders should be regarded as a criminal charge for the purposes of the Convention. See T Stahlberg and H Lahmann, 'A Paradigm of Prevention: Humpty Dumpty, the War on Terror, and the Power of Preventive Detention in the United States, Israel, and Europe' (2011) 59 *American Journal of Comparative Law* 1051, 1076.

[62] *Engel v Netherlands* (n 1) [85].

that the ECtHR in *Engel* had to adopt a very narrow interpretation of liberty since the applicants argued that the sanctions imposed on them constituted a violation of their Article 5 rights.[63] This led the ECtHR to interpret liberty in the context of Article 5. Consequently, in order for a sanction to meet the threshold set by *Engel* it must severely restrict the perpetrator's physical liberty.[64] Accordingly, if we were to adopt the *Engel* approach as to the meaning of liberty, then we would only associate criminal punishment with imprisonment, home curfews and any other kinds of sanction which significantly limit the perpetrators' freedom of movement.

Although imprisonment is regarded as a paradigmatic form of criminal sanction and freedom of movement as a fundamental right, this does not necessarily mean that our analysis should be restricted only to the most severe types of sanction. Imprisonment is just one out of the many weapons in the criminal law's arsenal that can be used against those who offend. A defendant who is found guilty of a criminal offence can be ordered to pay a fine, he can be required to compensate the victim for the harm suffered or he can receive a community sentence.[65] As part of this process, the sentencing court must take into consideration an array of other external factors to the wrong committed, such as the rehabilitation of the perpetrator and his financial circumstances.[66] This means that sanctions imposed for the commission of a criminal offence can take various forms and vary considerably both in terms of their nature and severity.

The narrow interpretation of liberty adopted in *Engel* may in fact facilitate further subversions to the criminal law rather than prevent them. Focusing on imprisonment alone might encourage the introduction of civil preventive measures, such as the TPIMs and the injunction, through which non-custodial sanctions can be imposed. Although these non-custodial sanctions can severely restrict the perpetrator's liberty (not necessarily his physical liberty), based on *Engel*, these measures should not be regarded as criminal rules. To prevent possible subversions to the criminal law, therefore, liberty should be interpreted more widely than in *Engel*. This will allow us to expand our analysis beyond traditional forms of criminal sanctions, such as custodial sentences, and examine whether alternative sanctions can also be regarded as a form of criminal punishment.

To illustrate further what is problematic about the third limb of the anti-subversion doctrine (and therefore make the case for an alternative approach), it would be instructive to compare how this was applied in the cases of *M* and *Ezeh*. In *Ezeh*, the ECtHR noted that additional days of custody imposed on the appellants, that is 40 days for the first appellant and seven for the second, 'cannot

[63] ibid [56].
[64] ibid [61]–[64].
[65] Sentencing Act 2020, Part 7 (Chapter 1) and Part 9 (Chapter 2) respectively.
[66] ibid ss 57(2) and 124(1) respectively.

be regarded as sufficiently unimportant or inconsequential as to displace the presumed criminal nature of the charges against them'.[67] In *M*, the Strasbourg Court held that depriving someone of most of his property (and in effect labelling him a criminal) is not so severe 'as to warrant its classification as a criminal penalty for the purposes of the Convention'.[68] The above decisions beg the question whether seven days of additional custody is indeed a more severe sanction than seizing most of an individual's assets while publicly condemning him as someone who lives off the proceeds of organised crime. A possible solution here would be to avoid the imposition of a specific threshold altogether and focus on whether the sanction in question simply interferes with the perpetrator's liberty.

The formulation of the anti-subversion doctrine can clearly be regarded as a positive development since it constitutes an explicit acknowledgment by the ECtHR that non-criminal measures can operate as de facto criminal rules. In doing so, however, the ECtHR decided to adopt a quite conservative approach by focusing solely on the most extreme examples of indirect criminalisation, that is sanctions that severely restrict the perpetrators' freedom of movement. This is, of course, in stark contrast to the variety of sanctions that can currently be imposed on those found guilty of an offence. To address this, a more inclusive approach should be adopted that would focus on whether the sanction in question simply interfered with the perpetrator's liberty.

## 3.3. RECONCEPTUALISING CRIMINALISATION

Our discussion so far has focused on the main challenges faced by both the way criminalisation has been conceptualised in the academic literature and through the anti-subversion doctrine. The main purpose of this analysis was to examine whether these existing accounts can provide a single viable test for distinguishing criminal from non-criminal rules bearing in mind that some supposedly non-criminal measures are susceptible of indirect criminalisation. As seen earlier, for many prominent legal philosophers, what distinguishes the criminal law from other forms of regulation is the imposition of punishment. For them, in order for a legal sanction to be regarded as criminal punishment: (i) it must allow for the imposition of 'hard treatment'; and (ii) it must intentionally and publicly communicate censure. Although this account accurately represents the normative difference between the punishment imposed for paradigmatic criminal offences, such as the unlawful infliction of grievous bodily harm, and the penalty imposed for breach of a non-criminal rule, such as the compensation that someone is ordered to pay to another party following a breach of their contractual agreement, it has been argued that it fails to take into consideration

[67] *Ezeh and Connors v United Kingdom* (n 50) [129].
[68] *M v Italy* (n 53) [98].

the prospect of *indirect* criminalisation since it is based on the assumption that censure is tied exclusively to the criminal label. In order to examine whether criminalisation occurs indirectly, it is essential to look beyond the label attached to each legal rule and scrutinise the true nature of the sanctions imposed (or threatened to be imposed) on those who are found in breach of the rule at hand.

As far as the anti-subversion doctrine is concerned, I argue that although this was a step in the right direction, an alternative test is needed. The main reason for this is twofold. First, the anti-subversion doctrine requires an examination of the legislature's intentions with regard to the legal rule at hand, that is the first limb of the test. Although the Strasbourg court reiterated that particular attention should be paid to the second and third parts of the test, on many occasions the ECtHR itself has been extremely reluctant to actually look beyond the official label attached to the legal rule under scrutiny. This was also the case with the House of Lords in *McCann* which paid particular attention to the legislature's original intentions with regard to the ASBO. Second, concerns have been raised regarding the third limb of the test and the severity threshold that needs to be met for the penalty imposed to amount to a form of punishment. As noted above, a very narrow interpretation of liberty was adopted in *Engel* which fails to take into account the entire array of sanctions that can currently be imposed upon a guilty verdict. I argue that this narrow interpretation of liberty adopted by the ECtHR in *Engel* can in fact encourage subversions to the criminal law rather than prevent them.

The above criticisms led me to the conclusion that a new working definition of criminalisation is needed through which we can distinguish criminal from non-criminal rules irrespective of the label attached to them. Similar to the accounts of criminalisation examined earlier, central to the working definition formulated below is the assumption that criminal rules are those rules which result in the imposition of criminal punishment. Criminal punishment comprises of two main prerequisites, both of which must be satisfied in order for the legal rule under scrutiny to constitute a form of criminalisation. The two prerequisites of this working definition are:

(i) The implementation of the legal rule must result in the imposition of a sanction which interferes with the perpetrator's liberty.
(ii) The sanction imposed and/or threatened to be imposed on the perpetrator must publicly and purposefully communicate state censure.

As we shall see below, this working definition of criminalisation cannot predetermine whether the injunction and/or other civil preventive measures are criminal in nature. Rather, it requires us to scrutinise the implementation of each measure on an individual basis to examine whether it satisfies both prerequisites.[69]

[69] I will further discuss this need to assess each case individually during my evaluation of the working definition of criminalisation in section 3.3.3.

### 3.3.1. To Interfere with the Perpetrator's Liberty

Central to both accounts of criminalisation scrutinised earlier is the need for the sanction imposed to restrict the perpetrator's liberty through the imposition of 'hard treatment'. What qualifies as 'hard treatment' though? As seen earlier, based on the anti-subversion doctrine, the sanction imposed needs to amount to a deprivation of the perpetrator's physical liberty if it is to satisfy the third limb of this three-part test.[70] Drawing a precise distinction between sanctions that deprive someone's physical liberty and those which do not can, however, be particularly challenging and problematic. This distinction becomes even more complicated when scrutinising the imposition of non-custodial restrictions on the perpetrator's liberty, such as those imposed through the issue of an injunction or a TPIMs notice. If we set the severity threshold that needs to be met too high, then it is likely that our test will further facilitate the introduction of supposedly non-punitive interventions that can severely undermine (but not deprive) people's liberty. It is for this reason that a more inclusive interpretation of 'hard treatment' is needed, focusing on any sanction that interferes with the perpetrator's liberty. What does liberty entail though?

As Moore rightly contends, liberty can be interpreted in various ways due to the fact that it can 'mean a lot of things to a lot of different people'.[71] According to him, to be left free without any interference by the state is not always desirable since this will allow people to 'do evil'.[72] It is for this reason that for contractarians, as members of the community we must accept some deprivation of our liberty, such as restricting our freedom to 'do evil', in order for the state to guarantee to us a number of other more important and valuable freedoms, such as to protect us from others' evil behaviour.[73] On this view, not 'all instances of coercion are equally objectionable'.[74] Road users, for instance, must accept a deprivation of their liberty by driving on a particular side of the road, in exchange for a more secure road network. Liberty, therefore, should be interpreted as a set of valuable freedoms rather than as an all-encompassing abstract term.[75] To this end, a distinction must be drawn between those freedoms which are valueless, such as the freedom to 'do evil'/the right of nature, and those which are worthwhile, such as the right to life.[76] A potential solution

[70] See section 3.2.2.

[71] M Moore, 'Liberty's Constraints on What Should be Made Criminal' in A Duff et al (eds), *Criminalization: The Political Morality of the Criminal Law* (Oxford, Oxford University Press, 2014) 184.

[72] ibid 184. See further R Dworkin, *Taking Rights Seriously* (London, Duckworth, 1996).

[73] J Rousseau, *The Social Contract* (Hertfordshire, Wordsworth, 1998). See further, ch 2, section 2.2.

[74] D Husak, 'The Presumption of Freedom' (1983) 17 *Noûs*) 345, 357; J Feinberg, *Social Philosophy* (Englewood Cliffs, NJ, Prentice-Hall, 1973) 7–8.

[75] J Raz, *The Morality of Freedom* (New York, Oxford University Press, 1986) 11.

[76] ibid 16–17.

here would be to draft a list of basic/fundamental liberties which form the backbone of every contemporary liberal society. Raz was critical of this approach pointing out that a 'list of basic liberties is a matter of contention' and that only a handful of freedoms, such as the right to family, can certainly be included in such a list.[77] Instead, Raz proposed a distinction based on the 'contribution [that these freedoms] have to the ideal of personal autonomy'.[78] Based on his account, if a particular freedom, such as the freedom of religion, is capable of enhancing one's autonomous life, then it would be justifiable to hold 'members of the society at large to be duty-bound … to provide [individuals] with the social environment necessary' to exercise their religion.[79]

Although Raz's assertion that a list of basic/fundamental freedoms can be a very contentious matter appears to be reasoned, this approach should not be dismissed outright. In many jurisdictions, such as in the United States, an indication as to what is regarded as a basic/fundamental freedom can be provided through a closer examination of the rights protected under the Constitution. In the absence of a written constitution, such as in the case of England and Wales, our focus could shift to other authoritative sources of law. For example, for England and Wales the main focus can be on the rights protected through the Human Rights Act 1998 (HRA 1998). The HRA 1998 incorporated most of the rights and freedoms guaranteed under the ECHR, such as the freedom of expression and the protection of property.[80] The enactment of the HRA 1998 indicates that these rights and freedoms are to be regarded as basic/fundamental for this society since they reflect its core values and principles. For the purposes of this working definition, liberty is conceptualised in terms of those rights and freedoms guaranteed to every citizen in this jurisdiction through the HRA 1998. It is worth reiterating that it is not my intention to formulate a normative political theory in this study. Instead, my main objective is to formulate a single viable test through which instances of indirect criminalisation can be identified.

The final aspect of the first prerequisite relates to the required threshold that the restrictions on one's liberty must meet to qualify as a potential form of criminal punishment. As discussed earlier, in *Engel* the ECtHR held that only when the perpetrator is 'kept under lock and key' can the sanction imposed against him be regarded as a form of punishment.[81] As mentioned above, the imposition of such a high threshold cannot only cause ambiguities as to the threshold that needs to be met for the hard treatment imposed to satisfy this first prerequisite, but it can also facilitate the introduction of even more measures that are susceptible to indirect criminalisation. For these reasons, I argue that a working definition of criminalisation should not require the sanction imposed to *severely*

[77] ibid 246.
[78] ibid.
[79] ibid 247.
[80] Art 10 and Art 1 of the First Protocol of the ECHR respectively.
[81] *Engel v Netherlands* (n 1) [61]–[64].

restrict the perpetrator's liberty in order to potentially qualify as a form of criminal punishment. In fact, it should include no such requirement at all. Simply put, if the sanction under scrutiny interferes with the perpetrator's liberty as this was defined above, then the first prerequisite is satisfied. The degree of deprivation should therefore be irrelevant for the purpose of determining whether the first prerequisite is satisfied.

The imposition of a severity threshold can exclude from our assessment penalties imposed through supposedly non-punitive interventions that are more liberty intrusive than sanctions imposed following conviction for a criminal offence. Is, for instance, the imposition of a home curfew following the issue of a TPIM notice a less burdensome restriction on the perpetrator's liberty than a fine imposed for a road traffic violation or a community sentence? Clearly, not. Where do we draw the line then? This is not to suggest that only lengthy custodial sentences amount to 'hard treatment'. Instead, it is to highlight the breadth of the sanctions that can be imposed on those who are convicted of a criminal offence while highlighting the need for the adoption of a more flexible approach that will truly enable us to look beyond the official label attached to each legal rule and to examine its true nature. This, however, means that the net of potential criminal rules is cast very wide and thus the role of the second criterion becomes even more important in terms of identifying those rules which can result in the imposition of criminal punishment.

### 3.3.2. It Must Publicly and Purposefully Communicate State Censure

The second prerequisite of this working definition is that the sanction imposed (or threatened to be imposed) *publicly* and *purposefully* communicates state censures. That is, it publicly and purposefully expresses the state's condemnation towards the perpetrator and his conduct. Regardless of the level of hard treatment imposed, what really distinguishes criminal sanctions from other types of sanctions imposed by law is their ability to publicly condemn on behalf of the entire community both the offender and the wrong committed.[82] To formally criminalise a particular kind of behaviour is to publicly and purposefully condemn it.[83] Through criminalisation a message is conveyed to society that the behaviour at hand is so blameworthy that it is worth criminalising.[84] Accordingly, to be found guilty of an offence is to be publicly and purposefully condemned by the state as a serious moral wrongdoer. As we saw in section 2.2,

[82] A Duff, *The Realm of Criminal Law* (Oxford, Oxford University Press, 2018) 19; Z Hoskins, *Beyond Punishment: A Normative Account of the Collateral Legal Consequences of Conviction* (New York, Oxford University Press, 2019) 46.

[83] Duff (n 82) 22–23.

[84] S Kadish, *Blame and Punishment: Essays in the Criminal Law* (New York, Macmillan, 1987) 23 and 73.

direct criminalisation can be used by the state as a means of reminding/educating members of the public about the core principles and values that underpin society. It is due to the moral message conveyed through criminalisation that a criminal conviction can result in the stigmatisation and social ostracisation of the perpetrator by the rest of the community.[85] This account provides an accurate description of how *direct* criminalisation communicates censure. Nonetheless, it provides no guidance as to how censure can be communicated *indirectly* through the implementation of non-criminal interventions. This was one of the main reservations expressed about the way criminalisation is conceptualised in the academic literature.[86]

As far as *indirect* criminalisation is concerned, our starting point should not be the label attached to the legal rule at stake, but its implementation. The fact that the legislature decided not to classify a particular rule as criminal, indicates that its intention was not to publicly condemn the behaviour regulated. As discussed earlier, however, certain non-criminal rules, such as the injunction, appear to allow for the imposition of sanctions akin to criminal punishment, albeit 'civil' in nature. In order to examine whether these measures operate as de facto criminal rules, it is necessary to look beyond the label attached to them by the legislature and investigate how this was implemented in practice. If the implementation of civil measures does not publicly and purposefully communicate state censure towards the perpetrator and his conduct, then the second prerequisite of the working definition is not satisfied. However, if there is evidence to suggest that at least one of the *purposes* of the sanction imposed was to inflict pain and there are public forms of stigmatisation attached to it, then this will satisfy the second prerequisite of the working definition. In determining whether this was indeed the case, we need to examine more closely the manner in which the sanction was imposed.

State actors, such as the police, can publicly and purposefully communicate censure through various ways. For this reason, an exhaustive list of how censure can be publicly and purposefully communicated (when moving away from direct criminalisation) by and/or on behalf of the state cannot be provided. Instead, it is necessary to assess each case on its own merits and examine whether the sanction imposed on the perpetrator aimed at his public denunciation. To illustrate this, consider the following hypothetical scenario. Suppose that Sam is a suspected terrorist and that a home curfew has been imposed on him through a TPIMs notice.[87] Here, it is important to remind ourselves that for the issue of

[85] For more on the collateral consequences of a criminal conviction see Hoskins (n 82) ch 1.

[86] See section 3.2.1

[87] The reason why I am referring here to the TPIMs instead of the injunction is twofold. First, I elaborate further on how the injunction can be implemented in a manner that results in the public and purposeful condemnation of those subjected to it below (see ch 4, section 4.3.2.2). Second, as discussed earlier, other civil preventive measures, such as the TPIMs, raise similar considerations as those raised by the ASBOs and now the injunction. Hence, it proves instructive to refer to the TPIMs here in order to illustrate this further (see ch 1, section 1.3).

a TPIMs notice the suspected terrorist need not be convicted of any offence. The Secretary of State needs only to establish a prima facie case against that individual and that the allegations against him are not 'obviously flawed'.[88] It follows that the intention of the legislature was not to label the TPIMs as criminal measures. Rather, the legislature's intention is for these measures to prevent terrorism-related activities. Nonetheless, the police's counter-terrorism unit decided to publicise Sam's story along with his personal details as a means of reassuring the public that action has been taken against a potential terrorist. In this press release colourful language was used against Sam and his behaviour. Following this press release Sam was stigmatised by the rest of the polity as a terrorist sympathiser and aider. Although the main objective of this press release was to reassure the public, it is evident that it also sought to publicly condemn Sam. Clearly, the public denunciation of Sam was not incidental. Rather, the use of colourful language suggests that this was amongst the purposes of this press release.[89] In this case, the second prerequisite of the working definition is satisfied and thus the home curfew imposed on Sam should be regarded as criminal punishment.[90]

Thus far, this chapter has scrutinised both the academic literature on criminalisation and the anti-subversion doctrine formulated by the ECtHR in *Engel*. The main objective of this analysis was to explore whether these accounts can lead to a single viable test based on which we can distinguish criminal from non-criminal rules. Upon closer scrutiny of these accounts, certain problems and inconsistencies have been identified. These problems and inconsistencies necessitated the formulation of a working definition of criminalisation. The test formulated above does not constitute a complete departure from the pre-existing accounts of criminalisation. Rather, these accounts have formed the basis for this new test the main objective of which is to identify potential instances of indirect criminalisation regardless of the label attached to the legal rule at hand. In the remainder of this chapter an evaluation of this working definition will be provided.

### 3.3.3. Evaluation of the Working Definition

The working definition of criminalisation formulated above can be criticised on four grounds. First, it can be criticised for being potentially over-inclusive since

[88] Terrorism Prevention and Investigation Measures Act 2011, s 6(3)(a).

[89] In *YB and others v Turkey* (48173/99), the ECtHR held that statements made by state officials at a press conference through which they suggested that the applicant was guilty of murder violated the applicant's right under Art 6(2) ECHR, that is the presumption of innocence. This was the first time the ECtHR acknowledged that someone's right to be presumed innocent until proved guilty can be violated by public officials other than national courts. See further B Rainey et al, *The European Convention on Human Rights*, 7th edn (Oxford, Oxford University Press, 2017) 316–17.

[90] I will elaborate further on how the working definition of criminalisation can be applied in practice in ch 4, section 4.3.2.

it can cover any kind of sanction which slightly interferes with someone's liberty, as defined above. This can be attributed to the first prerequisite of the working definition which requires mere interference with the perpetrator's liberty. Although at first sight this criticism appears to be well founded, it is essential to reiterate that for a sanction to be regarded as a form of criminal punishment both prerequisites must be satisfied. If the sanction imposed interferes with the perpetrator's liberty but does not *publicly* and *purposefully* communicate state censure, then the second prerequisite will not be satisfied and the test will not be made out. Moreover, it must be borne in mind that this assessment does not relate to the justifiability of criminalisation. Rather, this working definition assists us to determine whether the restrictions imposed on the perpetrator amount to criminal punishment and thus constitute a form of criminalisation. The issue as to whether criminalisation can be warranted should form part of a different exercise at a later stage.

Second, concerns can be raised about the fact that if this working definition of criminalisation is to be adopted, then a detailed examination of each and every legal rule and its implementation will be needed. In the context of the ASB tools and powers, a case-by-case analysis of every injunction or a Criminal Behaviour Order will be needed to determine whether in each case the restrictions imposed meet both prerequisites of the working definition of criminalisation. In some cases, we might conclude that the implementation of the injunction amounts to criminalisation whereas in some other instances this might not be the case. This of course highlights once again the ambiguous scope of the law in this area and the extensive degree of discretion given to local enforcement agents and the courts regarding the implementation of the injunction.[91]

Third, another reservation that can be raised relates to the need to examine how the legal rule in question has been implemented in the past. In effect, this means that we can only assess whether the legal rule in question has been operating as a de facto criminal measure after the perpetrator has already been punished in the absence of enhanced criminal procedural protections. At first sight, therefore, this working definition cannot really assist in preventing the indirect criminalisation of certain kinds of behaviour. Rather, it only manages to identify instances where non-criminal rules resulted in the imposition of criminal punishment.

Although this working definition cannot prevent all instances of indirect criminalisation, it can still be used by courts to assess how similar rules as the one in question have been implemented in the past in order to determine its likely status. If there is evidence to suggest that on numerous occasions the implementation of the injunction has resulted in the indirect criminalisation of certain kinds of behaviour, then the court can take additional steps to ensure that this will not happen in the future. For instance, if there is evidence to suggest that

[91] See ch 1, section 1.4.2 and section 1.4.3.

local enforcement agents in question have previously issued press releases as a means of publicly condemning young individuals against whom an injunction was issued, the court can issue a 'section 39 order (Children and Young Persons Act 1933) prohibiting publication' of the perpetrator's details, such as his name and address.[92] Moreover, the working definition formulated above can be a very useful tool for local enforcement agents who can reflect on the way they utilise the injunction examining whether this has resulted in the indirect criminalisation of the perpetrators' conduct.[93]

Finally, although this working definition of criminalisation can be a very useful tool for legal theorists to determine whether the implementation of non-criminal rules resulted in the indirect criminalisation of certain kinds of behaviour, it has to be admitted that cases like *Engel* and *McCann* illustrate that this approach is unlikely to be adopted by courts. As seen earlier, in both cases, emphasis was placed on the legislature's intentions about the legal rules in question. In *McCann*, the fact that the ASBO was introduced as a means of preventing ASB was one of the main factors which led the House of Lords to conclude that this was a civil rather than a criminal order.[94] In addition to this, due to time and resource constraints it seems unlikely that the courts will adopt an approach which would require a very detailed analysis of each and every case. Instead, it will seem more sensible and practicable for courts to favour a more general approach similar to the one adopted in *McCann*. The above is not to argue that courts should not revise their current approach for scrutinising rules which are susceptible to indirect criminalisation. Rather, it is to point out that a shift to a new approach similar to the one advanced above, is unlikely to occur primarily due to practical considerations.

Notwithstanding the above-mentioned limitations, the main advantage of this working definition is its ability to look beyond the official classification of legal rules. This enables us to focus on the nature of the sanctions imposed and investigate whether the implementation of a legal rule has resulted in the indirect criminalisation of certain kinds of behaviour regardless of the label attached to this rule by the legislature. For the purposes of this study, this working definition can assist us in determining whether the implementation of the injunction's first limb by local practitioners and the police resulted in the indirect criminalisation of certain types of ASB.

[92] Home Office, *Anti-social Behaviour, Crime and Policing Act 2014: Reform of Anti-social Behaviour Powers – Statutory Guidance for Frontline Professionals* (London, Home Office, 2021) 32.

[93] As mentioned in ch 1, certain civil preventive measures that have been introduced in other jurisdictions, such as the gang injunctions in the United States, are also susceptible to indirect criminalisation. Consequently, the working definition of criminalisation formulated for the purposes of this book can be utilised by local enforcement agents in other jurisdictions who face similar challenges as well.

[94] *R (on the application of McCann)* (n 3) [72].

The working definition of criminalisation formulated in this chapter allows for the adoption of a more holistic approach to criminalisation by taking into consideration both *direct* and *indirect* criminalisation. This enables us to scrutinise not only the implementation of the injunction, but the use of any legal rule which, in theory, allows for the imposition of restrictions akin to criminal punishment. Through this working definition of criminalisation, we will also be in a better position to identify and prevent instances of *indirect* criminalisation. Consequently, even if this working definition of criminalisation is not formally adopted for reasons of practicality by courts (for example, due to the need to closely examine the implementation of the legal rule in question), it remains an essential device for legal commentators who wish to examine more closely measures susceptible to indirect criminalisation. Moreover, it can be a valuable tool for local enforcement agents who might wish to use this as a means of ensuring that they have those safeguards in place that prevent (or at least minimise the possibility of) indirect criminalisation.

## 3.4. CONCLUSION

Identifying whether a particular kind of conduct has been criminalised indirectly poses many practical and philosophical challenges for criminal law theorists, criminologists, courts and law enforcement agents. For example, apart from the need to formulate a single viable test that will enable courts to look beyond the official label attached, concerns can be raised as to whether it would be appropriate for anyone other than the legislature to determine how each legal rule should be classified.[95] Is it appropriate, for instance, for courts to completely disregard the official classification of the instrument at hand? What impact will this have on the separation of powers between the legislative and the judicial branch?

The main objective of this chapter was not to address every normative and practical challenge posed by indirect criminalisation. What it tried to do was to formulate a working definition of criminalisation that will enable legal commentators, courts and local enforcement agents to determine whether the implementation of the injunction (and other civil preventive measures that are susceptible to indirect criminalisation) resulted in the indirect criminalisation of certain types of ASB. To this end, an empirical examination of the implementation of the injunction is needed bearing in mind the conditions that must be satisfied in order for it to amount to a form of indirect criminalisation. Although the need to prevent certain undesirable kinds of conduct and to protect members of the public from any unjustifiable interference with their liberty by others

[95] L Zedner, 'Penal Subversions: When is a Punishment not Punishment, Who Decides and on What Grounds?' (2016) 20 *Theoretical Criminology* 3, 4.

should be a priority for the liberal state, we still need to be mindful of how this is to be achieved. The purposeful labelling of potentially punitive interventions as non-criminal simply to circumvent the enhanced procedural protections offered to those facing criminal prosecution is antithetical to the essence of and has no place in a liberal society.

# 4

# *A Theoretical Analysis of the Injunction*

## 4.1. INTRODUCTION

THE IMPETUS FOR formulating a working definition of criminalisation in chapter three emanated from the challenges posed by how criminalisation is conceptualised both in academic discourse and through the anti-subversion doctrine.[1] In particular, one of the main concerns raised about these pre-existing accounts of criminalisation is their inability to effectively look beyond the official classification of non-criminal rules and examine whether they are operating as de facto criminal measures. As far as Feinberg and Husak's conceptualisation of criminalisation is concerned, the main reason for this is the fact that these accounts aimed to articulate the normative distinction between criminal punishment and the penalties imposed through other mechanisms of social regulation. These normative accounts were not intended to assist courts to identify instances of indirect criminalisation. As for the anti-subversion doctrine, concerns were raised about its focus on the legislature's original intentions with regard to the legal instrument under scrutiny, that is the first limb of the test, and the high severity threshold that the sanction imposed needs to meet, that is the third part of the test, in order for this to be regarded as a punitive measure.[2] The working definition of criminalisation formulated in chapter three overcomes the above-mentioned concerns by adopting a more flexible approach. It was argued that in order for the penalty imposed to amount to criminal punishment: (i) it must interfere with the perpetrator's liberty; and (ii) it must *publicly* and *purposefully* communicate state censure. The formulation of this working definition of criminalisation will enable me to look beyond the official label attached to the Part 1 injunction of the Anti-social Behaviour, Crime and Policing Act 2014 and investigate whether the implementation of its first limb resulted in the indirect criminalisation of certain kinds of anti-social behaviour (ASB). The importance of this investigation is twofold.

First, if there is evidence to suggest that indeed the injunction's first limb has been operating as a de facto criminal measure, then it is necessary to ensure that

[1] See ch 3, section 3.2.
[2] The second part of the test focuses on the nature of the legal rule at hand. See ch 3, section 3.2.2.

those against whom it is issued are at least afforded the same level of protection as those facing criminal prosecution. Second, if the injunction's first limb is operating as a de facto criminal measure, then we must subject it to the same level of theoretical critique as criminal rules. Before examining empirically, the implementation of the injunction's first limb, it is essential to scrutinise further the relevant legal framework and investigate whether it is possible for the injunction (as this appears on the statute book) to be used in a manner that would satisfy both prerequisites of my working definition of criminalisation.

Chapter four begins by scrutinising the current law on ASB and the most important amendments brought in by the 2014 Act. This will provide us with a more in-depth understanding of the law relating to ASB while laying the foundations for the theoretical analysis of the injunction's first limb. Central to this analysis is the shift from the hybrid Anti-social Behaviour Order (ASBO) to what appears to be a purely civil injunction and whether this undermines any potential for indirect criminalisation. As we shall see later, although the shift to a purely civil injunction appears to mitigate many of the concerns raised about the ASBO, the criticisms raised about the first limb of the order and whether the restrictions imposed during this initial stage of the process can constitute a form of punishment in their own right remain largely unaddressed. Chapter four then proceeds to investigate if the injunction (as this appears on the statute book) can be implemented in a manner that would satisfy both prerequisites of the working definition of criminalisation formulated in chapter three. Although it is concluded that the injunction can be implemented in a manner that satisfies both prerequisites of my working definition of criminalisation, it is imperative to be mindful of the significant degree of discretion granted to local enforcement agents and the courts regarding its implementation. The importance of this lies in the fact that the implementation of the injunction can vary considerably across England and Wales. Consequently, even if there is evidence to suggest that on at least some occasions the first limb of the injunction operated as a de facto criminal measure, this is not necessarily reflective of how this instrument was used in other parts of the country.

## 4.2. ADDRESSING ANTI-SOCIAL BEHAVIOUR

Before examining the injunction's first limb with reference to the working definition of criminalisation, it is important to examine how the law on ASB developed through the years and what changes the enactment of the 2014 Act brought in this area.[3]

[3] As noted in ch 1, section 1.3, the main focus of this study is the injunction's first limb. However, where appropriate reference will also be made to the Criminal Behaviour Order (CBO) and any other informal interventions used by local enforcement agents to address ASB at a local level.

### 4.2.1. A Critique of the ASBO

The legislature chose initially to address ASB through the introduction of the ASBO under section 1 of the Crime and Disorder Act 1998. The ASBO constituted a two-stage criminalisation process where a civil order was issued against an individual who behaved in an anti-social manner.[4] That is the first stage of the process. During this initial stage of the process, the court examining the application for the issue of an ASBO could impose any restrictions deemed *necessary* on the perpetrator in order to prevent further ASB in the future.[5] If an ASBO was issued, then the defendant was prohibited 'from doing anything described in the order'.[6] Breach of these restrictions without reasonable excuse constituted a criminal offence, the maximum sentence for which was five years' imprisonment and a fine, that is the second stage of the process.[7]

Although the ASBO was portrayed by the New Labour government as an effective mechanism through which ASB could be addressed without resorting to the ineffective and resource-intensive criminal law,[8] the order was heavily criticised by human rights activists and legal commentators. For instance, one of the most heavily contested and controversial features of the ASBO was the statutory definition of ASB under section 1(1)(a) of the 1998 Act.[9] In particular, the statutory definition of ASB was characterised as 'sweeping and vague'[10] since it could capture almost any kind of behaviour as long as this was 'likely to cause harassment, alarm or distress' to other people.[11] The main focus of the ASB's statutory definition was the actual and/or likely impact that someone's behaviour could have on others rather than the actual nature of the behaviour in question. In effect, this meant that any kind of conduct could potentially be regarded as anti-social even if this was otherwise lawful.[12] The importance

[4] A Simester and A von Hirsch, 'Regulating Offensive Conduct through Two-Step Prohibitions' in A von Hirsch and A Simester (eds), *Incivilities: Regulating Offensive Behaviour* (Oxford, Hart Publishing, 2006) 213.

[5] Crime and Disorder Act 1998, s 1(6).

[6] ibid s 1(4).

[7] ibid s 1(10)(b).

[8] Tony Blair, 'Britain's Liberties: The Great Debate' *Guardian* (23 April 2016), available at: www.theguardian.com/commentisfree/2006/apr/23/humanrights.constitution.

[9] See further, ch 1, section 1.4.3.

[10] A Ashworth et al, 'Neighbouring on the Oppressive: The Government's "Anti-Social Behaviour Order" Proposals' (1998) 16 *Criminal Justice* 7, 14, 9.

[11] It should be borne in mind though that the court examining the application for the issue of an ASBO could only impose such an order if it was satisfied that this was *necessary* for the prevention of further ASB. Hence, even if someone's conduct 'caused or was likely to cause harassment, alarm or distress' to others, an ASBO could not be imposed on them unless the court was satisfied that this was a necessary response. In *R v Jones* [2006] EWCA Crim 2942, for instance, the Court of Appeal held that the ASBOs imposed on the appellants were 'wrong in law' since there was no evidence to suggest that they would behave in an anti-social manner in the future. Consequently, there was no need for the imposition of an ASBO against the appellants.

[12] P Ramsay, 'What is Anti-social Behaviour' [2004] *Criminal Law Review* 908, 921. This argument also applies to other civil preventive measures, such as the Football Banning Orders. See further

of this was heightened by the fact that breach of the order without reasonable excuse constituted a criminal offence carrying a lengthy custodial sentence. In theory, therefore, some relatively minor ASB followed by a breach of the restrictions imposed could result in the imposition of a lengthy custodial sentence.[13] Although the punishment imposed for breaching an ASBO could be justified on the offender's failure to reassure other members of the polity about their security,[14] this does not change the reality of the situation. That is that the ambiguous scope of ASB's statutory definition along with the significant magnitude of discretion afforded to courts and local enforcement agents regarding the implementation of the ASBO allowed the net of social control to be extended to 'all spheres of life'.[15] This is a stark reminder of the need to be mindful of how the prevention of crime and of other undesirable kinds of conduct is to be achieved and at what cost in terms of liberty and autonomy.

Another highly controversial feature of the ASBO was its hybrid nature.[16] In *McCann*, the House of Lords explicitly stated that the first and the second limb of the process are independent and therefore the sentence imposed for breach of the order could not 'be based on the aggregate impact of the entire course of conduct'.[17] Instead, as Ramsay points out, in determining the sentence that must be imposed for breach of the ASBO the court had to focus on the 'seriousness of conduct in terms of the harassment, alarm or distress involved in breach[ing]' the order rather than on the seriousness of the conduct that led to the issue of the order in the first place and/or the cumulative impact of the perpetrator's behaviour.[18] Although, therefore, the perpetrator's initial ASB that led to the imposition of an ASBO should not be taken into consideration when passing sentence for breach of the order, this did not change the fact that some minor ASB followed by a breach of the order constituted a criminal offence which carried a lengthy custodial sentence.[19]

Finally, of particular concern was the severity of the restrictions that could be imposed on the liberty of those against whom an ASBO was issued. As Duff

M James and G Pearson, '30 Years of Hurt: The Evolution of Civil Preventive Orders, Hybrid Law, and the Emergence of the Super-Football Banning Order' [2018] *Public Law* 44, 52–53.

[13] G Pearson, 'Hybrid Law and Human Rights – Banning and Behaviour Orders in the Appeal Courts' (2006) 27 *Liverpool Law Review* 125, 129–30.

[14] P Ramsay, *The Insecurity State: Vulnerable Autonomy and the Right to Security in the Criminal Law* (Oxford, Oxford University Press, 2012) 2.

[15] D Stephen, 'The Responsibility of Respecting Justice: An Open Challenge to Tony Blair's Successors' in P Squires (ed), *ASBONation: The Criminalisation of Nuisance* (Bristol, Policy Press, 2008) 321–22.

[16] See ch 1, section 1.4.1.

[17] Ramsay, *The Insecurity State* (n 14) 49–50.

[18] ibid 44–45.

[19] As the case of John Garcia shows, who following a breach of an ASBO issued against him faced deportation to the Philippines, the potential consequences of breaching such an order could be far reaching due to the criminal nature of the ASBO's second limb. See further, Nigel Morris, 'Deported to the Philippines: Man whose Crime was Breaching Asbo' *Independent* (8 January 2008), available at: www.independent.co.uk/news/uk/home-news/deported-to-the-philippines-man-whose-crime-was-breaching-asbo-768791.html.

and Marshall put it, the issue of an ASBO allowed for the imposition of restrictions that could be so severe that they could amount to a form of punishment in their own right, albeit 'not subject to the kind of constraint that could legitimate them as punishments'.[20] It is for this reason that I argue that the first limb of the ASBO (and therefore of the injunction) could constitute a form of *indirect* criminalisation regardless of whether the order was breached.

What also appeared to be problematic about the administration of ASB was the use of certain informal interventions by local enforcement agents before applying to court for the issue of an ASBO. Evidence from a study conducted by Crawford et al suggests that the 'ASBOs represent[ed] only the very tip of a much larger structure of proactive ASB interventions'.[21] Their study focused not only on the issue of the ASBO, but they also scrutinised the pre-ASBO stage and the use of formal warning letters and Acceptable Behaviour Contracts (ABCs)[22] issued to young individuals.[23] Evidence from that study suggests that sometimes young people were 'forced' to sign ABCs out of fear of losing their accommodation.[24] What is important for our purposes is the nature of the restrictions imposed on those against whom these informal interventions were used and whether they amount to a form of criminal punishment in their own right.

### 4.2.2. Scrutinising the 2014 Amendments

Despite efforts from the Labour government to encourage the use of the ASBO and the post-conviction ASBO (CrASBO) in the early 2000s, the orders soon fell out of favour with local enforcement agents.[25] The reluctance of local enforcement agents to utilise the orders along with the alleged need for the adoption of

[20] A Duff and S Marshall, 'How Offensive Can You Get? in A von Hirsch and A Semester (eds), *Incivilities: Regulating Offensive Behaviour* (Oxford, Hart Publishing, 2006) 80.

[21] A Crawford et al, '"It ain't (just) what you do, it's (also) the way that you do it": The Role of Procedural Justice in the Implementation of Anti-social Behaviour Interventions with Young People' (2017) 23 *European Journal on Criminal Policy and Research* 9, 12.

[22] ABCs are informal agreements signed between local enforcement agents and people whose behaviour has been regarded as anti-social as a means of nipping 'the problem behaviour in the bud before it escalates'. Simply put, rather than applying to court for the issue of an ASBO/injunction, local enforcement agents invite individuals who behave in an anti-social manner to sign such as a contract. Through these contracts the alleged perpetrator might agree to refrain from doing certain things, such as behaving in a particular way, and/or to engage in certain activities, such as attending anger-management sessions. See Home Office, *Putting Victims First: More Effective Responses to Anti-social Behaviour* (London, Home Office, 2012) 1.18.

[23] Crawford et al (n 21) 14–16.

[24] ibid 19.

[25] K Brown, 'Punitive Reform and the Cultural Life of Punishment: Moving from the ASBO to its Successors' (2020) 22 *Punishment & Society* 90, 91, 107; Home Office and Ministry of Justice, *Statistical Notice: Anti-social Behaviour Order (ASBO) Statistics – England and Wales 2013* (2014) 2, available at: assets.publishing.service.gov.uk/government/uploads/system/uploads/attachment_data/file/355103/anti-social-behaviour-order-statistical-notice-2013.pdf.

a more flexible, effective and victim-oriented approach[26] led to the enactment of the 2014 Act which brought significant changes in the law on ASB.[27]

The most important amendment brought by the 2014 Act has been the repeal and replacement of the ASBO by a purely civil injunction.[28] In particular, breach of the injunction constitutes a civil contempt of court rather than a criminal offence.[29] As a result of this, those found in breach of their injunctions cannot be arrested immediately unless a power of arrest has been attached to the injunction. Due to the hybrid nature of the ASBO, if the police had evidence which proved that an individual breached their order, then they could arrest the perpetrator immediately. This is not the case, however, under the new scheme. The court examining the application for the issue of an injunction can attach a power of arrest to it only if it is satisfied that: (i) the respondent used or threatens to use violence against others; or (ii) that 'there is a significant risk to others' due to the respondent's behaviour.[30] If a power of arrest is attached to the injunction, then the police can arrest the perpetrator without a warrant.[31] Otherwise, the police must apply for the issue of a warrant. This shift towards a purely civil approach also means that breach of the injunction will not appear on the perpetrator's criminal record.[32] Previously, breach of the ASBO constituted a recordable offence and those who breached the terms of their orders had to carry the stigma of a criminal conviction. That said, breach of the injunction will be treated as a civil contempt of court[33] carrying a maximum penalty of two years' imprisonment and an unlimited fine.[34] However, it should be noted that the full array of sentencing options that are available to a criminal court when passing sentence for the commission of an offence, such as the imposition of a community sentence, are not available when someone is found in contempt of court.[35] Although the sentence imposed following a breach of an injunction, that is the second limb of this process, is beyond the scope of this book, it would be interesting to examine what impact this limited availability of sentencing options has both in terms of the actual penalty imposed on those found in contempt of court and the overall effectiveness of this instrument.[36]

[26] Home Office, *Putting Victims First* (n 22) 3–4.

[27] See Table 4.1 for an overview of the most important changes made by the 2014 Act.

[28] See ch 1, section 1.4.2.

[29] Home Office, *Anti-social Behaviour, Crime and Policing Act 2014: Reform of Anti-social Behaviour Powers – Statutory Guidance for Frontline Professionals* (London, Home Office, 2021) 33.

[30] Anti-social Behaviour, Crime and Policing Act 2014, s 4(1).

[31] Home Office, *Anti-social Behaviour, Crime and Policing Act 2014* (n 29) 33.

[32] National Police Records (Recordable Offences) Regulations 2000, reg 3(1)(a). See, further, *Cobra Golf Ltd v Rata* [1998] Ch 109.

[33] It should be noted that there are differences in how contemnors are treated compared with those who serve a custodial sentence for committing a criminal offence. See further, Ramsay, *The Insecurity State* (n 14) 63.

[34] Home Office, *Anti-social Behaviour, Crime and Policing Act 2014* (n 29) 33.

[35] *Palmer* [1992] 1 WLR 568.

[36] Courts dealing with contempt proceedings, for instance, in the vast majority of cases might prefer the issue of a fine reserving the imposition of a custodial sentence for the most serious cases

At first sight the repeal and replacement of the ASBO by what appears to be a purely civil instrument can be regarded as a positive development since it seems to address many of the concerns raised about its predecessor's hybrid nature. This move to a purely civil instrument should be approached with caution though since the proximity of the injunction to the criminal law has been officially distanced. As a result of this, the implementation of the injunction might attract less attention and outside scrutiny enabling both courts and local enforcement agents to use this tool as a means of criminalising indirectly what they consider to be ASB.[37] This is evidenced by the government's decision not to collect data regarding the implementation of the injunction.[38] The importance of this lack of scrutiny lies in the potential punitive nature of the injunction the implementation of which might, as we shall see below, result in the indirect criminalisation of various kinds of ASB.[39] As Ramsay rightly points out, 'the manipulation of the procedural boundary is more striking' following the 2014 amendments.[40] This is further evidenced by the fact that the issue of an injunction can result in the imposition of even more burdensome restrictions on the liberty of those subjected to it than the ASBO. This is due to the introduction of positive requirements.[41]

Under the 1998 Act those against whom an ASBO was issued could only be prohibited from doing anything mentioned in the order. If there was, for example, evidence to suggest that Samantha, who was an alcoholic, was congregating with

since there is no 'middle ground' in terms of sentencing. This reluctance of the courts to impose a custodial sentence might undermine the deterrent effect of the injunction.

[37] Under the Crime and Disorder Act 1998, in order for an ASBO to be imposed on someone, the relevant authority had to submit an application to the magistrates' court. In contrast to this, under the 2014 Act, an injunction can (in the case of an adult) only be issued by the High Court or the county court. What this means is that applications for the issue of an injunction are examined by more experienced and better qualified judges, something that mitigates against some of the concerns raised about the implementation of the injunction attracting less attention and outside scrutiny. (For a more comprehensive analysis of the potential implications of this change in the forum of the applications made, see K Brown, 'Replacing the ASBO with the Injunction to Prevent Nuisance and Annoyance: A Plea for Legislative Scrutiny and Amendment' (2013) 8 *Criminal Law Review Issue* 623.) Although at first sight this change in the forum appears to undermine the force of my argument, as we shall see in ch 6, in most cases the regulation of ASB at a local level takes place in the shadows with local enforcement agents using an array of informal interventions before resorting to formal legal action against those who behave in an anti-social manner. It is for this reason that legal commentators, local enforcement agencies, the government and the public at large still need to be mindful of how the ASB tools and powers are used at a local level. The fact that there has been a shift from the hybrid ASBO to what appears to be a 'purely' civil injunction should not distract us from the potential punitive nature of this new instrument.

[38] Even if data about the total number of successful applications made for the issue of a Part 1 injunction was collected, this might not have been an accurate reflection of how (and to what extent) these are utilised in practice due to the various informal interventions used by local enforcement agents before applying to court for the issue of an injunction. As we shall see in ch 6, in fact, in most cases local enforcement agents do not resort to formal legal action against those who behave in an anti-social manner.

[39] Brown, 'Punitive Reform and the Cultural Life of Punishment' (n 25) 104.

[40] Ramsay, *The Insecurity State* (n 14) 64.

[41] Anti-social Behaviour, Crime and Policing Act 2014, s 1(4)(a).

others in the town centre after midnight behaving in an anti-social manner, then the court examining the application for the issue of an ASBO could allow for the imposition of a home curfew during night hours on her to prevent her from behaving in the same way in the future. The imposition of restrictions alone, however, could not necessarily address the underlying causes of Samantha's ASB and thus provide permanent relief to those affected. Evidence suggests that the imposition of exclusion zones or other forms of prohibitions did not provide long-term relief from ASB. Rather, according to a number of studies,[42] such as the one conducted by Matthews et al, the imposition of these prohibitions led to the 'displacement of crime and anti-social behaviour both within' the same town and nearby places.[43] Instead of addressing the underlying causes of ASB, these prohibitions encouraged the perpetrators to move to a different area where they would be able to continue causing problems uninterrupted.[44]

The 2014 Act sought to provide local agencies with a more effective legal framework which would enable them to address the underlying causes of ASB.[45] To this end, under the new scheme a court examining an application for the issue of an injunction or of a CBO can impose both negative and positive requirements on the perpetrators.[46] In the case of Samantha, for instance, she can be prohibited from entering the town centre and at the same time be ordered to attend an alcohol rehabilitative programme. Thus, the 2014 Act starts from the premise that the imposition of some bland prohibitions on the perpetrators cannot be a sufficient response to ASB.[47] As the Home Office points out, local enforcement agents are provided with the necessary discretion needed 'to tailor the positive requirements in each case to address the respondent's individual circumstances, behaviour and needs'.[48]

Although the introduction of these positive requirements has the potential of addressing the underlying causes of low-level criminality and ASB, it also raises

[42] See, eg, A Edwards and G Hughes, 'Resilient Fabians? Anti-Social Behaviour and Community Safety work in Wales' in P Squires (ed), *ASBO Nation: The Criminalisation of Nuisance* (Bristol, Policy Press, 2008) 63–64.

[43] R Matthews et al, *Assessing the Use and Impact of Anti-Social Behaviour Orders* (Bristol, Policy Press, 2007) 4.

[44] As Sager and Jones point out, this was particularly evident in the case of prostitution where the imposition of exclusion zones simply resulted in the relocation of the problem. See T Sager and H Jones, 'Crime and Disorder Act 1998: Prostitution and the Anti-social Behaviour Order' [2001] *Criminal Law Review* 873, 881.

[45] Home Office, Anti-social Behaviour, Crime and Policing Act 2014 (n 29) 4.

[46] Anti-social Behaviour, Crime and Policing Act 2014, s 1(4)(a) and Sentencing Act 2020, s 330(b) respectively.

[47] Evidence from a study conducted by Lewis et al suggests that positive obligations were already used at the pre-ASBO stage by some local practitioners and the police. This is in line with the findings of this study which will be discussed in more detail in ch 6, section 6.3. See S Lewis et al, 'Nipping Crime in the Bud? The use of Anti-social Behaviour Interventions with Young People in England and Wales' (2017) 57 *British Journal of Criminology* 1230, 1236.

[48] Home Office, *Anti-social Behaviour, Crime and Policing Act* 2014 (n 29) 30.

concerns as to the constraints placed on the perpetrators' liberty and whether these can constitute a form of criminal punishment in their own right. This assumption should be examined in light of the conditions that need to be met in order for an injunction to be issued. As the 2014 Act appears on the statute book, the issue of an injunction seems much easier now when compared to the ASBO. As shown in Table 4.1, under the 1998 Act, an ASBO could only be issued if the court examining the application was satisfied that the order was 'necessary to protect relevant persons from further anti-social acts' by the defendant.[49] In contrast to this, under section 1(3) of the 2014 Act, the court examining an application for the issue of an injunction must consider 'it just and convenient to grant the injunction for the purpose of preventing' further ASB. In reality, though, this change of terminology is unlikely to have any impact on the daily administration of ASB at a local level. As Brown points out, 'statistics have shown courts granting 98 per cent of ASBO applications' even with that higher threshold.[50] Consequently, even with the imposition of what appears to be a lower threshold it seems highly unlikely for this to have any significant impact on the implementation of the injunction.

**Table 4.1** The impact of the 2014 amendments on the law on anti-social behaviour

| **Applying for the issue of an ASBO** | | | | |
|---|---|---|---|---|
| **Triggering behaviour** | **The legal test** | **Requirements** | **Duration** | **Breach** |
| Behaviour that 'caused or was likely to cause harassment, alarm or distress to one or more persons not of the same household as [the defendant] himself'. | 1. The defendant behaved in an anti-social manner; and<br>2. The magistrates' court had to consider the issue of an ASBO '*necessary* to protect relevant persons from further ASB'. | Through the issue of an ASBO, the magistrates' court could 'prohibit the defendant from doing anything described in the order'. | Each ASBO lasted for a minimum period of two years. | Breach of the requirements imposed without reasonable excuse constituted a criminal offence which carried a maximum penalty of five years' imprisonment and a fine. |

*(continued)*

[49] Crime and Disorder Act 1998, s 1(1)(b).
[50] Brown, 'Replacing the ASBO' (n 37) 628.

Table 4.1 *(Continued)*

| Applying for the issue of an injunction | | | | |
|---|---|---|---|---|
| **Triggering behaviour** | **The legal test** | **Requirements** | **Duration** | **Breach** |
| Conduct that:<br>1. 'caused or is likely to cause harassment, alarm or distress to any person';<br>2. is 'capable of causing nuisance or annoyance' in a housing-related context; or<br>3. is 'capable of causing nuisance or annoyance' to anyone. | 1. The respondent behaved in an anti-social manner; and<br>2. The court 'considers it *just and convenient* to grant the injunction for the purpose of preventing the respondent from engaging in ASB'. | Through the issue of an injunction, the court can prohibit the respondent from and/or require the respondent to do anything described in the injunction. | For adults there are no minimum or maximum requirements.<br>For those under the age of 18, the injunction can last for a period of no more than 12 months. | For adults, breach of the injunction without reasonable excuse constitutes a civil contempt of court which carries a maximum penalty of two years' imprisonment and an unlimited fine.<br>For those under the age of 18, breach of the injunction without reasonable excuse constitutes a civil contempt of court and can result in a detention order (only for those between 14 and 17 years) or a supervision order with a supervision, curfew or activity requirement. |

Another really important change brought in by the 2014 Act relates to ASB's statutory definition. The ASBO dealt with conduct that 'caused or was likely to cause harassment, alarm or distress to one or more persons not of the same household as himself'.[51] Section 1(5) of the 1998 Act explicitly excluded though

[51] Crime and Disorder Act 1998, s 1(1)(a).

conduct that the defendant could show 'was reasonable in the circumstances'. This meant that even if the defendant's conduct actually caused 'harassment, alarm or distress' an ASBO could not be imposed on them, if he could show that his behaviour was reasonable based on the circumstances that existed at the time.[52] The presence of section 1(5) 'forced', according to Ramsay, local enforcement agents to assess each potential incident of ASB objectively disregarding conduct that was reasonable in the circumstances.[53] The injunction's scope extends well beyond that of its predecessor. It covers three different kinds of ASB,[54] that is: (i) 'conduct that has caused, or is likely to cause, harassment, alarm or distress to any person' regardless of whether they live in the same household as the perpetrator herself; (ii) 'conduct capable of causing nuisance or annoyance to a person in relation to that person's occupation of residential premises'; and (iii) 'conduct capable of causing housing-related nuisance or annoyance to any person'.[55] It is also worth noting that section 2 of the 2014 Act does not include a clause similar to section 1(5) of the 1998 Act. In theory, therefore, the injunction does not only cover a wider range of conduct than the ASBO,[56] but most importantly it can deal with behaviour that was reasonable at the time. In reality, it seems highly unlikely for local enforcement agents to apply to court for the issue of an injunction where the conduct at hand was clearly reasonable in the circumstances. That said, it is not just about whether the injunction is actually used against behaviour that was reasonable in the circumstances, but it is also about the broad and ambiguous drafting of the law which allows this to happen. This omission of the legislature to explicitly exclude from the scope of the law behaviour that was reasonable in the circumstances is further testament of the contemporary liberal state's willingness to sacrifice individual liberty in the name of crime/ASB prevention.

Moreover, while an ASBO lasted for a minimum period of two years, under the 2014 Act there is no minimum or maximum requirements with regard to the duration of an injunction when dealing with an adult.[57] If an application for the issue of an injunction is made against a minor though, this can last no longer than 12 months.[58]

Finally, it is worth noting that under the new legal framework there has been a change in the forum of the proceedings for the issue of an injunction.

[52] Ramsay, *The Insecurity State* (n 14) 31.

[53] ibid 32.

[54] It is worth reiterating here that other tools and powers, such as the CBO and the Community Protection Notices (CPN), focus on different types of ASB. See further, ch 1, section 1.4.3.

[55] Anti-social Behaviour, Crime and Policing Act 2014, s 2(1).

[56] This can be attributed to the fact that the injunction is the consolidation of various measures, such as the ASBO and the ASB injunction, into a single multipurpose instrument. See House of Commons, *Anti-Social Behaviour, Crime and Policing Bill: Explanatory Notes* [HL Bill 52] (2013) para 13.

[57] Crime and Disorder Act 1998, s 1(3).

[58] Anti-social Behaviour, Crime and Policing Act 2014, s 1(6).

Applications for the issue of an ASBO were examined by the magistrates' court[59] whereas under the 2014 Act in the case of an adult the application for the issue of an injunction is examined by the county court or the High Court and for those under the age of 18 by the youth court.[60]

At first sight, under the new legal framework the ASBO, the hybrid nature of which attracted most of the criticism, has been repealed and replaced by a purely civil instrument. Nonetheless, the introduction of positive obligations make, at least in theory, the first limb of this two-step method of regulation potentially even more restrictive than before. Although breach of the injunction does not constitute an offence, the 2014 Act appears to allow for the imposition of more restrictions on the perpetrators' liberty when compared with the pre-2014 legal framework. This expansion in the kinds of restrictions that can be imposed on the perpetrators' liberty should of course be examined in light of section 1(3) of the 2014 Act which makes (at least based on how the law appears on the statute book) the issue of an injunction much easier than before. The importance of this study, therefore, does not only remain unaffected by the repeal and replacement of the ASBO, but it is instead heightened by the potentially more restrictive nature of the injunction's first limb.

As far as the CrASBO is concerned, this was repealed under Part 2 of the 2014 Act by the CBO which retains the two-stage criminalisation process.[61] Similar to the CrASBO, the CBO is a post-conviction order which can only be imposed on those found guilty of an offence. As with the pre-2014 legal framework, there is no need for the offence that triggers the issue of a CBO to be associated with the perpetrator's ASB. Moreover, similar to the injunction, both positive and negative requirements can be imposed on those against whom such an order is issued.

## 4.3. A FORM OF CRIMINALISATION?

Thus far, the main objective of this chapter has been to scrutinise the current law on ASB and the most important amendments brought by the 2014 Act. An equally important objective has been to reflect on these amendments in order to demonstrate that despite the move to a civil injunction, it is important to remain mindful of the restrictions imposed both prior to the use of any formal interventions, and during the initial stage of this two-stage regulatory process. The importance of this assessment is heightened by the fact that under the 2014 Act the first limb of the injunction is potentially even more restrictive than its predecessor. It is also clear from the above analysis of the 2014 amendments that

[59] S Hoffman and S Macdonald, 'Should ASBOs be Civilised?' [2010] *Criminal Law Review* 457, 463–65.

[60] Anti-social Behaviour, Crime and Policing Act 2014, s 1(8).

[61] Following the enactment of the Sentencing Act 2020, provisions relating to the CBO are now found in Part 11 (Chapter 1) of the 2020 Act.

the nature and severity of the requirements that can be imposed on those against whom an injunction is issued can vary considerably depending on how local enforcement agents decide to use the significant degree of discretion granted to them. In the remainder of this chapter, I will examine the current law in this area with reference to the working definition of criminalisation formulated in chapter three. The underlying objective of this analysis is to explore whether the injunction's first limb can be implemented (based on how the law appears on the statute book) in a manner that can result in the *indirect* criminalisation of certain kinds of behaviour.

### 4.3.1. The Legislature's Objectives

To obtain an enhanced understanding of the ASB tools and powers, it is essential to begin our analysis of these measures by examining in more detail the legislature's main objectives with regard to the 2014 amendments. According to the Conservative–Lib Dem coalition government which was the main driving force behind the 2014 amendments, the new ASB legal framework has two primary objectives. First, the 2014 Act aims to provide a more effective and flexible legal framework to local communities.[62] As the Home Office maintains, ASB can be best addressed through early interventions by using informal pre-enforcement tools, such as through the signing of an ABC. For this reason, it has been argued that local enforcement agents should be afforded more discretion in order to be able address ASB swiftly and effectively without the need to resort to any form of legal action against the perpetrator.[63]

Second, the new legal framework does not only seek to *prevent* low-level criminality and ASB, but it also aims to adopt a more victim-oriented approach.[64] For Duggan and Heap, what is important about the 2014 amendments is that what started as an attempt to address neighbour disputes 'has [now] transformed into an area which currently focuses on protecting vulnerable and/or repeated victims from a wide range of ASB types' including hate motivated ASB.[65] As the Home Office explains, 'agencies should recognise/consider the debilitating impact that persistent or repeated anti-social behaviour can have on its victims, and the cumulative impact if that behaviour persists over a period of time'.[66] This acknowledgement of ASB's potential impact has led to the conclusion that victims and their needs should be prioritised.[67]

[62] House of Commons (n 56) para 13.
[63] Home Office, *Putting Victims First* (n 22) 1.19.
[64] Home Office, *Anti-social Behaviour, Crime and Policing Act 2014* (n 29) 4.
[65] M Duggan and V Heap, *Administrating Victimisation: The Politics of Anti-Social Behaviour and Hate Crime Policy* (Basingstoke, Palgrave Macmillan, 2014) 8.
[66] Home Office, *Anti-social Behaviour, Crime and Policing Act 2014* (n 29) 5.
[67] ibid 5–6.

The first issue to be addressed here is what the adoption of a more victim-oriented approach entails and how this can affect the administration of ASB. In the context of hate crimes, Iganski contends that a victim-oriented approach must be adopted as a means of conceptualising crimes of this nature.[68] Based on his account, if a victim of an assault felt that the perpetrator's conduct was motivated by ethnic or religious prejudice,[69] then this behaviour should be treated from the outset as a hate incident.[70] On this view, a hate crime is to be conceptualised subjectively based on how the victim perceived the perpetrator's behaviour rather than based on an objective interpretation of the incident at hand. This approach, according to Iganski, enables us to understand the actual impact of hate crimes on victims and through this enhanced understanding be in a better position to repair the harm suffered.[71] It follows that a victim-oriented approach does not only aim to repair the harm suffered by the victim, but it also allows them to actively engage in certain parts of the process.

In the context of ASB, one of the most important developments towards the adoption of a more victim-oriented approach has been the enactment of the provisions under Part 6 of the 2014 Act which aim to give victims a more active role in terms of managing and shaping ASB strategies at a local level.[72] As the title of Part 6 suggests, its main objective is to promote 'local involvement and accountability' through the introduction of two new tools: (i) the Community Remedy; and (ii) the Community Trigger. Greater local involvement, in this context, is to be achieved by allowing local communities to develop their own unique Community Remedy. The Community Remedy is an 'out-of-court punishment' tool available for those who have committed minor criminal offences and ASB.[73] A statutory duty under section 101(1) of the 2014 Act has been imposed on every Police and Crime Commissioner[74] to draft a list of possible actions that the perpetrator might be asked to do (after consulting with local

[68] P Iganski, *Hate Crime and the City* (Bristol, Policy Press, 2008) 1.

[69] Crime and Disorder Act 1998, s 28.

[70] Iganski (n 68) ch 1.

[71] ibid ch 6.

[72] Home Office, *Anti-social Behaviour, Crime and Policing Act 2014* (n 29) 5–6.

[73] ibid 18.

[74] Police and Crime Commissioners were introduced under s 1 of the Police Reform and Social Responsibility Act 2011. Each police area (see Sch 1 of the Police Act 1996) has its own Commissioner who is directly elected by members of the public. The role of the Commissioners includes, inter alia, the formulation of a police and crime plan and the appointment of the relevant Chief Constable (for more on the role of the Commissioners, see Association of Police and Crime Commissioners, 'Role of the PCC', available at: www.apccs.police.uk/role-of-the-pcc/). As Jones and Lister point out, the introduction of the Commissioners appears to represent 'a major reversal in the long-term trend of centralisation of policing in England and Wales'. Nonetheless, central influence over policing matters remains high mainly due to the fact that most of each police force's funding comes from the central government. Also, for national bodies such as the Association of Chief Police Officers, the main task is to set certain minimum standards that need to be maintained across all police forces. See, further, T Jones and S Lister, 'Localism and police governance in England and Wales' (2019) 16 *European Journal of Criminology* 552.

enforcement agents and the public) 'when a community resolution is to be used', such as offering a written apology to the victim.[75] Victims should be invited to choose what they think the most appropriate action in each case should be.[76] As far as the Community Trigger is concerned, its main objective is to enable victims to ask for a review of a potential incident of ASB.[77] This will essentially 'compel agencies to respond to ASB' and address what really matters to their community while enabling victims to actively engage with local ASB strategies.[78]

At first glance, a victim-oriented approach in this context appears to provide local communities with the necessary flexibility needed to address what really affects the victims' lives and have their voices heard. The adoption of a victim-oriented approach though is not a panacea to ASB and low-level criminality especially when the measures introduced are susceptible to indirect criminalisation.[79] Rather, such an approach can result in the introduction of more punitive interventions while significantly expanding the net of social control in the name of victim protection. This can be attributed to the phenomenon of penal populism and its potential adverse effects on crime policies. What is problematic about this phenomenon is that 'policy measures are constructed in ways that privilege public opinion over the views of criminal justice experts and professional elites'.[80] The reason for this lies with politicians' desire to gain public support, something which is often achieved through populist statements, such as the slogan 'tough on crime and tough on the causes of crime'.[81] This often leads to the adoption of a more punitive approach towards crime, such as the introduction of lengthier custodial sentences.[82] As argued before, although the liberal state has a duty to prevent crime, we need to be mindful of how this is to be achieved and at what cost in terms of individual liberty.[83] As Ericson explains, in contemporary Western societies criminalisation is risk-driven.[84] Imaginary risks are overemphasised by politicians in order to create a sense of uncertainty and insecurity amongst the public.[85] As a result of this sense of uncertainty and insecurity, society is more eager to accept less liberty for greater security.[86]

[75] Home Office, *Anti-social Behaviour, Crime and Policing Act 2014* (n 29) 20.

[76] ibid 18.

[77] ibid 9.

[78] Home Office, *Putting Victims First* (n 22) 3.

[79] Duggan and Heap (n 65) 3.

[80] D Garland, *The Culture of Control: Crime and Social Order in Contemporary Society* (Chicago, IL, University of Chicago Press, 2001) 142.

[81] Tony Blair, 'The Full Text of Prime Minister Tony Blair's New Year Message, Given at Trimdon Colliery Community Centre, Co Durham' (1999), available at: news.bbc.co.uk/1/hi/uk_politics/582621.stm.

[82] Garland (n 80) 168–70.

[83] See ch 2, section 2.2.

[84] R Ericson, *Crime in an Insecure World* (Cambridge, Polity Press, 2007) ch 1.

[85] ibid 70.

[86] J Simon, *Governing Through Crime: How the War on Crime Transformed American Democracy and Created a Culture of Fear* (New York, Oxford University Press, 2007) 3–4.

Although the adoption of a more punitive approach is not always based on expert evidence, it is often justified on the basis that this is in line with what victims and the general public demand.[87] For Duggan and Heap, the underlying rationale for meeting society's expectations lies in the inability of the state to 'guarantee the prevention of crime … [and for this reason politicians] might instead seek to address (or deflect some of the responsibility for) existing victims' expectations, experiences and needs'.[88] As Garland explains, however, 'the voice [victims] are given is not necessarily theirs [since they have] been carefully stage-managed to ensure that it fits the political message of which it now forms a part'.[89]

What can be problematic about the adoption of a victim-oriented approach in the context of ASB is that victims and their alleged opinions/demands can be used by local politicians and enforcement agents as a Trojan Horse for the adoption of a more punitive stance towards low-level criminality and ASB. This more punitive approach can, for example, be in the form of tougher restrictions on the liberty of those against whom an injunction or a CBO is issued. As part of this more punitive approach, the scope of the ASB measures can also be extended to behaviour which goes well beyond what was originally intended by the legislature expanding the net of social control 'to potentially "'all spheres of life'".[90]

The above is not to suggest that a victim-oriented approach will inevitably result in the adoption of a more punitive stance towards low-level criminality and ASB. Rather, it is to reiterate that the stated objectives of the government and the label attached to a particular legal rule by the legislature should not automatically determine whether the rule in question is criminal or non-criminal. The introduction and implementation of a victim-oriented strategy should not be used as a Trojan Horse for *indirect* and/or unwarranted criminalisation. Although the injunction has been presented by the legislature as a purely civil measure which aims to prevent ASB via the adoption of a victim-oriented approach, it is still necessary to examine whether its implementation amounts to a form criminalisation regardless of its officially stated objectives. The label attached is indicative of the legislature's intentions with regard to the legal rule at hand, but the main criterion should be how this legal rule has been implemented in practice and whether this led to the criminalisation of certain kinds of behaviour. This is not to undermine the importance of the legislature's intentions. These can be further scrutinised at a later stage during the theoretical critique of the injunction's first limb especially if there is evidence to suggest that this has been operating as a de facto criminal measure. My main objective in this monograph is to examine whether the implementation of the injunction resulted in the indirect criminalisation of certain kinds of ASB.

[87] A Bottoms, 'The Philosophy and Politics of Punishment and Sentencing' in C Clarkson and R Morgan (eds), *The Politics of Sentencing Reform* (Oxford, Oxford University Press, 1995) 40.

[88] Duggan and Heap (n 65) 34.

[89] Garland (n 80) 143.

[90] Stephen (n 15) 321–22.

### 4.3.2. Applying the Working Definition of Criminalisation

At a theoretical level, we can investigate whether the injunction's first limb has been operating as a de facto criminal measure by analysing the relevant statutory provisions in light of the working definition of criminalisation formulated in chapter three. To reiterate it here, I argued that in order for a legal sanction to amount to criminal punishment and thus constitute a form of criminalisation it must:

(i) Interfere with the perpetrator's liberty.
(ii) Publicly and purposefully communicate state censure.

To facilitate my analysis, I will rely on the following two hypotheticals scenarios. **A**, Andrew and his friends live at the outskirts of the town, but during the weekends they tend to meet at a particular park in the town centre where they get drunk and use abusive language towards other members of the public. **B**, Caroline, who is an alcoholic, tends to congregate with a number of rough sleepers in the town centre. During weekends, Caroline and her friends tend to get drunk and use abusive language towards other members of the public.

#### *4.3.2.1. Restrictions on Liberty*

In order for the first prerequisite of the working definition of criminalisation to be satisfied, it must be proved that the implementation of the legal rule at stake interfered with the perpetrator's liberty. Liberty, in this context, is to be interpreted as a set of basic/fundamental freedoms to which every individual in this jurisdiction is entitled to through the HRA 1998.[91] These freedoms include, amongst others, freedom of movement, freedom of expression, the right to enjoy our property and every other right and freedom guaranteed through the HRA 1998.

As seen earlier, under the 2014 Act both positive and negative obligations can be imposed on those who behave in an anti-social manner.[92] To illustrate how this can be used in practice, let us revisit the above hypotheticals. Suppose that local enforcement agents successfully applied for the issue of an injunction against both Andrew and Caroline. The court has decided that both of them should be prohibited from being drunk in a public space and from using abusive language towards other members of the public. Andrew has also been prohibited from visiting the park where he tends to meet with his friends, while Caroline is prohibited from entering the entire town centre. In addition to these negative obligations, the court has decided that a positive obligation should also be imposed on Caroline to attend an alcohol-related treatment. As part of her

[91] See ch 3, section 3.3.1.
[92] See section 4.2.2.

treatment, Caroline is required to attend lengthy daily sessions for four months with a specialist in the late afternoon at her local alcohol rehabilitation centre. For the court, this is the only way to permanently address Caroline's behaviour.

What is important for the purposes of our analysis here is whether the requirements imposed on Andrew and Caroline can satisfy the first prerequisite of the working definition of criminalisation. As far as Andrew is concerned, he can claim that there has been an interference with his liberty, since he is not allowed to enter that particular park. This can satisfy the first prerequisite of the working definition since this negative obligation interferes with Andrew's freedom of movement under Article 5 ECHR. As noted earlier, the interference with one's liberty need not be significant to satisfy the first prerequisite.[93] Mere interference with one's ability to move freely in places which are open to the rest of the public would be sufficient in this context. Using abusive language towards other members of the public though can hardly qualify as a basic/fundamental freedom since no such right is guaranteed through the HRA 1998.

Although this may appear to extend the reach of the working definition of criminalisation too far, it should be remembered that both prerequisites must be satisfied in order for the restriction imposed on Andrew to amount to criminal punishment. The working definition formulated in chapter three purposefully avoids the imposition of a severity threshold that each restriction must meet in order for the first prerequisite to be satisfied.[94] This was attributed to the need to avoid any unnecessary ambiguities as to what qualifies as severe interference with someone's liberty. This omission allows us to move beyond paradigmatic forms of criminal punishment, such as imprisonment, and include into our assessment alternative forms of legal sanctions, such as the imposition of exclusion zones similar to the one imposed on Andrew.

As far as Caroline is concerned, she cannot argue either that using abusive language towards other members of the public constitutes a basic/fundamental freedom. Her exclusion, however, from the entire town centre satisfies the first prerequisite of the working definition of criminalisation as this interferes with her freedom of movement, according to Article 5 ECHR. Moreover, due to her exclusion from the town centre, Caroline can argue that she is unable to associate with her friends who live in that area, potentially interfering with her rights under Article 11 ECHR.

In relation to the positive obligation imposed on Caroline, it is again necessary to examine the impact that the injunction will have on her liberty and whether compulsory attendance at this treatment interferes with one of her fundamental freedoms and rights. At first glance, it is evident from the facts in scenario **B** that these positive obligations will have a significant impact on Caroline's life. Caroline, for instance, will be unable to spend time with her

[93] See ch 3, section 3.3.1.
[94] See ibid.

daughter (or anyone else) because she has to spend her afternoons at the local alcohol rehabilitation centre. Although in this case the imposition of this positive obligation aims to address the underlying causes of Caroline's ASB, it also interferes with her ability to enjoy her 'private and family life', that is Article 8 ECHR.

It follows from the above theoretical analysis of how the injunction can be implemented in practice that despite its civil nature there is clearly a potential for it to be used in a manner that would satisfy the first prerequisite of my working definition of criminalisation. In practice, of course, this working definition requires a case-by-case analysis of the requirements imposed on the perpetrators to determine whether they actually interfere with their liberty. Moreover, the above discussion highlights the significant degree of discretion afforded to local enforcement agents and the courts regarding the nature and extent of the requirements that can be imposed on those against whom the injunction is used.

#### *4.3.2.2. To Communicate Censure*

The requirements imposed on Andrew and Caroline will only amount to criminal punishment if both prerequisites of the working definition are satisfied. It is, therefore, essential to investigate whether the implementation of the injunction's first limb can result in the public and purposeful denunciation of both Andrew and Caroline. Failure to satisfy both prerequisites will result in the classification of these requirements as mere 'sanctions'" that interfere with the perpetrators' liberty.

As far as the first limb of the injunction is concerned, our analysis should start with the ASBO and the concerns raised under the old scheme regarding the way it purposefully communicated censure, stigmatising those individuals against whom such an order was issued. One of the main criticisms raised against the implementation of the ASBO related to the 'naming and shaming' practices followed in certain areas by local practitioners and the police.[95] One of the most illustrative examples was the 'wall of shame' in Guildford where pictures and information about those who received an ASBO were posted 'for public information'.[96] Although the publication of certain information about those against whom an ASBO was issued could facilitate the better policing of the orders and the reintegration of the perpetrators into the community, the 'naming and shaming' practices used by local enforcement agents led to a 'campaign of vilification' which resulted in the further isolation of those who were 'already excluded'.[97]

[95] See, for instance, the concerns expressed by a number of legal commentators and non-governmental organisations to the Home Affairs Committee regarding the 'naming and shaming' practices used by certain local authorities. See Home Affairs Committee, *Anti-social Behaviour: Fifth Report of Session 2004–2005* (London, The Stationery Office, 2005) para 223.

[96] P Squires and D Stephen, 'Rethinking ASBOs' (2005) 25 *Critical Social Policy* 517, 523.

[97] ibid 523.

The practice of publicising the recipients' personal details was challenged in *R (on the application of Stanley) v Commissioner of Police of the Metropolis*.[98] In this case the claimants, who were young and had a long history of violence and ASB, sought a judicial review of their local Community Safety Partnership's (CSP) decision to distribute 'leaflets and publicise other materials' which contained their pictures and other personal information following the issue of ASBOs against them.[99] Although proceedings for the issue of these ASBOs had been covered extensively by local and national press, according to the claimants, the publication of this information by their local CSP was unlawful and in breach of their right to 'private and family life' under Article 8 ECHR.[100]

The defendants submitted that it was not their intention to punish or victimise the claimants and they sought to justify the publication of this information on three grounds: (1) 'to restore public confidence, (2) to assist in enforcing the ASBOs, and (3) to deter others and maintain peace in the community'.[101] In dismissing the claimants' application, the trial judge held that although colourful language was issued against the claimants, the publication of this information was *necessary* for the enforcement of the orders.[102] It was, therefore, acknowledged that local residents should have been informed about the identity of the claimants and the restrictions imposed on them in order to be able to identify and report any possible violations of the orders. Nevertheless, the trial judge highlighted the need for 'publicity [to be] confined to what is reasonable and proportionate'.[103]

In effect, the decision in *Stanley* was echoed by the Home Office's guidance on publicising ASBOs which explicitly stated that the main objective of this practice is the prevention of further ASB rather than to punish those against whom an order was issued.[104] According to the Home Office, the publication of certain information was an essential tool for local enforcement agents against ASB since the ASBOs could only be effective if those affected by this behaviour were made aware of the terms of the orders.[105] It was also argued that the publication of certain information would deter others in the future from behaving in a similar way.[106]

[98] *R (on the application of Stanley) v Commissioner of Police of the Metropolis* [2004] EWHC 2229.

[99] 'Other materials' included information publicised on the CSP's website concerning the claimants. The leaflets were distributed in the exclusion zone included in the ASBOs issued against them. *R (on the application of Stanley)* (n 98) [1].

[100] *R (on the application of Stanley)* (n 98) [16].

[101] ibid [31].

[102] ibid [40].

[103] ibid [42].

[104] Home Office, *Publicising Anti-social Behaviour Orders* (London, Home Office, 2005) 2.

[105] ibid.

[106] Home Office, *A Guide to Anti-Social Behaviour Orders and Acceptable Behaviour Contracts* (London, Home Office, 2003) 50–51.

A similar approach regarding the publication of the perpetrators' details has also been adopted by the 2014 Act. As explained in the Statutory Guidance, informing the public about the issue of an injunction is vital in terms of both enforcement and heightening the public's confidence in local enforcement agencies.[107] Moreover, similar to the pre-2014 era, it is for the local authorities and the police to decide whether the recipient's details should be publicised.[108] For cases involving young persons, section 39 of the 2014 Act gives the court examining an application for the issue of an injunction 'the discretion to restrict the publication of certain information in order to protect the identity of the child or young person, for example: his or her name, address, school, etc'.[109]

Though the effectiveness of the injunction depends largely on public involvement, I argue that publicising the perpetrators' pictures and personal information can under certain circumstances result in their social reprobation, especially in cases involving young persons. Similar to those found guilty of an offence, members of the public are likely to view those against whom an injunction has been issued as serious moral wrongdoers who are worthy of reprobation. Simply put, members of the public can perceive the publication (especially in cases where very colourful language is used) of this information as an invitation by the state and its agents to condemn both the perpetrators and their behaviour. This will inevitably result in the stigmatisation of the perpetrators and possibly to their social ostracisation.[110] In a study conducted by Matthews et al with ASBO recipients and their families, for instance, one of the interviewees noted that after receiving an ASBO they were constantly accused by the local community and the police of various offences they had not actually committed.[111] Furthermore, based on the findings of that study many of the ASBO recipients noted that they struggled with employment and accommodation, something which further highlights the stigmatising effect that the imposition of the order had.[112]

The potentially stigmatising effects of ASBOs can be attributed directly to the 'naming and shaming' of the perpetrators. In *Stanley*, the relevant CSP did not only publicise the pictures and the personal details of the claimants, but they also decided to use colourful language against them in order to highlight the severity and blameworthiness of their actions. For instance, on the CSP's website which was widely accessible by all members of the public, the claimants were 'described as thugs and bully boys engaging in animalistic behaviour'.[113] This was not a mere appeal for information in case there was a breach of the

[107] Home Office, Anti-social Behaviour, Crime and Policing Act 2014 (n 29) 32.
[108] ibid.
[109] House of Commons (n 56) para 123.
[110] Squires and Stephen (n 96) 523.
[111] Matthews et al (n 43) 51.
[112] ibid 53.
[113] *R (on the application of Stanley)* (n 98) [24].

ASBOs issued against these young individuals. Instead, the wording used and the extensive publication of these materials beyond what was absolutely necessary for the enforcement of the order suggest that the CSP sought to *publicly* and *purposefully* censure the claimants for their behaviour.

The pressing question here is whether the mere publication of certain information regarding both the perpetrators and the restrictions imposed on them would automatically satisfy the second prerequisite of the working definition of criminalisation. The fact that some 'naming and shaming' practices have been used as a means of deterrence or to inform the public about an order does not necessarily mean that these were not also used to purposefully condemn the perpetrators and their behaviour. This is not to dispute the need to inform those immediately affected by ASB about the restrictions imposed on the perpetrators. Rather, it is to argue that if this process of informing the public aimed, inter alia, to *publicly* communicate state censure, then the second prerequisite of the working definition will be satisfied.

As with *Stanley*, the starting point is to examine the language used by local enforcement agents. The use of colourful language, for instance, against the perpetrators would clearly satisfy the second prerequisite since the purpose of publicity is not just to inform the public about the perpetrator's behaviour, but is to publicly condemn them for their conduct. Moreover, as part of our investigation we can also scrutinise the extent of this 'naming' and whether its underlying objective is to facilitate enforcement or to communicate censure. To illustrate this, let us revisit scenario **A**. Suppose that after the issue of the injunction against Andrew, his local CSP decided to hold a press conference and distribute leaflets across the entire town which contained information about the restrictions imposed on Andrew along with a picture of him. According to the relevant CSP, the extensive publicity was deemed necessary to facilitate the enforcement of the injunction. Andrew's behaviour, however, affected only a very small part of the community, that is those who used or lived near the park. Informing the entire community about Andrew's behaviour appears to be a rather disproportionate response.[114] In this case, the *purpose* of this extensive publicity is not only to facilitate the effective policing of the injunction, but it is also to *publicly* condemn Andrew. Such a scenario could potentially satisfy the second prerequisite of the working definition of criminalisation and the restriction imposed on Andrew would have constituted criminal punishment.

Suppose now that instead of informing the entire local community, the CSP decided only to inform local enforcement agents and those who had been affected by Andrew's behaviour. Clearly, in the latter scenario, the purpose of

[114] In 2007, for instance, Transport for London publicised the name of a young person against whom an ASBO was issued. It is evident from the information provided and the language used that Transport for London's sole purpose was not the effective enforcement of the order. See Transport for London, 'TfL obtains its first ASBO against Graffiti Menace' (2007), available at: tfl.gov.uk/info-for/media/press-releases/2007/september/tfl-obtains-its-first-asbo-against-graffiti-menace.

sharing information is to facilitate the effective policing of the injunction, rather than to publicly condemn Andrew. It is less likely that this case would satisfy the second prerequisite of the working definition of criminalisation. Similarly, if Andrew was publicly condemned through the actions of the local media, rather than through the actions of state actors, such as local enforcement agents, then this would also be unlikely to satisfy the second prerequisite of the working definition of criminalisation. In order for the second prerequisite to be satisfied, it is essential for state condemnation to be *publicly* and *purposefully* communicated.

## 4.4. CONCLUSION

Although the ASBO was repealed and replaced by what appears to be a purely civil instrument, it is evident through the above analysis of the relevant legislation that the injunction's first limb is potentially more restrictive than the first limb of the ASBO. The main reason for this is that the 2014 Act allows for the imposition of both negative and positive requirements on those against whom an injunction is issued. Moreover, the fact that the injunction has a significantly broader scope than its predecessor means that even more kinds of behaviour can be regulated through this allegedly civil intervention. The importance of this is heightened by the potential punitive nature of the injunction.

As the close (theoretical) examination of the injunction revealed, it is possible for this measure to be implemented in a manner that would satisfy both prerequisites of my working definition of criminalisation. Although at a theoretical level this appears to be possible, it should be borne in mind that the implementation of the injunction can vary significantly across England and Wales primarily due to the significant degree of discretion granted to courts and local enforcement agents regarding both the scope of the injunction and the nature of the requirements that can be imposed.

The theoretical analysis of the injunction and the possibility of criminalising *indirectly* a wide range of behaviour through its implementation, reiterates the need to examine empirically how the injunction's first limb has been used by local enforcement agents. The data collected through this empirical study can then be examined in light of the working definition of criminalisation formulated in chapter three to determine whether the injunction should be regarded as a criminal measure. If there is evidence to suggest that indeed the injunction has been operating as a de facto criminal rule, then it is necessary for it to be subjected to the same theoretical critique as criminal offences. The outcome of this analysis will also have an impact on whether, and on what basis, the injunction can be justified.

# 5

# *A Qualitative Analysis of the 2014 Amendments*

## 5.1. INTRODUCTION

THE IMPETUS FOR this book was the proliferation of civil preventive measures during the last two decades in many Western jurisdictions. Although the stated objective of these measures is the prevention of certain types of criminality, they formally lie outside the ambit of the criminal law. The importance of this lies in the fact that those subjected to these measures, such as the Part 1 injunction of the Anti-social Behaviour, Crime and Policing Act 2014 and the Terrorism Prevention and Investigation Measures (TPIMs), fall in a legal lacuna with fewer rights and less protection than those prosecuted for the commission of a criminal offence. The proliferation of civil preventive measures matters, because as we saw earlier these instruments allow for the imposition of severe restrictions on the liberty of those against whom they are used. These restrictions can be so severe that they can amount to a form of criminal punishment in their own right resulting in the indirect criminalisation of the behaviour regulated.

In order to investigate further the phenomenon of indirect criminalisation I chose to focus on the Anti-social Behaviour Order's (ASBO) successor. I did so for two main reasons. First, I decided to focus on the injunction because of the breadth of its scope. As we saw earlier, the broad and ambiguous statutory definition of anti-social behaviour (ASB) covers a wide range of behaviour from everyday neighbour disputes to serious forms of criminality.[1] The law affords a significant magnitude of discretion to courts and local enforcements agents not only to decide what kinds of conduct can be regarded as anti-social, but also to determine the nature and severity of the requirements that can be imposed on those against whom an injunction is issued. What this means is that the implementation of the injunction can vary considerably from one area to another depending on how courts and local enforcement agents decide to exercise their discretion. For instance, what might be regarded as ASB in one part of the country can go unnoticed in another. The importance of this is heightened by the

[1] See ch 1, section 1.4.3.

potential punitive nature of the injunction.[2] Second, of particular concern were the 2014 amendments and the repeal and replacement of the hybrid ASBO by what appears to be a purely civil injunction. Although at first sight this seems to be a positive development, this move to a purely civil response should be approached with caution since it might result in less attention and outside scrutiny allowing the injunction to operate in the shadows as a de facto criminal rule.

The main objective of this study was to examine whether indeed the injunction has been operating as a de facto criminal measure resulting in the indirect criminalisation of certain kinds of ASB. To this end, I had to formulate a working definition of criminalisation that would enable me to look beyond the official label attached to the injunction. Moreover, I had to investigate empirically whether the implementation of the injunction resulted in the indirect criminalisation of certain kinds of ASB. Surely, a doctrinal analysis of the injunction can assist us to identify some of the normative and/or practical challenges posed by the law laying the foundations for a more in-depth examination of these issues.[3] A purely doctrinal analysis, however, fails to take into consideration how the law has been implemented in practice and the impact that this has 'in the world external to the black letter box'.[4] This omission matters because there can be significant discrepancies between the way the law appears on the statute book and the way it is implemented by law enforcement agents on the ground.[5] It was precisely for this reason that I decided to scrutinise the implementation of the injunction's first limb through an empirical study which would allow me to examine the relevant legislation in its social rather than solely its theoretical context, investigating whether the implementation of the injunction satisfies both prerequisites of my working definition of criminalisation.[6] The decision to conduct an empirical study is not to underplay the importance of doctrinal research. As Ramsay explains, a 'researcher needs to spend sufficient time in order to be reasonably on top of the subject before commencing the empirical research'.[7] Rather, the above is to point out that the theoretical analysis of the law might not always accurately reflect how it has been implemented in practice, especially in cases where the law in question has been broadly drafted, providing a significant degree of discretion to law enforcement agents and the courts as to its implementation.

[2] See ch 4, section 4.3.2.

[3] T Hutchinson, 'Doctrinal Research: Researching the Jury' in D Watkins and M Burton (eds), *Research Methods in Law* (Abingdon, Routledge, 2013) 15.

[4] ibid.

[5] C McCrudden, 'Legal Research and the Social Sciences' (2006) 122 *Law Quarterly Review* 632, 637.

[6] ibid 634.

[7] I Ramsay, 'Why is There so Little Empirical Corporate Law Research? A Comment' (1996) 3(1) *Canberra Law Review* 110, 112.

Chapter five begins by providing an overview of the empirical study conducted for the purposes of this monograph focusing particularly on its limitations and the contribution that it makes to the extant academic literature on criminalisation and ASB. I then proceed to present the first set of my empirical findings regarding the implementation of the injunction. The findings presented in this chapter relate to two main pillars. The first pillar relates to how ASB is conceptualised by local enforcement agents at a local level. I thought that if there was evidence to suggest that the injunction was in fact operating as *a de facto* criminal measure, then it would be imperative to examine what kinds of behaviour are criminalised through this process. As we shall see, there was evidence to suggest that the decisions of local enforcement agents to classify someone's behaviour as anti-social was informed by a number of factors, such as the limited availability of resources, that tended to narrow the scope of the law. The second pillar focuses on the 2014 amendments and whether these had any impact on the daily administration of the injunction. In particular, the data collected relate to the shift to a purely civil injunction and the introduction of positive obligations.

## 5.2. THE SCOPE OF THIS STUDY

Before presenting the empirical findings of this study, it is imperative to elaborate on its scope, its limitations and its contribution to the academic debates on criminalisation and ASB. The importance of this task lies in the rich pre-existing academic literature on the ASB tools and powers, especially at a theoretical level.[8] The initial decision to tackle ASB through a hybrid method of social control, for instance, was criticised by a number of academics, such as Duff, and Ashworth and Zedner, who argued that the ASBO was guilty of blurring the normative distinction between the criminal and the civil law.[9] Other critics of the ASBO, such as Cornford, focused on the alleged over-inclusiveness of ASB's statutory definition and the possibility of extending the reach of social control to behaviour which is 'merely offensive'[10] and/or to 'minor infractions commonly associated with young people'.[11]

At an empirical level, a number of small-scale studies have already been conducted focusing on specific aspects of the ASBO and related measures. Bullock and Jones, for instance, scrutinised the use of Acceptable Behaviour

[8] See ch 1, section 1.4.1.

[9] A Duff, 'Perversions and Subversions of Criminal Law' in A Duff et al (eds), *The Boundaries of the Criminal Law* (Oxford, Oxford University Press, 2010) 99–101; A Ashworth and L Zedner, 'Preventive Orders: A Problem of Undercriminalisation?' in A Duff et al (eds), *The Boundaries of the Criminal Law* (Oxford, Oxford University Press, 2010) 83.

[10] A Cornford, 'Criminalising Anti-social Behaviour' (2012) 6 *Criminal Law and Philosophy* 1, 3.

[11] S Lewis et al, 'Nipping Crime in the Bud? The use of Anti-social Behaviour Interventions with Young People in England and Wales' (2017) 57 *British Journal of Criminology* 1230, 1231.

Contracts (ABCs) in the London Borough of Islington.[12] According to their findings, although 43 per cent of the ABCs signed in Islington had been breached, this method of informal intervention had been very successful with many young people.[13] Based on their findings, there was a significant reduction in the levels of ASB committed by those who signed an ABC.[14]

In another study conducted by Koffman, the main objective was to examine empirically whether the 'ASBO and other measures' used by local enforcement agents in East Brighton targeted particular social groups, such as young people.[15] Based on his findings, 80 per cent of the ASBOs in this area were issued to people aged 20 or below.[16] Nonetheless, in most of the cases the ASBO was reserved for the most prolific perpetrators rather than as a first resort measure against ASB.[17] An equally important finding of this study was that the ASBO was used on many occasions to address behaviour which was already proscribed by criminal law.[18]

In another small-scale study, Matthews et al focused on the use of the ASBO and its impact on the perpetrators, the victims and local communities.[19] That study found that the issue of the order had different impacts on those against whom it was issued in terms of their future behaviour. While some of them viewed the issue of an ASBO as a 'wake-up call', others perceived the ASBO as a 'weaker alternative' to prosecution.[20] This study also revealed that the issue of an ASBO had a significant societal effect on both the perpetrators and their families. Evidence from this study suggests that both the perpetrators and their families were stigmatised by the rest of society.[21] The researchers also found an increased reliance by local enforcement agents on the post-conviction ASBO (CrASBO), rather than on the ASBO.[22]

In a study published in 2010, Donoghue examined the administration of both the ASBO and the CrASBO across Britain from a socio-legal perspective focusing on how due process considerations and 'judicial power and discretion intersect[ed] to shape' the implementation of these measures.[23] One of the most important findings of that study was that many members of the judiciary were

[12] K Bullock and B Jones, *Acceptable Behaviour Contracts Addressing Antisocial Behaviour in the London Borough of Islington* (London, Home Office, 2004).

[13] ibid 35.

[14] ibid 37.

[15] L Koffman, 'The Use of Anti-social Behaviour Orders: An Empirical Study of a New Deal for Communities Area' [2006] *Criminal Law Review* 593, 599.

[16] ibid 599–600.

[17] ibid 600.

[18] ibid 601.

[19] R Matthews et al, *Assessing the Use and Impact of Anti-Social Behaviour Orders* (Bristol, Policy Press, 2007).

[20] ibid 33–34.

[21] ibid 51.

[22] ibid 18.

[23] J Donoghue, *Anti-social Behaviour Orders: A Culture of Control?* (Basingstoke, Palgrave Macmillan, 2010) 88.

concerned about the fact that they could only impose negative obligations on those against whom an ASBO or a CrASBO was to be issued.[24] According to her findings, there was evidence to suggest that on many occasions judges were aware of the underlying causes of the perpetrator's behaviour, such as alcohol and drug addiction, and that the imposition of bland prohibitions could not permanently address the behaviour at hand.[25] The study also found a lack of cooperation amongst the various local enforcement agents.[26]

Finally, Crawford et al conducted a large-scale study in four different sites in England between 2008 and 2012 and examined 'the use of formal ASB warning letters, ABCs and ASBOs and the interrelations between these tools and the wider preventive and support services allied to them'.[27] Based on their findings, the use of the above-mentioned measures in the sites under investigation was in contrast to their preventive nature since those against whom these measures had been used had 'already engaged in serious or persistent offending'.[28] Moreover, although that study confirmed the existence of 'a pyramidal system of regulation' with regard to the administration of ASB, it found that in each site there were 'myriad variations' in terms of 'the numbers of tiers in the pyramidal structure'.[29]

This study examined the implementation of the post-2014 regime on ASB across two counties in England. As part of this project, between May 2015 and April 2016 29 interviews were conducted with local practitioners and police officers who had an everyday interaction with ASB and had been responsible for the implementation of the relevant tools and powers.[30] In particular, 19 interviews were conducted in Site A (10 with local practitioners and nine with police officers) and 10 in Site B (six with local practitioners and four with police officers).[31] It should also be noted that due to the criticisms raised about the potential punitive nature of the injunction, a decision was taken to conceal the true identity of the research participants, their institutions and the names of the actual sites investigated. To this end, the research participants' true identities were replaced by a three-part unique reference code to protect them from the consequences that may flow from their participation in this study.[32]

[24] ibid 128–30.

[25] ibid.

[26] ibid 99–100.

[27] See A Crawford et al, '"It ain't (just) what you do, it's (also) the way that you do it": The Role of Procedural Justice in the Implementation of Anti-social Behaviour Interventions with Young People' (2017) 23 *European Journal on Criminal Policy and Research* 9; Lewis et al (n 11).

[28] Crawford et al (n 27) 1237.

[29] ibid 1238.

[30] It should be noted that the injunction entered into force in March 2015.

[31] For a more detailed account of the methodology adopted, see ch 1, section 1.6.

[32] M Israel and I Hay, 'Research Ethics in Criminology' in D Gadd et al (eds), *The Sage Handbook of Criminological Research Methods* (London, Sage Publications, 2012) 504–05.

The first part of the code, such as 'Int 1', is a random number assigned to each participant and it is not reflective of the order in which each interview took place. The second part of the code, such as 'LP', refers to the research participant's occupation, that is 'PO' for police officers and 'LP' for local practitioners. The third part of the code, such as 'Site A', refers to the site where the interview took place.

The contribution of this empirical study to the current academic literature on ASB and criminalisation is threefold. First, in contrast to the above-mentioned empirical studies, which focused on the pre-2014 tools and powers, this is the first empirical data collected (that I am aware of) on the 2014 amendments. This empirical study provides an insight into how ASB is managed and addressed after the repeal and replacement of the ASBO and explores how local enforcement agents have utilised positive obligations.[33] It should be borne in mind that the use of these measures can vary considerably from one area to another due to the extensive discretion afforded to local enforcement agents regarding both the scope of the law in this area and the nature of the sanctions that can be imposed on those who behave in an anti-social manner.[34] Thus, it is necessary to approach the findings of this study with caution since they might not be representative of how the ASB tools and powers have been implemented across the country. Rather, they are only representative of the two sites under scrutiny.

Second, it is important to bear in mind that the implementation of the 2014 amendments and of the ASB legal framework in general are examined through the lenses of indirect criminalisation and in light of the working definition of criminalisation formulated in chapter three. Although at a theoretical level the ASBO's first limb was criticised for allowing for the indirect criminalisation of a wide range of behaviour, this is the first study that examines empirically the validity of this claim. The importance of this examination is heightened by the earlier theoretical analysis of the 2014 amendments through which I demonstrated how the injunction can result in the indirect criminalisation of certain kinds of ASB, albeit a purely civil response.[35]

Third, beyond indirect criminalisation, the findings of this study can contribute to the growing literature on localism, that is the delegation of power from the centre to local governments, discussed, albeit briefly in chapter one. Although in chapter one localism was discussed primarily in the context of criminal law, the findings of this study can shed light on how local authorities utilise the powers and discretion afforded to them when dealing with ASB.

[33] Under the 2014 Act a number of other tools and powers have been introduced as well, such as the Community Remedy and the Community Trigger. These measures are beyond the reach of this study. See ch 1, section 1.5.

[34] See ch 4, section 4.3.

[35] See ch 4, section 4.3.2.

## 5.3. CONCEPTUALISING ANTI-SOCIAL BEHAVIOUR AT A LOCAL LEVEL

One of the most concerning features of the pre-2014 legal framework was the statutory definition of ASB which, according to its critics, expanded (at least based on how it appeared on the statute book) the net of social control to everyday 'trivial, sub-criminal, or nuisance behaviour'.[36] As noted earlier, this can be attributed to the fact that the statutory definition of ASB focused on the actual and/or potential impact of someone's behaviour on others rather than on the nature of the wrong committed.[37] The government sought to defend the broad drafting of the statutory definition on the basis that each local community faces its own problems and they should be allowed a certain magnitude of discretion in order to be able to address what really matters to them.[38]

Under the current statutory definition, ASB ranges from conduct which causes mere 'nuisance and annoyance' to behaviour that causes 'harassment, alarm or distress'.[39] The flexibility of the statutory definition is further evidenced by the fact that the 2014 Act has retained the 'caused or likely to cause' clause. This enables local enforcement agents to adopt a proactive approach by 'highlight[ing] to [suspected perpetrators] that if they continue or escalate their behaviour what action can be taken' against them.[40]

The ambiguous limits of the statutory definition were confirmed when research participants were asked about how they would personally define ASB. In both sites, the majority of the participants felt that it was quite difficult to conceptualise ASB precisely or provide examples of behaviour that would definitely fall within the ambit of the statutory definition. As one police officer noted, 'almost everything fits under the ASB legislation'.[41] This was further evident by the participants' responses when asked to provide some examples of behaviour that could possibly be regarded as anti-social in their own localities. It was clear from the examples provided that ASB could range from behaviour which on the face of it appears to be part of everyday life to conduct which is already proscribed by criminal law. As a local practitioner noted:

> There are a lot of types of behaviour that we do not like or as a society we say are unacceptable such as noise, nuisance, it could be drug dealing for some people, substance abuse for other people who find it quite upsetting and anti-social.[42]

This statement also highlights the subjective nature of ASB. What can be regarded as anti-social by one person might be ignored as harmless behaviour by

[36] Koffman (n 15) 611–12.
[37] See ch 1, section 1.4.3.
[38] Home Office, *More Effective Responses to Anti-social Behaviour* (London, Home Office, 2011) 1.
[39] Anti-social Behaviour, Crime and Policing Act 2014, s 2(1).
[40] Int 17-LP-Site B.
[41] Int 12-PO-Site B.
[42] Int 4-LP-Site A.

another. It is for this reason that I argue that the implementation of the injunction, including how ASB is conceptualised at a local level, can vary considerably across the county.

As far as the lower end of the spectrum is concerned, it was clear that ASB covers primarily behaviour which appears to be part of everyday social interaction and not directly regulated by law, such as 'drinking [alcohol and] ... being loud' while being in a public place.[43] Although consuming alcohol in a public space is not prohibited by law, local enforcement agencies can seek to prevent people from doing this if it leads to ASB.[44] Local enforcement agents can use, for instance, a Public Spaces Protection Order (PSPO) to prohibit the consumption of alcohol in a particular area if they deem this as one of the underlying causes of ASB.[45] Although the use of the 2014 Act as a means of regulating otherwise legal activities appears to be contentious, it is clear that the ASB provisions provide a further flexible tool to local enforcement agents since these measures do not require the formalities of direct criminalisation. Most importantly, as we will see below, local enforcement agents will take into consideration a number of factors before labelling someone's behaviour as anti-social, something that significantly narrows the scope of the injunction.

### 5.3.1. Impact and Persistence

Most of the interviewees noted that the regulation of otherwise legally permissible activities through these measures can be attributed to the *impact* that these activities had on others, as against the actual nature of the conduct in question. Several interviewees highlighted the fact that while some activities appear, in isolation, to be of a trivial nature, their cumulative effect on people's lives can in fact be devastating. On many occasions, ASB 'will determine where people want to live, it will determine their friendships, their family [and] it can put strains on relationships'.[46] Moreover, as the case of Fiona Pilkington illustrates,[47] victims of prolonged ASB 'have gone on to commit suicide because they felt that what they were reporting had no impact and they were dismissed'.[48]

[43] Int 3-LP-Site A.

[44] Being disorderly in a public space while drunk constitutes an offence under s 91 of the Criminal Justice Act 1967.

[45] Under s 58 of the 2014 Act a local authority can issue such an order as a means of addressing or preventing a certain kind of behaviour in a public space which has or is likely to have a 'detrimental effect on the quality of life of those in the locality'. Breach of the order or failure to comply with the requirements of an order constitutes an offence under s 67 and can result in the issue of a fixed penalty notice (s 68 of the 2014 Act). See further J Woodhouse and P Ward, 'Drinking in the Streets' (2015) 4, available at: researchbriefings.parliament.uk/ResearchBriefing/Summary/SN05117.

[46] Int 16-LP-Site A.

[47] See further, ch 1, section 1.4.3.

[48] Int 4-LP-Site A.

Although 'there [was] no specific number of incidents' required in order for local enforcement agents to classify someone's behaviour as anti-social,[49] it was clear from the data collected that either the perpetrator's behaviour must have a significant effect on victims' lives 'over a period of time' or that its impact had been so severe that immediate action was needed.[50] As one of the participants put it:

> We are going to review [each incident] and if we think that it is too high or has been going on for a long time and nothing that we have done seems to have worked ... we will then look at enforcement.[51]

The above testimonies suggest that the key factor that is considered when determining whether something is classified as ASB is its actual or potential impact on others, which is often marked by persistent and repetitive conduct. This approach is in line with the Home Office's guidelines regarding the way ASB is to be conceptualised at a local level. According to these guidelines, 'the right response in each case will depend on a range of factors, but most importantly, on the needs of the victim and the impact the behaviour is having on their lives'.[52]

### 5.3.2. Discretion and Common Sense

According to half of the interviewees, the focus on the impact that certain kinds of behaviour have on others also helps to explain the reason why similar activities can be treated differently, that is as non-anti-social, depending on the context in which they take place. One police officer explained:

> Having a house party where no one can hear it for three miles is not going to be anti-social. But if you put that same incident ... in the middle of a town centre it is likely to cause harassment, alarm or distress ... So, same people doing the same thing, different locations, massively different impact.[53]

This need for a flexible legal framework was further evident when participants were asked about the 2014 amendments with regard to the way ASB is defined. As mentioned before, under the 2014 Act the definition of ASB (applicable to the Part 1 injunction) has been extended in two ways when compared with the one applicable to the ASBO.[54] First, the consolidation of a number of instruments,

[49] Int 19-PO-Site A.

[50] Int 24-LP-Site A.

[51] Int 19-PO-Site A. It should be noted that most of the participants used the term 'enforcement' to describe the process of taking formal legal action against someone, such as applying for the issue of an injunction or of a Criminal Behaviour Order (CBO).

[52] Home Office, *Putting Victims First: More Effective Responses to Anti-social Behaviour* (London, Home Office, 2012) 1.3.

[53] Int 26-PO-Site A.

[54] See ch 4, Table 4.1.

such as the Anti-social Behaviour Injunction, into a single multi-purpose injunction has led to the expansion of ASB to behaviour that causes 'nuisance and annoyance' in a housing-related context.[55] Second, under the 1998 Act, ASB was defined as conduct which 'caused or was likely to cause harassment, alarm or distress to one or more persons not of the same household as himself'.[56] This was modified by section 2 of the 2014 Act and now includes behaviour that 'causes or is likely to cause harassment, alarm or distress to any person'.[57]

As many of the participants noted, the 'same household as himself' clause caused ambiguities and 'grey areas' especially when the alleged incident of ASB took place in hostels and houses of multiple occupancies.[58] The abolition of this clause was regarded as a positive development by most of the research participants who perceived this as a necessary amendment. According to one local practitioner, 'it is broadening the net … the behaviour can be monitored wider' and this allows them to determine the scope of the law based on the issues faced locally.[59]

The great magnitude of discretion afforded to local enforcement agents regarding the way ASB is to be conceptualised at a local level conforms to the government's promise for a new legal framework that will be capable of 'provid[ing] faster, more visible justice for victims and communities … and that act[s] as a real deterrent'.[60] For the majority of the participants this flexibility in the statutory definition, particularly the 'likely to cause' clause, was vital for the protection of vulnerable victims since it enabled them to adopt a more proactive approach towards ASB. This allowed local enforcement agents to intervene at an early stage and 'stop [the perpetrators'] ASB rather than leave them to escalate'.[61] According to a police officer, 'by keeping "likely" to occur it gives us greater scope to assess cases and put measures if we need to protect those vulnerable members of community'.[62]

This does not necessarily mean that the police or local practitioners applied for the issue of an injunction in cases where someone's behaviour was only *likely* to cause 'harassment, alarm or distress'. To be used in this way would have constituted a significant and possibly unjustifiable expansion of the scope of the law in this area. Nevertheless, as Sanders and Young explain, 'the importance of legal powers [given to the police] is not so much that they are *actually* invoked frequently, but that they could be'.[63] On this view, what is important about the

[55] House of Commons, *Anti-Social Behaviour, Crime and Policing Bill: Explanatory Notes* [HL Bill 52] (2013) para 13.

[56] Crime and Disorder Act 1998, s 1.

[57] Anti-social Behaviour, Crime and Policing Act 2014, s 2(1)(a).

[58] Int 5-LP-Site A.

[59] Int 6-LP-Site A.

[60] Home Office, *Putting Victims First* (n 52) 1.

[61] Int 6-LP-Site A.

[62] Int 12-PO-Site B.

[63] A Sanders and R Young, 'Police Powers' in T Newburn (ed), *Handbook of Policing*, 2nd edn (Cullompton, Willan Publishing, 2008) 281.

'likely to cause' clause is not so much its actual implementation, but that it *can* be used by law enforcement agents at their own discretion when this is deemed necessary. Although based on the data collated in both sites, local enforcement agents had not actually used the ASB tools and powers to regulate behaviour which did not actually cause any of the above-mentioned negative experiences to other people, we still need to ensure that these measures are only used against behaviour that is really problematic and has an adverse impact on people's quality of life.

Notwithstanding the significant magnitude of discretion afforded to local enforcement agents to determine what kinds of behaviour should be regarded as anti-social, most of the research participants highlighted the need for their 'response to be measured' and to focus on behaviour that does not fall within the realm of everyday social interaction.[64] For instance, as a local practitioner argued:

> If it is simply that someone is having children and their children are using their own back garden and they are causing nuisance to their neighbours because they do not want to hear children, then that is not ASB and we will not deal with that. That is living sound.[65]

Although the majority of the participants held that a certain degree of flexibility is necessary when dealing with ASB, four interviewees, two from each site, highlighted the risks associated with the broad drafting of the statutory definition by characterising it as 'frighteningly subjective'.[66] According to one local practitioner:

> It is becoming potentially quite powerful for local authorities for addressing behaviours that they just decide they do not like … my concern for that is that it could be used inappropriately and disproportionately against people who maybe do not have a voice, [such as] members of the street community.[67]

Moreover, some participants noted that the broad statutory definition of ASB created a lot of misconceptions amongst members of the public as to nature of the behaviour dealt with through these measures, something which led to higher expectations as to what local enforcement agents can achieve through the implementation of the relevant tools and powers. Some interviewees, for example, noted that members of the public tend to perceive these measures as a 'panacea in solving their problems'.[68] Consequently, some members of the public believed that the scope of the law in this area should be extended in order to address what they personally believed to be anti-social. In theory, this can be further facilitated

[64] Int 11-PO-Site B.
[65] Int 16-LP-Site B.
[66] Int 8-LP-Site B.
[67] Int 4-LP-Site A.
[68] Int 17-LP-Site B.

through the introduction of the Community Trigger which imposes an obligation on local enforcement agents to formulate a review procedure with regard to the public's complaints relating to ASB.[69] This can possibly put extra pressure on local enforcement agents to extend the net of social control to 'potentially "all spheres of life"'.[70] These increased expectations do not only impose a higher burden on local enforcement agencies which have to administrate them, but they can also have a negative impact on society's tolerance level and interpersonal relationships. An expansion in the net of social control can encourage people to report/complain about behaviour which would have been previously ignored or considered to be part of everyday social interaction. As a result of this, the way can be paved for the introduction of even more far-reaching interventions that can further restrict individual liberty in the name of ASB prevention. The following testimony is a good illustration of the possible adverse consequences of these increased expectations:

> What we find is that we will get residents who report issues with their neighbours without having to address them themselves and as you know as soon as the landlord gets involved you can end up breaking up a relationship.[71]

The above testimonies clearly highlight a really important struggle that lies at the heart of practice with local enforcement agents trying to manage the public's expectations while trying to adopt a common sense approach regarding the implementation of the ASB tools and powers. The concerns raised above, therefore, regarding the expansion of the net of social control to 'all spheres of life' through the implementation of ASB tools and powers are not evidenced empirically. Rather, it was evident that local enforcement agents used the discretion granted to them in a sensible manner focusing only on behaviour that had a real impact on others. As discussed earlier, however, what is important about the powers granted to law enforcement agents is not always the way they are currently used. Instead, what really matters, according to Sanders and Young, is the fact that these powers are available to them if they wish to invoke them.[72] Although Sanders and Young are referring here to the ability of police officers to search people even without making use of the powers granted to them by law, their argument is readily applicable in the context of the ASB tools and powers as well.[73] Although in both sites ASB has not been conceptualised in an arbitrary manner, it is still necessary to formulate mechanisms through which we can ensure that changes in the implementation of these measures will not result in the expansion of the net of social control.

[69] For more on the Community Trigger, see ch 4, section 4.3.1.

[70] D Stephen, 'The Responsibility of Respecting Justice: An Open Challenge to Tony Blair's Successors' in P Squires (ed), *ASBO Nation: The Criminalisation of Nuisance* (Bristol, Policy Press, 2008) 321–22.

[71] Int 16-LP-Site B.

[72] Sanders and Young (n 63) 281.

[73] ibid.

### 5.3.3. Focusing on Victims and their Experiences

In Site A, there was strong evidence to suggest that victims' perceptions were central to the way ASB was conceptualised. It was evident from the data collected that if the complainant was negatively affected by someone's behaviour or if they deemed their behaviour as anti-social, then the investigation of this incident would start from the premise that it constituted ASB. The next testimony is illustrative of this victim-oriented approach adopted in Site A in terms of conceptualising ASB: 'it is a victim-led, victim/witness-led process. When a victim reports us that they have felt harassment, alarm or distress then that very much informs whether we are going to take it on as a case'.[74] A similar approach was also adopted by the relevant police force. According to one of its members, 'a common theme within policing is … that it is actually better to deal with something as it has been identified rather than to justify why it is not anti-social'.[75] For this reason, 'if there is a hate element to it then [the victim's] perception [of the behaviour in question] is really important because there is a perception that it is a hate incident. It is a hate ASB and then we will deal with it accordingly'.[76]

The above is not to suggest that local enforcement agencies structured their investigation and response solely on the alleged victim's perception of an incident in the absence of any other credible evidence. As one of the participants pointed out, 'if we obtain evidence … that suggests otherwise we will then make adjustments to that' effect.[77] Instead, it illustrates the importance attributed by these institutions in Site A to victims and the possible adverse consequences that persistent low-level criminality and ASB can have on them. This is in line with the government's promise to depart from the 'one size fits all' approach of the past.[78] As the Home Office explains, 'anti-social behaviour is a fundamentally local issue, one that looks and feels different in every area, in every neighbourhood and to every victim'.[79] Accordingly, the views of the victims should not be dismissed outright since what might appear to be of trivial nature to local enforcement agents, can have a devastating effect on the complainant's life.

As far as Site B was concerned, three out of the 10 participants from this site noted that they would take into consideration whether the alleged victim perceived a particular kind of behaviour as anti-social. However, the overall impression from this area was that a victim's perception of an incident would not affect significantly, or at least not to the extent that this did in Site A, the way

[74] Int 5-LP-Site A.
[75] Int 28-PO-Site A.
[76] Int 29-PO-Site A.
[77] Int 21-PO-Site A.
[78] Home Office, *Putting Victims First* (n 52) 3.
[79] ibid.

local enforcement agents conceptualise ASB. As noted by a police officer, 'if we are getting repeated calls about the same thing … we are going to look at it to determine [whether we] actually need to do something about it because there is a risk to the public'.[80]

From a victim's perspective, an approach similar to the one adopted in Site A, offers assurance to the complainants that their reports 'are taken seriously' by the authorities and that they are not going to be dismissed outright without any further investigation.[81] Moreover, as with 'hate crimes', focusing on the alleged victim's perception of an incident can increase the public's confidence in law enforcement agencies, tackle under-reporting and ensure that equal protection is offered to every social group.[82] Although the adoption of a more victim-oriented approach by local enforcement agents echoes the government's promise of 'putting victims first',[83] recourse to this approach should not be viewed as a panacea in addressing ASB.[84] As Duggan and Heap rightly point out, victims and their needs should not be used as a Trojan Horse for the adoption of a more punitive response to ASB, such as the imposition of more severe restrictions on the liberty of those subjected to these measures.[85] According to Sanders and Jones, in the context of criminal trials 'all too often the rights of the accused are portrayed as obstacles in the way of fair treatment for victims'.[86] For this reason, according to them, we must be mindful of the 'trade-off[s]' between the rights of the accused and the needs of the victim.[87] Our main objective should be to strike a fair balance between the two. Individual liberty should not be seen as antagonistic to security but as one of the fundamental values underpinning every contemporary liberal state.

In the context of ASB, this shift towards a victim-oriented approach can be used as a means to expand the net of social control to behaviour that falls within the remit of everyday interaction, such as 'kids playing football in the street'.[88] As Crawford et al contend, adopting a more inclusive approach in terms of the way ASB is to be defined can result in a 'regulatory overload [and to] net widening'.[89]

The concerns expressed by Duggan and Heap are further justified by the significant variations in communities' tolerance levels reported particularly in

[80] Int 14-PO-Site B.

[81] Home Office, *Putting Victims First* (n 52) 3.

[82] HM Government, *Action Against Hate: The UK Government's Plan for Tackling Hate Crime – 'Two Years on'* (2018) 7, available at: assets.publishing.service.gov.uk/government/uploads/system/uploads/attachment_data/file/748175/Hate_crime_refresh_2018_FINAL_WEB.PDF.

[83] Home Office, *Putting Victims First* (n 52) 3.

[84] See ch 4, section 4.3.1.

[85] M Duggan and V Heap, *Administrating Victimisation: The Politics of Anti-Social Behaviour and Hate Crime Policy* (Basingstoke, Palgrave Macmillan, 2014) 3.

[86] A Sanders and I Jones, 'The Victim in Court' in S Walklate (ed), *Handbook of Victims and Victimology* (Cullompton, Willan Publishing, 2007) 282–83.

[87] ibid.

[88] Int 2-LP-Site A.

[89] Crawford et al (n 27) 15.

Site B. Evidence collected from this site suggests that people in more affluent areas and/or areas with lower crime rates tend to be less tolerant towards ASB. In contrast to this, in areas with high crime rates people tend to report only the most serious incidents of ASB 'because they have to deal with [criminality] on a daily basis … it becomes part of their normal lives'.[90] The following statement is illustrative of a number of responses given by many research participants in Site B through which these variations were highlighted: 'you will find this in the more affluent areas. The lowest level of ASB will be reported there'.[91] It follows that the way different social groups perceive and approach ASB can vary considerably since this is influenced by their socio-economic background. This becomes particularly problematic where a strict victim-oriented approach, that is no other factors are taken into consideration in determining whether someone's behaviour should be regarded as anti-social, is adopted by local enforcement agents. As explained earlier, this could not only lead to the unjustifiable expansion of the net of social control, but it can also result in the targeting of certain social groups, especially those whose voices are not often heard. That said, it would be wrong to assume that the adoption of a more victim-oriented approach in this context would inevitably lead to the expansion of the net of social control. As we shall see below, the ambit of the law in this area is shaped by a number of factors, most of which tend to narrow it down rather than expand it.

### 5.3.4. Review Procedure

As mentioned above, the interview data suggested that the main factor that practitioners used to determine whether someone's behaviour was to be classified as anti-social is its *impact* on other members of the community. The findings of this research also echo the findings of previous studies which revealed both an overlap between ASB and criminality and the possibility of regulating otherwise permissible legal activities through the implementation of these measures.[92] This was an expected discovery primarily due to the way ASB is defined under section 2 of the 2014 Act. As seen earlier, one of the main criticisms against ASB's statutory definition is its reliance on the impact or likely impact of someone's behaviour rather than on the nature of the conduct at hand.[93] That said, it was evident from the data collected for the purposes of this study that the relevant measures were only utilised in serious cases where the behaviour in question was impactful and most commonly repetitive. The behaviour at hand had to be more than merely offensive or to cause something more than mere discomfort in order for it to fall

[90] Int 4-PO-Site B.
[91] Int 13-PO-Site B.
[92] See, eg, Lewis et al (n 11) 1237–38.
[93] See ch 1, section 1.4.3.

within local enforcement agents' mandate. As one of the participants from Site B noted, each complaint/incident 'has to be taken by a degree of common sense because again lots of different people find lots of different things offensive'.[94] The adoption of this common sense approach was also evident in Site A with one local practitioner explaining that 'people have their eccentricities. I do not have any problem with those eccentricities ... but if your habit is having an impact on the community and it is affecting people's lives then something needs to be done about it'.[95] As this local practitioner then mentioned, 'although [the ASB provisions] have been described as being draconian, in my mind they are only asking people to behave in a reasonable manner'.[96] Overall, there was little to no evidence to suggest that these measures were used in either Site A or B in an irrational manner against behaviour which was merely offensive, caused mere discomfort or behaviour that was part of daily social interaction.

This finding is further strengthened by the fact that in most of the participating institutions the initial decision to classify someone's behaviour as anti-social 'goes through several layers of review'.[97] As a police officer put it, 'it is not just one officer on their own' who decides whether the behaviour at stake should fall within the ambit of the ASB legislation.[98] Rather, as the following testimony elucidates, cases were constantly reviewed both internally and externally:

> We have discussions on a weekly basis about the behaviour that has been reported and we have a team discussion about whether we would class that as ASB and secondly whether it is something that falls within the remit of our team. Then we go to wider city meetings, the multi-agency assessment and targeting meetings. So, we kind of get wider city consent as to what ASB is.[99]

It is evident from the above testimonies that there was a review procedure in place through which local enforcement agencies tried to strike a fair balance between victims' needs and expectations and behaviour which was really worth addressing. Although an internal review procedure was not available in three housing associations, it was noted by the research participants from these institutions that they tend to collaborate closely with their local Community Safety Partnerships. One of them also mentioned that their institution participates sometimes in 'wider city meetings' as well.

Taken as a whole, it was evident from the interviews conducted in both sites that behaviour is not arbitrarily labelled as anti-social. The concerns raised earlier, therefore, regarding the expansion of the net of social control to 'all spheres of life' through the implementation of the ASB measures, especially of

[94] Int 9-LP-Site B.
[95] Int 24-LP-Site A.
[96] Int 24-LP-Site A.
[97] Int 28-PO-Site A.
[98] Int 12-PO-Site B.
[99] Int 5-LP-Site A.

the injunction, were not borne out by the evidence. The broad and ambiguous drafting of ASB's statutory definition, though, still enables local enforcement agents to use the law in an arbitrary manner if they want to. Consequently, it is imperative to formulate mechanisms through which it can be ensured that the implementation of the law will not result in the unjustifiable expansion of the net of social control. As I will argue in chapter seven, the data presented here can be further scrutinised by local enforcement agents and policymakers to identify those factors that contributed to the adoption of a more sensible approach in the sites under study and incorporate those principles into their existing policies.

### 5.3.5. Availability of Resources

It was clear from the data collected from both sites that the implementation of the ASB legal framework relied heavily on the amount of resources available at a local level. In 19 interviews the lack of resources and/or the costs of implementation of these measures were highlighted as one of the main factors that local enforcement agents would take into consideration when determining whether a particular incident should be regarded as anti-social. For instance, one local practitioner from Site A noted that:

> Because the resources are becoming a little bit more stretched, we try to prioritise the cases where there is a personal harm of ASB. We try to move away from the neighbour disputes and that sort of things.[100]

As the above account illustrates, the limited availability of resources has led local enforcement agents to concentrate on the most serious incidents reported to them. This is behaviour that is situated at the upper end of the ASB spectrum. As one police officer pointed out, 'there has to be a realistic understanding … we have reductions in the number of police officers. We have to focus on risk and harm'.[101] The foregoing testimonies accurately reflect a number of responses provided by participants who emphasised that the limited resources available for tackling ASB and criminality forced them to focus on behaviour that had a significant and detrimental impact on people's quality of life rather than on everyday incivilities, such as minor neighbour disputes.[102] The need to prioritise resources, however, does not necessarily prevent the inconsistent application of the ASB tools and powers. In areas with more resources, for instance, local enforcement agents might decide to interpret ASB more widely extending at the same time the scope of the injunction.

[100] Int 20-LP-Site A.
[101] Int 11-PO-Site B.
[102] As we shall see in the next chapter, evidence from this study also suggests that the amount of resources available was likely to have an impact on the procedure followed after someone's behaviour was labelled as anti-social.

Taken as a whole, it was evident from the interviews conducted in both sites that behaviour is not arbitrarily labelled as anti-social. Instead, in both sites the decision of local enforcement agents to classify someone's behaviour as anti-social is influenced by a number of factors, such as the limited availability of resources, which tend to significantly narrow the scope of the ASB tools and powers.

## 5.4. THE 2014 AMENDMENTS

During the second phase of the interview research participants were asked to comment on the 2014 amendments and whether, in their opinion, these had or would have any impact on the daily administration of ASB at a local level. In particular, emphasis was paid to the repeal and replacement of the ASBO by a purely civil injunction and the introduction of positive obligations. The reason why I decided to ask my research participants about the impact of the 2014 amendments was to examine if any of the concerns raised about the ASBO had been addressed, especially those relating to its hybrid nature and its inability to permanently address the underlying causes of ASB.

### 5.4.1. The Move to a Purely Civil Injunction

Although the ASBO's hybrid nature was one of its most contentious and heavily criticised features academically,[103] its abandonment attracted mixed responses from the research participants. For the majority of the participants the move to a purely civil injunction was unlikely to have any significant effect on the daily administration of ASB. According to the data collected during this study, there are three possible explanations for this. First, the majority of interviewees noted that the ASBO was just one out of the many tools and powers in their arsenal in dealing with ASB and criminality. As one of the interviewees noted, 'we have got offences with which we can still deal with people for and I am not overly concerned that the breach is not an offence anymore as long as we can still deal with it effectively'.[104] This is in line with the above findings and with the findings of previous studies which highlighted the overlap between ASB and criminality.[105]

Second, reference was made in both areas to the way courts used to deal with those who were found in breach of their ASBOs. Two participants from Site B argued that the shift to a purely civil mechanism was unlikely to have any impact

[103] See ch 1, section 1.4.1.
[104] Int 13-PO-Site B.
[105] Lewis et al (n 11) 1237; Koffman (n 15) 601.

on the way they were dealing with ASB since the ASBO 'was anyway a toothless tiger'.[106] According to one police officer, 'under the old legislation we would go back [to court] after breaches time after time and nothing would happen to that person. So, I do not think that it particularly concerns me'.[107] In contrast to this, two interviewees from Site A noted that they were 'quite confident'[108] that 'if you are having lots of breaches the next time they go back to court it will obviously be taken a lot more seriously'.[109] A possible explanation for these contradictory statements was, according to one police officer, that judges tend to treat (repeated) perpetrators differently:

> She breached it again within 4 days. So, she went back to court and unfortunately, we sat before a different judge and he actually deferred that case until January. But if she was to come back again in front of him, she would definitely get a custodial.[110]

Third, for some interviewees this shift towards a purely civil injunction was unlikely to have any real effect on certain individuals. According to them, the main reason for this was that some perpetrators would simply not comply with a court order or an injunction regardless of the possible consequences. One interviewee noted that 'you are still going to get the twenty per cent who did not care. They did not care because they had other issues'.[111]

Ten interviewees expressed their concerns as to whether a purely civil response will be as effective as the ASBO used to be in dealing with ASB. Many of the participants focused on the effectiveness of the ASBO as a 'bargaining tool for working with a person and getting them to understand the consequences of their behaviour'.[112] It had been suggested that the criminal nature of the ASBO's second limb acted as a leverage for the perpetrators to change their behaviour. Consequently, this shift to a purely civil method of regulation means that those who act in an anti-social manner are no longer provided with 'prudential reasons for desistence'.[113] More than a third of the interviewees argued that the abolition of the hybrid model will have a detrimental impact on the injunction's overall deterrent effect. As one police officer explained, 'it is a real shame … I think it has taken some of the bite away from the legislation'.[114]

Another cause for concern for many participants was the fact that a power of arrest is not automatically attached to an injunction. While breach of the ASBO constituted an offence and thus the police were able to immediately arrest anyone found in breach of his order, this is not the case with the new injunction.

[106] Int 14-PO-Site B.
[107] Int 14-PO-Site B.
[108] Int 4-LP-Site A.
[109] Int 7-LP-Site A.
[110] Int 18-PO-Site A.
[111] Int 8-LP-Site A.
[112] Int 4-LP-Site A.
[113] A von Hirsch, *Censure and Sanctions* (New York, Oxford University Press, 1993) 12.
[114] Int 12-PO-Site B.

Under section 4(1) of the 2014 Act, the institution applying for the issue of an injunction must demonstrate either that the respondent has a history of violence or that he poses 'a significant risk to others' in order for a power of arrest to be attached. According to some participants, obtaining a power of arrest is not as easy as it might appear to be:

> There is no point in even bothering looking at an injunction for him because he does not even care … In reality it will be unlikely to get a power of arrest attached to the injunction for him despite him having more aggravated offences on his record than anybody else in our city. The standard criminal justice has acted and it seems that it had no deterrent effect on him behaving in that way and an injunction without a power of arrest attached it would not have any effect. He is someone who actually if anything is to work is the imminence of arrest and significant sanction. An injunction would not do that.[115]

The above-mentioned concerns in conjunction with the limited amount of resources available led many of the participants to express their reservations as to whether they should be applying for the issue of an injunction. According to one of the interviewees, 'it makes me think what the point is. One of the things is that it costs a lot of money and if it is not a criminal offence, then for what purpose?'[116] This finding was further supported by a number of other testimonies based on which local enforcement agents are now more focused on getting a CBO rather than an injunction. As one interviewee pointed out, 'I think that there is more pressure to get a criminal order because (a) you have the power of arrest more or less kind of automatic and (b) in theory the court will cost less'.[117] This should be linked with our earlier discussion about the impact that the limited availability of resources had on the way ASB was conceptualised by local enforcement agents.[118]

This focus on the post-conviction order is not a new phenomenon. Between 2002 and 2013 the number of CrASBOs issued was almost twice the number of ASBOs.[119] The above finding, however, raises fundamental questions about the administration of justice which appears to be driven to a large extent by the amount of resources available at a local level rather than by principles of justice.

Most importantly, it undermines, at least to some extent, the preventive nature of the civil injunction. The introduction of the civil preventive measures was premised on the assumption that the state should be able to address ASB at

[115] Int 1-LP-Site A.
[116] Int 3-LP-Site A.
[117] Int 15-PO-Site A.
[118] See section 5.3.5.
[119] Home Office and Ministry of Justice, *Statistical Notice: Anti-social Behaviour Order (ASBO) Statistics-England and Wales 2013* (2014).

an early stage to prevent it from escalating to serious criminality.[120] The focus on the CBO, however, means that local enforcement agents will have to wait for someone to be found guilty of an offence to address their ASB. This is in line with the findings of Lewis et al who found that the implementation of the ASB tools and powers 'refute[s] the logical sequencing of prevention' because some of those against whom these measures were used had 'already engaged in serious or persistent offending'.[121]

### 5.4.2. The Introduction of Positive Obligations

The introduction of positive obligations under the 2014 Act was regarded by the government as a necessary addition to the new tools and powers since they 'allow professionals to respond to the underlying causes of anti-social behaviour'.[122] The perpetrator does not simply choose to act in an anti-social manner. Instead, in many cases the perpetrator's behaviour has deeper causes which cannot be addressed through the imposition of bland prohibitions. Through the introduction of positive obligations local enforcement agents are invited to engage with these underlying causes and provide perpetrators with the necessary support needed to address these causes.[123] In the case of an alcoholic, for example, these positive obligations can be utilised in order for the perpetrator to attend an alcohol-related treatment.

There was strong evidence to suggest from this study that the majority of the interviewees perceived this addition as a positive development, since it enables them to work with the perpetrators to address the underlying causes of their behaviour. As one of the interviewees pointed out, 'in a lot of cases you can only address ASB if you address the underlying causes … and sometimes I think people need to be pushed or even ordered to seek help with some things'.[124] In addition to this, it was noted by some interviewees that positive obligations can also be used to repair the harm caused to victims by, for instance, 'mak[ing] someone clean up street graffiti'.[125]

According to some of the participants, positive obligations were already used through the ABCs. A police officer explained that the ABCs were not just used to put restrictions on the perpetrator's behaviour, but they were used as

[120] A Crawford, 'Governing Through Anti-social Behaviour' (2009) 49 *British Journal of Criminology* 810, 816.

[121] Lewis et al (n 11) 1232.

[122] Home Office, *Anti-social Behaviour, Crime and Policing Act 2014: Reform of Anti-social Behaviour Powers – Statutory Guidance for Frontline Professionals* (London, Home Office, 2021) 25.

[123] ibid.

[124] Int 2-LP-Site A.

[125] Int 26-LP-Site A.

a means of referring people to 'juvenile services or attend this club six times a week'.[126] The foregoing testimony is consistent with the findings of Crawford et al who found that positive obligations were already imposed 'by way of support services to be accessed by the individual'.[127] Nevertheless, it was evident from the testimonies provided that for the majority of the participants the introduction of positive obligations is a step in the right direction. Although compulsory attendance at an alcohol-related treatment can be perceived as an interference with that person's liberty and autonomy,[128] this can be justified on the ground that these paternalistic interventions are capable of providing permanent rather than temporary relief to those affected by the perpetrator's behaviour.

Paternalism works from the premise that people sometimes need to be protected not just from others but also from themselves, either because they are not capable of making the right decision or because they might simply refuse to make it. Parents, for example, might not allow their children to ride their bikes in the city centre because they believe that they do not possess the necessary skills required to do so. This means that the children are not allowed to choose whether they will ride their bikes in the city centre or not. By the same token, under paragraph 83 of the Highway Code, a duty is imposed on every motorcyclist to wear a protective helmet. In theory, every motorcyclist is denied the opportunity to choose whether they wish to buy a protective helmet or not. Sam, for instance, might have been tempted not to buy a protective helmet simply to save some money. Under certain circumstances, therefore, a higher authority assumes that its subjects should be denied the opportunity to choose either because they are not capable or because they can be tempted not to make the right decision. For example, to prioritise their safety over the extra cost of buying a protective helmet.

The main cause for concern with regard to paternalistic interventions, therefore, is that they appear to undermine individual autonomy by denying those subjected to them the opportunity to choose freely what is in their best interest.[129] As Husak contends, however, paternalism as a reason for action is not prima facie objectionable.[130] For a legal paternalist, the interference of the state is usually justified on the grounds of 'welfare, good, happiness, needs, interests, or values of the person being coerced'.[131] To support his argument Husak uses the example of a patient who is driven to a hospital unconscious where lifesaving

[126] Int 29-PO-Site A.

[127] Crawford et al (n 27) 11.

[128] B Gert and C Culver, 'Paternalistic Behaviour' (1976) 6 *Philosophy & Public Affairs* 45, 46.

[129] ibid 46.

[130] D Husak, 'Paternalism' in A Marmor (ed), *The Routledge Companion to Philosophy of Law* (New York, Routledge, 2012) 469.

[131] G Dworkin, 'Paternalism' in R Wasserstorm (ed), *Morality and the Law* (Belmont, Wadsworth Publishing, 1971) 108.

surgery should be carried out.[132] The surgeon conducting the operation acts in a paternalistic manner. Thus, under certain circumstances paternalistic interventions can be justified especially when dealing with individuals who are not able to decide for themselves.

Similarly, the criminal law sometimes adopts a paternalistic approach to protect certain groups of individuals. To illustrate how paternalistic interventions operate, consider sections 9–15 of the Sexual Offences Act 2003 which proscribe the participation of a child in any sort of sexual conduct regardless of consent. The criminal law intervenes in this case in order to protect a specific group of people from taking what the state assumes to be the wrong decision. In this case, regardless of a minor's desire to engage in a sexual activity, the criminal law assumes a responsibility to protect that individual from harming himself.

As Simester and von Hirsch rightly point out, the justifiability of paternalistic interventions should also be examined in light of the mechanisms used by the state to achieve these desired outcomes.[133] For them, any paternalistic intervention by the state should take place through the civil rather than the criminal law due to criminalisation's coercive nature.[134] They contend that under certain circumstances the adverse effects of a criminal conviction, such as its stigmatising effect, can outweigh the effects of taking the wrong decision.[135] For them, if 'limited state intervention of a civil character [can be] justified, then recourse to the criminal law should not follow'.[136] On this view, the imposition of positive obligations through the implementation of the injunction appears to be less contentious than paternalistic interventions through punitive measures due to its civil nature. If there is evidence to suggest, however, that the injunction is operating as a de facto criminal intervention, then the justifiability of these paternalistic interventions can be called into question.

Although the prevention of crime is a worthwhile objective for the liberal state to pursue, we always need to be mindful of the impact that this will have on individual autonomy.[137] What distinguishes the liberal state from other kinds of political orders is that it promises to uphold both the security and the liberty of its citizens. Consequently, despite the potential benefits that these positive (and paternalistic) interventions can have in terms of addressing the underlying causes of ASB, it is imperative to examine whether the injunction has been operating as an ad hoc criminal rule.

[132] Husak (n 130) 468.

[133] A Simester and A von Hirsch, *Crimes, Harms, and Wrongs: On the Principles of Criminalisation* (Oxford, Hart Publishing, 2011) 148.

[134] ibid 160.

[135] ibid 157.

[136] ibid 160.

[137] See ch 2, section 2.2.

## 5.5. CONCLUSION

Despite the criticisms raised about the magnitude of discretion afforded to courts and local enforcement agents regarding the ambiguous scope of ASB's statutory definition, the 2014 amendments did little to mitigate these concerns. In fact, the 2014 Act extended the potential scope of the ASBO's successor even further while also allowing for the imposition of positive obligations. Based on the data collected though, the behaviour dealt with through these measures was *impactful* and in most of the cases *persistent*. This was due to the fact that the decision to classify someone's behaviour as anti-social was informed by a number of factors which partly compensated for the apparent broadness of ASB's statutory definition under section 2 of the 2014 Act. Some of these factors, such as the limited availability of resources, were beyond the research participants' control. Others though, such as the presence of a review procedure (both internal and external), were the product of good practice and they were equally instrumental in terms of limiting the scope of the law to behaviour that really had a negative impact on people's quality of life.

That notwithstanding, it has to be acknowledged that the 2014 Act still provides a considerable magnitude of discretion to local enforcement agents and courts as to the scope of the law in this area and the implementation of the relevant tools and powers. It is, therefore, possible for the implementation of these measures to vary considerably across England and Wales. Hence, the findings of this study might not accurately reflect how these measures are used in other areas. It should also be borne in mind that this study examined the implementation of the 2014 amendments from an enforcement perspective, that is it interviewed only local enforcement agents, not victims and/or those against whom an injunction (or an informal intervention) is issued. Perpetrators, for instance, might argue that the relevant legislation was used in an arbitrary manner against behaviour which is part of everyday human interaction.

As far as the shift to a purely civil injunction is concerned, this appears to assuage some of the criticisms raised about the ASBO and how this could be used to criminalise *indirectly* certain kinds of behaviour. Evidence from this study, however, suggests that this shift to a purely civil response was approached with a great deal of scepticism by many local enforcement agents who expressed their reservations as to the overall effectiveness of the injunction in terms of its ability to prevent further ASB. Looking forward, given the limited availability of resources and the reservations expressed by local enforcement agents about this shift to a purely civil response, it would be interesting to examine whether this will eventually result in the de facto abolition of the injunction.

In the next chapter, the remaining findings of this empirical study will be presented. The findings presented in the next chapter relate to the procedure followed by local enforcement agents after they are notified about a potential incident of ASB and whether this resulted in the indirect criminalisation of certain kinds of behaviour.

# 6

# *Implementing Anti-Social Behaviour Policies in Practice: An Empirical Evaluation of the ASBO's Successor*

## 6.1. INTRODUCTION

IN THEORY, THE repeal and replacement of the Anti-social Behaviour Order (ASBO) by a purely civil injunction appears to mitigate some of the concerns raised about its hybrid nature. For Brown, this shift towards what appears to be a less punitive approach to anti-social behaviour (ASB) was part of the Conservation–Lib Dem coalition government's efforts to re-brand the new ASB regime in an attempt to 'change the [negative] narrative associated with the ASBO'.[1] As part of this re-branding effort, the coalition government promised a more victim-oriented approach while providing local enforcement agents with the flexibility needed to deal with ASB swiftly and effectively.[2] Still though, this shift towards a purely civil injunction should be reflected upon with caution. The reason for this is twofold. First, the implementation of the injunction might not be subjected to the same level of judicial and academic scrutiny as the ASBO due to its civil nature. This is further evidenced by the government's decision not to collect data regarding the number of applications submitted for the issue of an injunction to courts. The importance of this omission is heightened by the prevalence of ASB. Data published by the Crime Survey for England and Wales suggests that 26 per cent of the adult population had experienced or witnessed some kind of ASB in the year ending in September 2021.[3] Second, as seen in chapter four, in theory, the implementation of the injunction can still operate as a de facto criminal measure, despite abandoning the hybrid model adopted under the Crime and Disorder Act 1998.

[1] K Brown, 'Punitive Reform and the Cultural Life of Punishment: Moving from the ASBO to its Successors' (2020) 22 *Punishment & Society* 90, 92.

[2] Home Office, *Putting Victims First: More Effective Responses to Anti-social Behaviour* (London, Home Office, 2012) 3.

[3] Office for National Statistics, *Crime in England and Wales, Coronavirus and Crime Tables – Year ending September 2021* (Office for National Statistics, 2022) table 1.

In this chapter, the remaining (two sets of) findings of the empirical study conducted with local practitioners and police officers in Site A and Site B are presented. The first set of findings relates to the procedure followed by local enforcement agents when notified about a potential incident of ASB.[4] As we shall see, central to the procedure followed in both sites is the level of risk posed by the perpetrator to the alleged victim and how this can best be managed and addressed. It is also worth noting that 'risk' had major implications not just in terms of the procedure followed before applying for the issue of an injunction, but throughout the whole process. Moreover, it is evident that the regulation of ASB takes place primarily in the shadows, since local enforcement agents try to use a range of informal interventions before applying to court for the issue of an injunction. The second set of data focuses on the requirements that local enforcement agents seek to impose on those against whom an application is made in court for the issue of an injunction. Although many research participants acknowledged how impactful these requirements can be on the liberty of the perpetrators, most of them firmly believed that they would only seek to obtain those requirements that are *necessary* and *proportionate* to the risk posed. In the final part of this chapter, I will scrutinise my findings in light of the working definition of criminalisation formulated for the purposes of this study. My objective is to examine whether the implementation of the injunction has resulted in the indirect criminalisation of certain kinds of ASB. As we shall see, although the implementation of the injunction *rarely* constituted a form of indirect criminalisation, and despite the methodological limitations of this study, it is imperative to further analyse the data collected in order to identify those factors that contributed to this. This will enable us to inform existing (or even formulate new) mechanisms through which instances of indirect criminalisation (in the context of ASB) can be prevented in the future.

## 6.2. PROCEDURE FOLLOWED AFTER BEING NOTIFIED ABOUT A POTENTIAL INCIDENT OF ANTI-SOCIAL BEHAVIOUR

The third section of the interviews focused on the procedure followed by local enforcement agents after someone's behaviour was labelled as anti-social until the point of applying to court for the issue of an injunction. It was not my intention to examine in depth any specific informal interventions used in the sites under study. Rather, the main objective of this section was to: (i) gain an insight into how incidents of ASB were managed in these sites; (ii) examine whether resorting to enforcement was a 'last resort' measure; and (iii) identify the basis for resorting to enforcement.

[4] It has to be noted, though, that the data collected do not cover the procedure followed by local enforcement agents after the perpetrator breached the injunction imposed on them.

### 6.2.1. Actuarial Justice

It was clear based on the evidence collected from both sites that the administration of ASB was primarily risk driven. When local enforcement agencies were notified about a potential incident of ASB a risk assessment was carried out to assess the level of risk faced by the victim. Central to this risk assessment was the impact that someone's behaviour had on others. This, of course, is in line with the government's promise for a more victim-oriented approach with regard to ASB.[5] It is also consistent with the more general shift in governmental policies towards preventive-led interventions discussed earlier.[6] As Zedner explains, these interventions aim 'to calculate, anticipate and forestall harms before they occur'.[7]

The next testimonies are illustrative of the procedure followed in both areas when a potential incident of ASB was reported to them and the importance attributed to the level of risk faced by victims. One interviewee from Site A noted that 'initially if a person phones up and says that they are suffering from this or the other, even from the telephone stage there is a risk assessment done by the call-taker'.[8] As another police officer from Site B explained, this risk assessment comprised of 'a series of questions which would be asked to the victims of ASB to identify what risk level they are at: being standard, medium or high'.[9] The risk-assessment carried out in both areas is in line with the Statutory Guidance issued by the Home Office. Based on these guidelines, it is considered as good practice for local enforcement agents to premise their investigation on the impact that the behaviour reported 'is having on the victim, particularly if repeated incidents of anti-social behaviour are having a cumulative effect on their well-being'.[10]

What was clear from the evidence collected in both areas was that the level of risk faced by the victim informed the entire procedure followed by local enforcement agents and not just the initial stages of their investigation. According to one police officer, the level of risk faced by the victim 'will [be] monitored until we have reduced that risk right down to a level where we can say actually "we have solved this problem. The person is no longer at risk"'.[11] As far as the high-risk cases are concerned, no significant variations were reported between

[5] Home Office, *Putting Victims First* (n 2) 3–4.

[6] See ch 1, section 1.1.

[7] L Zedner, 'Fixing the Future? The Pre-emptive Turn in Criminal Justice' in B McSherry, A Norrie and S Bronitt (eds), *Regulating Deviance: The Redirection of Criminalisation and the Futures of Criminal Law* (Oxford, Hart Publishing, 2009) 35.

[8] Int 21-PO-Site A.

[9] Int 12-PO-Site B.

[10] Home Office, *Anti-social Behaviour, Crime and Policing Act 2014: Reform of Anti-social Behaviour Powers – Statutory Guidance for Frontline Professionals* (London, Home Office, 2021) 23.

[11] Int 18-PO-Site A.

the two areas with regard to the procedure followed. Evidence collected from both areas suggests that high-risk cases were regarded as a top priority and were discussed at the local Community Safety Partnership's (CSP) multi-agency meetings which were held on a regular basis. As one police officer noted, 'once a week we will meet with the local authority and we will basically discuss all of our high-risk cases and just check that we are doing everything that we can in a timely manner and that we have not missed anything'.[12]

The role and importance attributed in both sites under study to the risk posed to victims was an unsurprising discovery mainly due to the prevalence of risk assessments in the development of crime policies since the late twentieth century.[13] This prevalence led to what Feeley and Simon describe as the evolution of 'new penology'.[14] Central to new penology is the 'retrospective orientation of the criminal justice process'.[15] As Garland explains, perpetrators are increasingly 'seen as risks that must be managed rather than rehabilitated'.[16] As a result of this, particular attention is paid by various criminal justice institutions, such as the police, to the level of risk posed by certain individuals rather than focusing exclusively on the nature of the wrong committed. In many jurisdictions,[17] risk calculating tools were incorporated in sentencing policies as a means of identifying and managing 'those offenders who pose a real and present risk of harm to others'.[18] In similar fashion, as we saw earlier,[19] in England and Wales, the ambit of the criminal law, especially with regard to terrorism-related activities, has been extended well beyond traditional inchoate liability to criminal offences 'targeted at non-imminent crimes'.[20]

The use of risk assessment tools to calculate the level of risk posed by those who behave in an anti-social manner appears to be a sensible approach, since

[12] Int 12-PO-Site B.

[13] P O'Malley, 'Crime and Risk' in P Carlen and A Leandro (eds), *Alternative Criminologies* (Oxford, Routledge, 2017) 223; D Garland, *The Culture of Control: Crime and Social Order in Contemporary Society* (Chicago, IL, University of Chicago Press, 2001) 12.

[14] M Feeley and J Simon, 'The New Penology: Notes on the Emerging Strategy of Corrections and its Implications' (1992) 30 *Criminology* 449, 449.

[15] L Zedner, *Security* (Oxford, Routledge, 2007) 1–2.

[16] Garland, *The Culture of Control* (n 13) 175.

[17] As far as England and Wales is concerned, risk assessment tools and multi-agency collaborations were first established as a means of dealing with domestic violence. As explained by Hoyle, the use of risk assessment tools can assist the various criminal justice agencies to identify 'those at risk of victimisation' at an early stage and therefore prevent domestic violence. This is mainly due to the fact that the relevant agencies rely on '[s]tructured decision approaches, using risk indices, [that] are superior to unstructured approaches because they promise broader and more accurate coverage of issues in assessing risk'. See further, C Hoyle, 'Will she be safe? A critical analysis of risk assessment in domestic violence cases' (2008) 30 *Children and Youth Services Review* 323, 328–29.

[18] M Ansbro, 'The Nuts and Bolts of Risk Assessment: When the Clinical and Actuarial Conflict' (2010) 49 *Howard Journal of Criminal Justice* 252, 252; K Hannah-Moffat, 'Punishment and Risk' in J Simon and R Sparks (eds), *The Sage Handbook of Punishment and Society* (London, Sage Publications, 2013) 2.

[19] See ch 1, section 1.1.

[20] J McCulloch and D Wilson, *Pre-Crime: Pre-emption, Precaution and the Future* (Oxford, Routledge, 2016) 5–6.

these tools usually operate on 'a standard set of criteria on which to base decisions of risk' and therefore eliminate any elements of subjectivity.[21] This enables local enforcement agents to assess more accurately the level of risk faced by those affected by the perpetrator's behaviour enabling them, at least in theory, to tailor their response based on the outcome of each assessment. Nevertheless, the outcome of these assessments should be approached with caution, especially when dealing with ASB, for a number of reasons.

First, the increased reliance on risk assessments in the 1990s played a pivotal role in the establishment of a 'culture of control', the main focus of which is how potential risks can be identified and excluded rather than reformed.[22] This shift from welfarism to crime management highlights an important tension faced by contemporary liberal societies, which not only need to reassure the public that potential risks are promptly identified and addressed, but also the need to deal with the underlying causes of criminality.

Second, it is worth reiterating here that in contrast to the pre-2014 era, there is no need for the court examining an application under Part 1 of the Anti-social Behaviour, Crime and Policing Act 2014 to consider the issue of an injunction (and therefore the imposition of certain restrictions on the liberty of the perpetrator) as a necessary means for the prevention of further ASB.[23] Instead, the court *only* needs to be satisfied that the issue of the injunction is a '*just and convenient*' response for the prevention of further ASB.[24] This lower threshold, in conjunction with an extensive reliance on risk assessments, can result in the imposition of significant and potentially *disproportionate* (bearing in mind what the perpetrator has actually done rather than what they *might* do in the future) restrictions on the liberty of those who are thought to pose a risk to others.

Moreover, although a risk-based approach can be beneficial in terms of identifying potential wrongdoers, as O'Malley rightly points out, this is also likely to create new risks, such as the social ostracisation of potential wrongdoers.[25] Finally (and most importantly), a risk-based approach can result in the expansion of the net of social control. As pointed out by Ansbro, when assessing the level of risk posed by someone, 'practitioners feel an understandable pressure to err on the side of caution' and they might therefore decide to use the injunction pre-emptively despite the perpetrator not actually causing harassment, alarm or distress.[26] As mentioned above, this can lead not only to the inconsistent

[21] J McCafferty, 'Professional Discretion and the Predictive Validity of a Juvenile Risk Assessment Instrument: Exploring the Overlooked Principle of Effective Correctional Classification' (2017) 15 *Youth Violence and Juvenile Justice* 103, 103–04.

[22] O'Malley, 'Crime and Risk' (n 13) 223.

[23] See ch 4, section 4.2.2.

[24] Anti-social Behaviour, Crime and Policing Act 2014, s 1(3).

[25] O'Malley, 'Crime and Risk' (n 13) 223.

[26] Ansbro (n 18) 259.

implementation of the law, but can also result in the imposition of disproportionate and potentially punitive restrictions on the liberty of those who are deemed to pose a risk to others.

As far as the sites under study are concerned, there was no evidence to suggest that the adoption of this risk-driven approach resulted in the pre-emptive and/or unjustifiable use of the relevant tools and powers. In fact, as seen in chapter five, the decision of local enforcement agents to classify someone's behaviour as anti-social is informed by a range of factors, such as the limited availability of resources and the adoption of a common sense approach, which tend to significantly restrict the scope of the relevant tools and powers. Moreover, many of the above-mentioned concerns raised regarding the use of risk assessment tools were partly mitigated by the adoption of a multi-agency and multidisciplinary approach.

### 6.2.2. A Multi-Agency Approach

Before illustrating how the adoption of this multi-agency and multidisciplinary approach mitigated some of the concerns raised above regarding the use of risk assessment tools, it will be instructive to elaborate further on the collaboration between the various enforcement agencies dealing with ASB at a local level. To begin with, it was evident from the data collected that the main objective of local enforcement agents, especially during the initial stages of their investigation, was to gather as much information as possible about the alleged perpetrator. This was not only achieved by conducting their own investigation, but also through their collaboration with other agencies and their information-sharing agreements. The next testimony is illustrative of the multi-agency approach adopted in both areas:

> We must make sure that other agencies are aware of that person … so it is really the case that a lot more agencies are involved now. Obviously in the past it was unstructured. The police would do their thing, the council would do their thing and it was not always connected to each other … with this new computer system we can put entries into the system which the council can read instantly.[27]

To emphasise the importance of these information-sharing agreements, one of the interviewees made reference to the tragic case of Fiona Pilkington:

> [W]e all knew a little bit about it and this is where the sharing of information comes in. Each individual person had bits and pieces but it was never joined up and brought together and hence the reason why this database was brought in.[28]

[27] Int 15-PO-Site A.
[28] Int 18-PO-Site A.

What was also important about this multi-agency approach was that high-risk cases were examined from various perspectives and a collective decision was taken as to the best way forward. Most of the participants made explicit reference to their collaboration with other local partners and its potential benefits. The importance of this strategy lies in the very nature of ASB, which on some occasions requires a multi-agency approach. This can be attributed to the fact that some people behave in an anti-social manner not simply by choice, but due to a number of deep-seated social problems that require careful attention.[29] Consequently, in order for local enforcement agents to be able to permanently address the perpetrator's behaviour, due attention and consideration must be paid to its underlying causes. To this end, local enforcement agents need to consult with other relevant institutions, such as the local mental health team, which might be in a better position to deal with the causes of ASB. This close collaboration with other agencies clearly enables local enforcement agents to assess more accurately both the needs and the risk posed by each perpetrator. Moreover, the adoption of this multi-agency and multidisciplinary approach not only added an extra layer of review in the whole process, but it was also instrumental in the adoption of a less enforcement-led stance towards ASB. The following narrative explains how the police's attitude towards homeless people changed following their collaboration with other local practitioners who had a social care background and more experience in dealing with this group of people. The narrative also illustrates how the adoption of this multidisciplinary approach mitigated against some of the above-mentioned concerns about the use of risk assessment tools:

> The police had a very negative attitude to them because they saw them as a bit of a pain where they were breaking up fights. So, it was always a crisis intervention. So, one of the cultural changes for the police back in those days was – we had to work together for two weeks solid and they had a no arrest policy and we got them to take off their hats, they still had uniform, to start breaking down those barriers which we found very difficult.[30]

The foregoing testimony demonstrates how the occupational background of local enforcement agents can influence their approach to ASB, and also highlights the impact that this might have on other enforcement agents.[31] Hence, despite the potential adverse effects that a risk-driven approach can have on the regulation of ASB, these were compensated (at least to some extent) by the adoption of a multi-agency and multidisciplinary approach in both sites.

[29] Home Office, *Anti-social Behaviour, Crime and Policing Act 2014* (n 10) 25.

[30] Int 3-LP-Site A.

[31] For a more elaborated analysis of the impact that this interaction between local enforcement agents from different backgrounds can have, see K Brown, 'The Developing Habitus of the Anti-social Behaviour Practitioner: From Expansion in Years of Plenty to Surviving the Age of Austerity' (2013) 40 *Journal of Law and Society* 375, 398.

### 6.2.3. An Effective Responsibilisation Strategy

Although under section 6 of the Crime and Disorder Act 1998 a duty is imposed on local authorities, the police and other public service providers to cooperate and formulate strategies through which they should address crime and disorder in their 'local government area', it was clear from the data collected from both sites that there was an effective 'responsibilisation strategy' in place.[32] As Garland explains, the 'responsibilisation strategy' refers to the process of connecting 'state agencies … with practices of actors in the "private sector" and "the community"' in order to delegate the responsibility of crime management and prevention to other relevant stakeholders.[33] According to one interviewee, 'if they are social housing tenants or private sector tenants we will get in touch with their landlord … because obviously landlords also have an obligation to deal with ASB'.[34]

As the following testimony demonstrates, this shift of responsibility can be partly attributed to the limited resources available to state agencies, such as the police, to deal with crime and ASB: 'there are not enough police officers as there used to be to deal with this and in theory you have partners who are trying to deal with it as well'.[35] That said, the delegation of responsibility to non-state actors and the public regarding crime management is not a new phenomenon.[36] Instead, it is a well-established form of governance through which society is regulated *indirectly*.[37] For O'Malley and Palmer, a possible explanation for the rise of this form of social control is that 'good governance came to be identified with dependency on expertise, as the locus of objective knowledge required for scientific and professional management of the social'.[38] The importance of this need to rely on expertise is even more apparent in the context of ASB, the regulation of which involves 'a diverse range of work [that] requires a comprehensive knowledge and skill set'.[39] On this view, the management of crime and ASB should be left to those who hold the necessary skills and experience needed. As one police officer explained, 'we will always look at a sort of multi-agency approach. If there are other agencies that can be involved in order to get them the kind of support they need in order to prevent them from committing further offences'.[40]

[32] Garland, *The Culture of Control* (n 13) 124.
[33] ibid.
[34] Int 9-LP-Site B.
[35] Int 8-LP-Site B.
[36] J Flint, 'Social Housing Agencies and the Governance of Anti-social Behaviour' (2002) 17 *Housing Studies* 619, 622; A Crawford, 'Governing Through Anti-social Behaviour' (2009) 49 *British Journal of Criminology* 810, 822.
[37] G Mythen, *Understanding the Risk Society* (Basingstoke, Macmillan, 2014) 53–54; K Bullock and N Fielding, 'Community Crime Prevention' in N Tilley and A Sidebottom (eds), *Handbook of Crime Prevention and Community Safety* (Oxford, Routledge, 2017) 89.
[38] P O'Malley and D Palmer, 'Post-Keynesian Policing' (1996) 25 *Economy and Society* 137, 140.
[39] Brown, 'The Developing Habitus of the Anti-social Behaviour Practitioner' (n 31) 388–89.
[40] Int 27-PO-Site A.

There was an impression that the procedure followed by local enforcement agents was well structured and complied with the statutory guidance issued by the Home Office.[41] This is not to suggest that local enforcement agencies simply tried to follow the Home Office's guidelines. Rather, there was an impression from both sites that the majority of the participants strongly believed that a multi-agency approach was the best way forward both in terms of information sharing and the administration of high-risk cases. This well-established multi-agency approach in both sites contradicts the findings of previous studies according to which there was 'a lack of joined-up approaches within and between partners'[42] and 'inconsistent attitudes towards information sharing'.[43] As discussed earlier, some possible explanations for this include the lack of resources and the realisation by local enforcement agents that on many occasions ASB is the precursor of a number of other issues that need to be addressed if a permanent solution is to be achieved.

Regardless of the true causes and alleged efficacy of this responsibilisation strategy, attention should be paid to its potential adverse consequences as well. For instance, not only can an extensive responsibilisation strategy dramatically transform the criminal justice system, but it can also have a profound effect on the relationship between the state and the public.[44] The risk is that the state no longer assumes responsibility for the (mis)management of crime and ASB, and instead accountability for failing crime prevention strategies can be shifted to non-state actors.[45] The result is that state agencies escape accountability for such matters and government institutions deflect blame that might otherwise be allocated by the public. Therefore, although the adoption of a multi-agency and multidisciplinary approach towards ASB is not a panacea, it can at least mitigate against some of the above-mentioned concerns raised about the potential misuse of the relevant tools and powers, such as the regulation of purely innocent kinds of behaviour.

## 6.3. ADDRESSING ANTI-SOCIAL BEHAVIOUR AT A LOCAL LEVEL

The impetus for initiating this research project came partly from the possible restrictions that can be imposed on someone's liberty during the initial phase

[41] Home Office, *Anti-social Behaviour, Crime and Policing Act 2014* (n 10).

[42] A Crawford et al, '"It ain't (just) what you do, it's (also) the way that you do it": The Role of Procedural Justice in the Implementation of Anti-social Behaviour Interventions with Young People' (2017) 23 *European Journal on Criminal Policy and Research* 9, 7.

[43] J Donoghue, *Anti-social Behaviour Orders: A Culture of Control?* (Basingstoke, Palgrave Macmillan, 2010) 99–100.

[44] D Garland, 'The Limits of the Sovereign State' (1996) 36 *British Journal of Criminology* 445, 454.

[45] Bullock and Fielding (n 37) 90.

of the two-stage regulation process rather than the sanction received if found in breach of the injunction. As Duff and Marshall contend, although breach of the ASBO (the second stage) constituted an offence, we should also be mindful of the restrictions/obligations imposed on those against whom an ASBO was issued (the first stage) because they had the potential to constitute a form of criminal punishment in their own right.[46] In order to test the validity of this contention, it is necessary to examine more closely the restrictions imposed on those against whom the ASB tools and powers are used. The findings of this analysis can then be examined with reference to the working definition of criminalisation formulated in chapter three, in order to investigate whether they indeed amount to criminal punishment.

### 6.3.1. Informal Interventions

As evidence from previous studies suggests, applying to court for the issue of an ASBO was not, in general, a first resort measure for local enforcement agents.[47] Instead, as a study conducted by Lewis et al revealed, the measures used at a local level to address ASB 'form[ed] a pyramidal system of regulation' with the ASBO being located at its apex.[48] Based on this 'pyramidal system', those whose behaviour was deemed as anti-social would initially receive a warning letter urging them to alter their behaviour.[49] Failure to comply with this warning letter would result in the issue of an Acceptable Behaviour Contract (ABC).[50] The final stage would include an application for the issue of an ASBO.[51] Based on their findings, although the existence of this 'pyramidal system' was confirmed, in practice they found that there were 'myriad variations' amongst the sites under investigation with some of them adding extra layers of regulation.[52]

This pyramidal system of social control is closely associated with Ayres and Braithwaite's model of responsive regulation.[53] Responsive regulation is based on the idea that it is more likely for the regulator, such as the police, to 'convince' the regulatee to comply, in this case stop behaving in an anti-social manner, if a pyramidal system of regulation is in place.[54] The rationale for this approach is

[46] A Duff and S Marshall, 'How Offensive Can You Get?' in A von Hirsch and A Simester (eds), *Incivilities: Regulating Offensive Behaviour* (Oxford, Hart Publishing, 2006) 80.

[47] L Koffman, 'The Use of Anti-social Behaviour Orders: An Empirical Study of a New Deal for Communities Area' (2006) 7 *Criminal Law Review* 593, 600.

[48] S Lewis et al, 'Nipping Crime in the Bud? The use of Anti-social Behaviour Interventions with Young People in England and Wales' (2017) 57 *British Journal of Criminology* 1230, 1238–39.

[49] ibid 1238–39.

[50] ibid.

[51] ibid.

[52] ibid.

[53] I Ayres and J Braithwaite, *Responsive Regulation: Transcending the Deregulation Debate* (New York, Oxford University Press, 1992) 4–7.

[54] ibid ch 2.

for the regulator to 'escalate to somewhat punitive approaches only reluctantly and only when dialogue fails. Then escalate to even more punitive approaches only when more modest sanctions fail'.[55] As Braithwaite maintains, if less punitive/coercive responses have been used first, then the regulation will be 'seen as more legitimate and procedurally fair [and therefore] compliance with the law is more likely'.[56] Moreover, the adoption of this approach can be a more expedient and cost-effective method of dealing with ASB since there might be no need for local enforcement agents to apply to court for the issue of an injunction against the alleged perpetrator(s).

Despite the different levels of ASB experienced, evidence collected by this study confirms the existence of a 'pyramidal system of regulation' in both sites, with the injunction located at its apex. In both sites, there was a genuine belief that applying to court for the issue of an injunction should generally be reserved as a *last resort* measure. According to one police officer, 'there are reasons for this behaviour so we need to look into it. I need to work with these people'.[57] Their initial objective, therefore, was to identify the underlying causes of ASB and 'try to look at a support network' for that individual.[58] As one local practitioner explained, 'taking it to court, for me personally is failure on what we can do otherwise to remove the ASB'.[59] The following testimony is representative of the approach adopted in both sites:

> When we go to court for an injunction, I want to be sure of two things. We can present the evidence that the person has behaved anti-socially, but also that we can show that everything else we have done and tried to address it because that is in a way what gives you the argument to argue for necessity or that is why it is reasonable to issue the order.[60]

Figure 6.1 is illustrative of the procedure followed by local enforcement agents in both sites with regard to the management of ASB. Initially, a risk assessment will be conducted in order to assess the level of risk posed by the alleged perpetrator. The next step will be an informal discussion with those involved in order to address the ASB. If this does not work, then a warning letter will be issued against the perpetrator, explaining the potential consequences of non-compliance with their requests. That said, it was evident that there had been some departure from out-of-court interventions which purely aim to achieve compliance through the threat of sanctions. In particular, there was strong evidence to suggest that in both sites local enforcement agents would examine the possibility of utilising certain restorative justice (RJ) processes,

[55] J Braithwaite, 'The Essence of Responsive Regulation' (2011) 44 *University of British Columbia Law Review* 475, 482.

[56] ibid 486.

[57] Int 18-PO-Site A.

[58] Int 11-PO-Site B.

[59] Int 10-LP-Site B.

[60] Int 2-LP-Site A.

with the majority of them noting that the most commonly used process was victim–offender mediation. To better understand the importance of incorporating RJ interventions into this process, it is imperative to engage (albeit briefly) with the principles underpinning these processes.

**Figure 6.1** The standard process of regulation followed in both sites

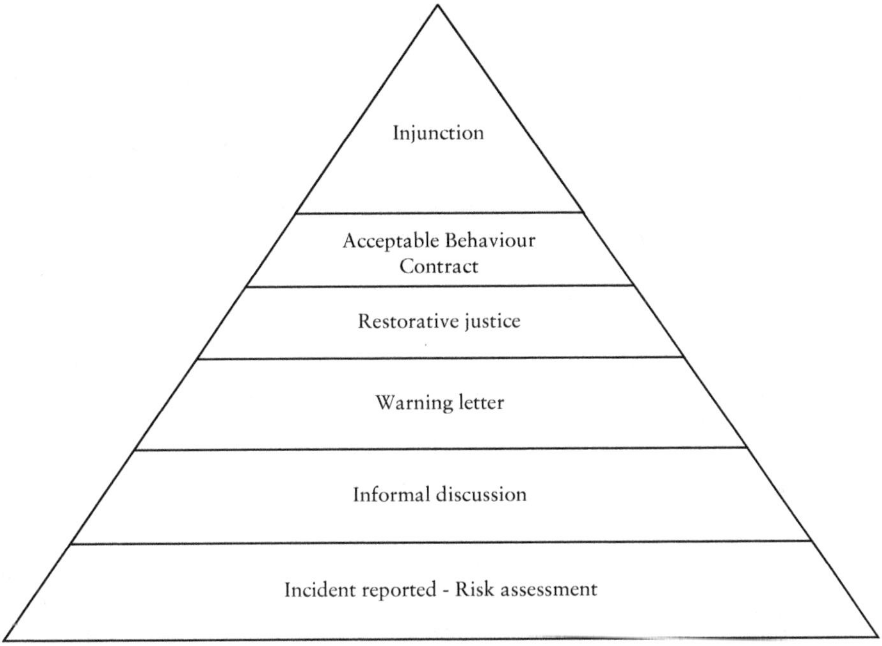


Central to any RJ process is the need for the relevant stakeholders to come together in order to discuss the behaviour in question and reach a commonly agreed solution.[61] As Johnstone and van Ness explain, what really distinguishes RJ from other forms of social control is that it departs from the state-centred administration of justice towards a more 'community-based reparative justice' model.[62] Consequently, what makes RJ processes appealing is their 'commitment to combating oppressive state structures of inhumane reliance on prisons'.[63] Thus, RJ offers an alternative to oppressive state interventions, such as criminal prosecution and in this case the possibility of taking formal legal action,

[61] A Ashworth, 'Social Control and "Anti-Social Behaviour": The Subversion of Human Rights?' [2004] *Law Quarterly Review* 263, 270.

[62] G Johnstone and D van Ness, 'The Meaning of Restorative Justice' in G Johnstone and D van Ness (eds), *Handbook of Restorative Justice* (Cullompton, Willan Publishing, 2006) 5.

[63] J Braithwaite, 'Setting Standards for Restorative Justice' (2002) 42 *British Journal of Criminology* 563, 564.

through which the wrong committed by the perpetrator can be addressed without the need to resort to the more coercive means of social control.

Although RJ processes share many characteristics, they can vary considerably both in terms of their structure and possible outcome. As to the former, some of these processes target the community at large rather than individual victims.[64] An example of this would be community conferences (or citizen panels) which primarily aim to address 'victimless' crimes which have a detrimental impact on the community's quality of life.[65] Another key objective of these conferences is to 'strengthen community solidarity'.[66] In contrast to community conferences, central to the victim–offender mediation is the participation of the victim who is given an active role in the management of their case.[67] As Walters explains, this type of mediation usually involves 'a single mediator who acts as an impartial facilitator of direct dialogue between the parties' involved.[68] Vital to this process is the need for the wrongdoer to assume 'responsibility for their actions and to repair the harms they have caused directly to the victim'.[69]

As to the latter, the outcome of every RJ practice can vary depending on the merits of each case.[70] For instance, in cases where no physical harm or any damage to the victim's property was caused, it might be decided that the perpetrator needs to offer an apology. Similarly, if damage was caused to the victim's property, it might be agreed that the perpetrator should repair the damage themselves or compensate the victim for it.[71]

The following testimony provided by a local practitioner in Site A, is illustrative of the adoption of a more RJ approach:

> We support people, additionally called victims, but we are trying to move away from that to a more restorative type of language and approach … We try to consider what restorative options might be. So, somebody has come to our attention for the first time and they are willing to engage we will try and look at restorative options. Will they be willing to write a letter of apology? Will they be willing to meet and have like a community conference with different parties there?[72]

A similar shift was also observed in Site B. As one of the interviewees pointed out 'we are using more of the RJ side of things … a lot of us have received RJ training and we are trying to get the local communities to solve the problem.

[64] J Dignan, 'The Victim in Restorative Justice' in S Walklate (ed), *Handbook of Victims and Victimology*, 1st edn (Cullompton, Willan Publishing, 2007) 311.

[65] L Kurki, 'Evaluating Restorative Justice Practices' in A von Hirsch et al (eds), *Restorative Justice and Criminal Justice* (Oxford, Hart Publishing, 2003) 304–05.

[66] ibid 311.

[67] ibid 311–13.

[68] M Walters, *Hate Crime and Restorative Justice: Exploring Causes, Repairing Harms* (Oxford, Oxford University Press, 2014) 37.

[69] ibid.

[70] ibid.

[71] ibid.

[72] Int 4-LP-Site A.

It is about trying to talk with your neighbours'.[73] It is also worth noting that explicit reference was made by most of the participants from Site B to the use of victim–offender mediation as one of the most common RJ practices used. As one ASB officer from a housing association pointed out, they have 'a contract with a mediator' and they tend to use their services especially when the behaviour at stake involves 'counter allegations' between neighbours.[74]

The importance of this shift towards a more RJ approach should not be underestimated. The use of victim–offender or community mediation in the context of hate crimes, for example, has been very successful in 'reducing [victims'] emotional harm and preventing further hate incidents from recurring'.[75] This was also confirmed by one local practitioner who argued that their 'best success rate is around mediation'.[76] Moreover, RJ provides victims of ASB with an opportunity to be heard, 'to play a part in repairing the harm and finding a positive way forward' without resorting to any formal legal action.[77] This enhanced role given to victims was not limited to their participation in mediation or any other form of RJ used. As seen before, especially in Site A, there was strong evidence to suggest that victims and their needs had a pivotal role in the management of their case.[78] The following testimony illustrates the victim's role in this process: 'we will not do anything without their permission. If they give us permission to address or talk to the person that they believe is causing the harm we will approach them as a team'.[79] The importance attributed to victims of ASB in this area was further evidenced by the fact that they were 'kept informed about what was happening with their case'.[80] As one of the interviewees pointed out, the fact that they were kept informed about the management of their case 'helped them [to] feel safer'.[81]

Beyond the potential benefits for the victims, the availability of RJ processes also adds an extra and less coercive layer to the pyramidal system of regulation used in both sites. Consequently, those who behave in an anti-social manner are provided with more opportunities to comply before local enforcement agents apply for an injunction to be issued.[82] It should be borne in mind though, that the use of RJ processes is contingent upon the willingness of both the perpetrator and those affected by their behaviour to participate.

[73] Int 8-LP-Site B.

[74] Int 16-LP-Site B.

[75] Walters (n 68) 239.

[76] Int 9-LP-Site B.

[77] Ministry of Justice, *Restorative Justice Action Plan for the Criminal Justice System for the Period to March 2018* (London, Ministry of Justice, 2014) 3.

[78] See ch 5, section 5.3.3.

[79] Int 4-LP-Site A.

[80] Int 2-LP-Site A.

[81] Int 1-LP-Site A.

[82] That said, further research is needed on the use of RJ for ASB, and its impact on the procedural and distributive justice of such cases.

Despite the move towards a purely civil injunction, it was evident from the data collected that in both sites the regulation of ASB takes place in the 'shadows', with local enforcement agents utilising an array of informal interventions before an application is submitted to the court for the issue of an injunction. Notwithstanding the potential benefits of responsive regulation, that is seeking to achieve compliance through less punitive interventions before resorting to formal (and potentially more punitive) legal action, it is apparent that robust review procedures must be put in place to ensure that these informal interventions are not operating as de facto criminal measures.

### 6.3.2. Dealing with High-Risk Cases

It was clear from the evidence collected by this study that in most of the cases 'a warning letter or a conversation with an individual or the alleged perpetrator will stop the behaviour' at stake.[83] If this was not enough to prevent further ASB, local enforcement agents would proceed to the next stage of the pyramidal system of regulation established. That said, evidence from both sites suggests that when the level of risk posed by that person was high, then the perpetrator would move through the above steps very quickly. One interviewee noted that 'if their behaviour is quite serious, we will move to enforcement quickly. If there is physical violence or if there is a hate element it will be much more likely to go to court and speed it up. So, we do look at the severity and the harm that is caused'.[84] This replicates the findings of previous studies based on which the use of formal legal action against those who behaved in an anti-social manner was neither a first nor a last resort measure.[85] Instead, this was done 'on a case-by-case basis … depending on the specific facts of the incidents reported'.[86]

Taken together, the above accounts suggest that applying to court for an injunction or a Criminal Behaviour Order (CBO) was generally reserved in both sites as a 'last resort' measure unless the level of risk posed by the perpetrator was high. As far as the injunction is concerned, if the behaviour in question was regarded as a high-risk incident, then local enforcement agents would not follow each step of the process outlined in Figure 6.1. As one local practitioner noted, 'if it is a high-risk case then we will create a separate action plan'.[87] Similarly, the overall impression from both sites was that if the perpetrator committed an offence and there was already a long history of persistent ASB and criminality, then they will apply for the issue of a CBO.

[83] Int 9-LP-Site B.
[84] Int 5-LP-Site A.
[85] Koffman (n 47) 601; Crawford et al (n 42) 1238–39.
[86] Int 3-LP-Site B.
[87] Int 16-LP-Site B.

### 6.3.3. Overlap between Anti-Social Behaviour and Criminality

As seen earlier, research participants were asked to define and provide examples of behaviour that they would classify as anti-social. For the majority, ASB can range from behaviour which on the face of it appears to be harmless and part of every social interaction (the lower end of the scale) to behaviour that is already proscribed by criminal law (the upper end of the scale). Some common examples cited by the majority of the participants included common assault and criminal damage. This study collected evidence on how participants and their institutions dealt with this kind of behaviour. In particular, police officers were asked whether an incident situated in the upper end of the scale would be dealt with as a criminal offence, as ASB, or a combination of the two, that is to apply for the issue of a CBO. Similarly, local practitioners were asked whether they would address this kind of behaviour themselves or if this was a matter for the police to deal with.

In Site A, the majority of the police officers noted that 'the criminal aspect will always take precedence'.[88] Simply put, if a criminal offence was committed, then the criminal justice route would be followed. As one police officer argued, this was the 'rule of thumb … when a criminal act' was committed.[89] This was reaffirmed by most of the local practitioners from Site A who argued that if an offence was committed, then the police would deal with it as a crime. One local practitioner noted, for instance, the following: 'I have met beggars making £500 per week easy … Sometimes it is money by deception. When I used to do targeted work with the police, nine out of ten times the police will deal with them as a beggar'.[90] Moreover, most of the police officers who participated in this study from Site A noted that if they are dealing with a prolific offender, then they will 'apply for a CBO in looking at ways of actually preventing that from happening'.[91] According to the majority of the police officers from Site A, the main reason for this is the inability of the criminal law to deal effectively with prolific low-level offenders. The following testimony is illustrative of the general dissatisfaction of police officers with the criminal law:

> They can be dealt with as crimes. However, as I said earlier, individuals who have been dealt with numerous times for harassment, public order offences and continue to offend, they continue to go before the court. Sometimes an injunction with a stronger power needs to be put in place to try and prevent that person … The CBO and the civil injunction hold a higher penalty and if it means that we have to deal with them with the higher penalty than the penalty for the criminal offence then so be it.[92]

[88] Int 15-PO-Site A.
[89] Int 15-PO-Site A.
[90] Int 2-LP-Site A.
[91] Int 23-PO-Site A.
[92] Int 18-PO-Site A.

In contrast to the foregoing testimony and what the majority of their colleagues argued, some police officers noted that they would use the ASB tools and powers as an 'addition to their criminal investigation. As a holistic approach to actually solving the problem'.[93] As most of the local practitioners from Site A pointed out, the criminal law alone cannot adequately address the underlying causes of criminality. One of the local practitioners, for instance, noted that 'going to prison it is such a short stain. It is not long enough in order to have the results that you need. To change someone's behaviour it takes time. It takes work. It does not happen overnight'.[94] Consequently, the use of a CBO is sometimes necessary to 'bring that long-term change' through the imposition of certain positive obligations.[95] Finally, one police officer noted that in the case of non-prolific offenders the injunction will be used as a means of diverting them away from criminality. Based on this testimony,

> if it is one off low-level then no we are no way near that … If there is a fifteen-year-old who does graffiti for a first time are we going to criminalise this person? Or is it better to make him face the victim and scrape this off the wall themselves?[96]

As far as Site B is concerned, mixed responses were received as well. For many of the participants, behaviour that constitutes an offence should and is dealt with by the police as a crime. As one police officer explained, if the behaviour at stake

> does not quite meet the criminal standard … [then] we will always try to see the civil application because they are quicker and therefore you get more effective turnaround for your victims. Whereas if you go on the back of a criminal conviction, then some cases might take a year if not more to actually be heard at court. And if you are waiting for that you still have that person playing up. It is not going to do anyone any favours.[97]

The officer then continued to explain that 'if there is a criminal offence that will be dealt with there and then. The ASB element and its tools and powers are coming in as a secondary, almost a support, measure to ensure that everything else is looked at as well'.[98] On this view, if a criminal offence was committed, then they would try to secure a conviction and if necessary, obtain a CBO.

For another group of participants from Site B, the use of the criminal law should be reserved as a last resort measure. One police officer noted that 'if we can deal with somebody without criminalising them, then this is ideally what we want to do'.[99] As one interviewee explained, their main objective was to

[93] Int 21-PO-Site A.
[94] Int 7-LP-Site A.
[95] Int 5-LP-Site A.
[96] Int 26-PO-Site A.
[97] Int 12-PO-Site B.
[98] Int 12-PO-Site B.
[99] Int 13-PO-Site B.

'divert [people away from criminality] rather than implementing the full power straight away'.[100]

The use of the CBO as a means of compensating for the inability of the criminal law to deal effectively with persistent low-level criminality raises a number of fundamental issues. One of the most important issues raised here is whether we can modify the criminal law in such a way as to make it effective against persistent low-level criminality without the need to resort to 'multiple sanctions and strategies of behaviour regulation'.[101] As far as the use of the injunction as an alternative to the criminal law is concerned, concerns can be raised as to the legitimacy of this approach and the fact that it constitutes a form of under-criminalisation.[102]

### 6.3.4. Requirements Imposed

The presence of the aforementioned system of regulation appears to provide perpetrators with ample opportunity to alter their behaviour, and demonstrates that applying to court for the issue of an injunction is usually reserved as a last resort measure. It should be borne in mind though that the pinnacle of the pyramid is enforcement, which can still result in the indirect criminalisation of certain kinds of ASB. Hence, despite the presence of this pyramid, it is still imperative to scrutinise the ramifications that enforcement can have on those who reach the apex of this system.

As expected, and in line with the findings of a previous study, according to many participants, the most common types of restriction imposed on those against whom these measures were used included: '(i) people being prohibited from doing certain things; (ii) going to certain places; (iii) be with certain people; and (iv) being out and about in certain times, ie curfews. I think geographical exclusion is the most common'.[103] One police officer, for instance, made reference to the case of a street drinker who was prohibited from entering a 'particular road … and not to have an open can in a public space'.[104]

As acknowledged by one interviewee, congregating with certain individuals, entering into specific parts of town or feeding pigeons 'appear to the surface to

[100] Int 10-LP-Site B.

[101] Lewis et al (n 48) 11.

[102] Ashworth and Zedner contend that when non-criminal mechanisms of social control are utilised to address behaviour that already falls within the ambit of the criminal law, then this constitutes a form of under-criminalisation. What is problematic about under-criminalisation is that it undermines the normative distinction between criminal and non-criminal legislation (see A Ashworth and L Zedner, 'Preventive Orders: A Problem of Undercriminalisation?' in A Duff et al (eds), *The Boundaries of the Criminal Law* (Oxford, Oxford University Press, 2010).

[103] Int 2-LP-Site A. See also R Matthews et al, *Assessing the Use and Impact of Anti-Social Behaviour Orders* (Bristol, Policy Press, 2007) 35.

[104] Int 15-PO-Site A.

be everyday lawful activities'.[105] Prohibiting someone from engaging in those otherwise lawful activities appears to be very contentions for two main reasons. First, certain activities, such associating with others, fall within the ambit of liberty as this was conceptualised in chapter three. Based on this formulation of liberty, rights and freedoms which are protected under the European Convention on Human Rights (ECHR) and brought into domestic law by the Human Rights Act 1998 should be regarded as basic and/or fundamental for this society. Accordingly, interference with these rights and freedoms will satisfy the first prerequisite of the working definition of criminalisation formulated for the purposes of this study.

Second, the imposition of the above-mentioned restrictions can be criticised for creating personalised prohibitions which only apply to certain individuals rather than to the society as a whole.[106] In theory, the creation of these personalised prohibitions allows local enforcement agents to criminalise *indirectly* specific groups of people while circumventing the enhanced procedural protections afforded to those facing the prospect of direct criminal punishment.

Most of the participants made particular reference to the imposition of positive obligations and their potential benefits. Some of the most commonly cited examples included: (i) attending drug or alcohol-related treatments; and (ii) engaging with the 'mental health services'.[107] As one police officer noted, positive obligations 'are very handy' since they can be used to address the underlying causes of the behaviour at hand.[108] The importance of this, according to many of the participants, lies with the fact that if 'someone is addicted to drugs and you just tell them to stop, then they will not stop' behaving in an anti-social manner.[109] For this reason, local enforcement agents tried to impose certain positive obligations that they deemed appropriate to address the underlying causes of the problem:

> If you have got somebody who has mental health issues, then you have to tackle the mental health issues rather than putting restrictions on their activities. You have to make sure that they engage with the mental health services, the psychiatric nurses, the doctors and anything else.[110]

Moreover, the foregoing account highlights once again the presence of a 'responsibilisation strategy' where local enforcement agents seek to 'enlist wider actors' in their ASB strategies.[111]

[105] Int 4-LP-Site A.
[106] A Gil-Robles, *Commissioner for Human Rights, on his Visit to the United Kingdom 4th–12th November 2004 for the Attention of the Committee of Ministers and the Parliamentary Assembly* (CommDH (2005)6) (Office for the Commissioner of Human Rights, 2005) 37, available at: wcd.coe.int/ViewDoc.jsp?id=865235.
[107] Int 8-LP-Site B.
[108] Int 15-PO-Site A.
[109] Int 16-LP-Site B.
[110] Int 8-LP-Site B.
[111] Crawford (n 36) 811.

Although the imposition of certain positive obligations aimed to address the underlying causes of ASB, it was a common belief amongst most of the participants that they had to convince the court examining their application that these obligations were both essential and that they had 'the necessary infrastructure in place to support' them.[112] As a local practitioner noted, if the necessary infrastructure and support mechanisms are not in place, then 'you will be setting the client up to fail'.[113]

### 6.3.5. The Purpose of Enforcement

It was evident from the data collected from both sites that one of the main purposes of enforcement, that is applying to court for the issue of an injunction or a CBO, was to address the underlying causes of ASB. In particular, 17 out of the 29 interviewees stated that enforcement was used as a means of working with the perpetrator to address the underlying causes of their behaviour. As the following testimony illustrates, if the perpetrator refused to utilise the services provided to them, then local enforcement agents could apply for the issue of an injunction or a CBO as a means of forcing the perpetrator to engage with the relevant service provider: 'For me [it] is about using enforcement as a tool to get people to engage in social care and make significant sustainable changes in their life style. That is the only way it will sit comfortably with me'.[114] As another local practitioner noted though, obtaining an injunction or a CBO is not a panacea for addressing the underlying causes of ASB: 'if we know that someone would never stick to anything, then we would never want to set up someone to fail'.[115] Rather, based on their account these measures should only be used if there is a *realistic* prospect of success.

The use of the injunction on purely paternalistic grounds can be criticised for denying perpetrators the opportunity to reject treatment. Rather than treating the perpetrator as a rational agent who is capable of deciding whether (and how) he should address the underlying causes of his behaviour, local enforcement agents seek through formal interventions (approved by courts) to dictate what they regard as the most appropriate treatment.[116] That said, this finding should be examined in light of the multi-agency and multidisciplinary approach adopted in both sites which enabled local enforcement agents to examine high-risk ASB from various perspectives. Participants in these multi-agency meetings

112 Int 17-LP-Site B.
113 Int 17-LP-Site B.
114 Int 3-LP-Site A.
115 Int 20-LP-Site A.
116 For a comprehensive analysis of the normative challenges posed by paternalistic interventions see D Husak, 'Paternalism' in A Marmor (ed), *The Routledge Companion to Philosophy of Law* (New York, Routledge, 2012).

had different skills, backgrounds and experience, all of which were brought together to reach a *collective* decision as to the best way forward. Moreover, the importance attributed to the underlying causes of ASB demonstrates that even when someone reaches the apex of this pyramidal system, they are still provided with an opportunity to change their behaviour.

Although certain interventions could amount to an interference with the perpetrator's liberty, for most interviewees this interference was *warranted* because there was always a connection between the perpetrators' past behaviour and the requirements imposed on them. For them, the objective of these interventions was not to 'prevent someone from having a normal life'.[117] Rather, their objective was to 'prevent them from conducting behaviour which is not acceptable'.[118] The following testimony provided by one police officer is illustrative of the majority's responses when asked about whether the restrictions imposed on the perpetrators result in the prohibition of otherwise lawful activities:

> If somebody has not stepped over the line, they will be allowed to carry on doing what they were doing. If they have stepped over the line to a point where we feel that we need to have some kind of order on them, then yes it would stop them doing something that might be legitimate to them, such as walking down the high street.[119]

To support the justifiability of these restrictions, most of the participants emphasised the need for these to be deemed as *necessary* and *proportionate*. As one local practitioner noted:

> We always say 'Is it necessary to ask for that restriction?' and 'is it proportionate to ask for that restriction?' These are the two questions we will ask ourselves in the whole preparation that is what we will be asking ourselves. If we do not feel that we have the evidence to support and say 'yes' to both of these questions, then we would not have included them. So, if somebody is just committing ASB in a particular street to exclude them from the whole city will not be proportionate.[120]

The foregoing accounts represent what the majority of the interviewees believed about the imposition of these restrictions. This finding contradicts with some of the theoretical concerns raised earlier regarding the issue of the injunction. The 2014 Act was criticised for imposing a lower threshold than the one imposed by the Crime and Disorder Act 1998. While under the 1998 Act an ASBO and the post-conviction ASBO could be issued only if it was regarded as a necessary means for the protection of those affected by the perpetrator's behaviour, under the 2014 Act the issue of the injunction needs only to be regarded as a 'just and convenient' measure for the prevention of further ASB. As far as the CBO is

[117] Int 19-PO-Site A.
[118] Int 19-PO-Site A.
[119] Int 14-PO-Site B.
[120] Int 4-LP-Site A.

concerned, its issue needs only to 'help in preventing the offender from' behaving in a similar manner in the future. Upon closer scrutiny of the findings of this study, it is evident that these criticisms do not reflect how the law had been implemented in the two sites under investigation.

To further support the need for these restrictions to be *necessary* and *proportionate*, many of the participants claimed that applying successfully to court for the issue of an injunction or a CBO is not an easy task. Instead, according to them, they 'need to justify'[121] these restrictions because ultimately the decision to 'impose certain restrictions on someone' lies with the court.[122] One interviewee noted, for instance, that in order to apply successfully to court 'you have to have hard core evidence and you have to have hard core statements. So, it is not an easy process to do. And you are not going to do it unless you can push it forward'.[123] As one local practitioner explained, 'we would not use the injunction … to shove a lot of things that are not actually relevant and judges are very strict on that. We would not even be able to bring that up. You would be hugely criticised'.[124]

The last two testimonies are consistent with the earlier finding of this study regarding the presence of a review procedure in both sites. As mentioned above, in both sites a multi-agency approach was adopted not only in terms of how ASB is to be conceptualised, but also in terms of how local enforcement agencies tried to address this kind of behaviour.[125] Evidence collected by this study revealed that this multi-agency approach also extended to the requirement(s) that local enforcement agents sought to impose on those who behaved in an anti-social manner. The following testimony provided by one police officer is illustrative of this multi-agency approach adopted in both areas:

> I will sit down with the Community Safety Team, with our colleagues and generally before we apply for a CBO, we will have a professionals' meeting and we will come up with a list of prohibitions … that would suit that individual.[126]

According to another interviewee, this pre-enforcement process is not as straightforward as it might appear to be since 'it is notoriously difficult to get all the agencies to agree' to these restrictions and/or obligations.[127]

Although local enforcement agents firmly believed that the requirements imposed were necessary and proportionate to the risk posed by the perpetrators, prohibiting someone from engaging in otherwise lawful activities can be criticised for creating personalised prohibitions which apply only to certain

[121] Int 15-PO-Site A.
[122] Int 2-LP-Site A.
[123] Int 11-PO-Site B.
[124] Int 16-LP-Site B.
[125] See ch 5, section 5.3.4.
[126] Int 23-PO-Site A.
[127] Int 28-PO-Site A.

individuals rather than to the whole of society. This clearly raises serious concerns about the actual (if there are any) limits of the ASB legal framework in terms of the restrictions that can be imposed on the liberty of those whose behaviour is regarded as anti-social, despite this shift to what appears to be a purely civil injunction. Moreover, it highlights the potential for these measures to be implemented inconsistently across England and Wales. That said, the adoption of the above-mentioned pyramidal system can contribute to the consistent implementation of the law, while the adoption of a multi-agency and multidisciplinary approach can act as a safety net against the misuse of these measures.

## 6.4. A FORM OF INDIRECT CRIMINALISATION?

During the interviews local enforcement agents were asked whether the use of formal legal action was used as a means of punishing those who acted in an anti-social manner based on their own understanding of punishment. For 23 out of the 29 interviewees, the restrictions imposed on the perpetrators did not amount to punishment. The following testimony provided by a local practitioner is illustrative of the majority's responses on this question: 'I have never thought an ASBO as a punishment for an individual. I always thought it as a means to protect individuals and the wider community from the behaviour of somebody'.[128] The foregoing testimony is consistent with the majority's belief based on which the main reason for resorting to enforcement was to prevent the perpetrator from behaving in the same manner in the future.

For the remaining six interviewees, the restrictions imposed on those who received an injunction or a CBO were 'quite punitive'[129] or included an 'element of punishment'.[130] As to the former, one police officer argued that the implementation of the relevant legislation 'can be quite punitive' because it enables local enforcement agents to address ASB 'as if it was an offence'.[131] As to the latter, three interviewees noted that 'although [the imposition of these restrictions] is a punishment in a sense', their main objective was 'to support and divert people from' ASB.[132]

Although local enforcement agents' views as to whether the issue of the injunction can be regarded as a form of punishment provide vital insights into how they personally view this statutory instrument, what really matters for the purposes of this study is whether the implementation of the injunction constitutes a form of punishment based on the working definition of criminalisation formulated in chapter three. It is worth reiterating here the two prerequisites

[128] Int 9-LP-Site B.
[129] Int 1-LP-Site A.
[130] Int 7-LP-Site A.
[131] Int 21-PO-Site A.
[132] Int 10-LP-Site B.

that need to be met in order for the requirements imposed through the implementation of the injunction to amount to criminal punishment:

(i) The implementation of the legal rule must result in the imposition of a sanction which interferes with the perpetrator's liberty.
(ii) The sanction imposed and/or threatened to be imposed on the perpetrator must publicly and purposefully communicate state censure.

### 6.4.1. Did the Requirements Imposed Interfere with the Perpetrator's Liberty?

As far as the first prerequisite of my working definition of criminalisation is concerned, it was evident from the data collected that on many occasions the requirements imposed (in the form of restrictions and/or positive obligations) did indeed interfere with the liberty of those against whom an injunction was issued. On many occasions, for example, those against whom an injunction was issued were prohibited from associating with certain individuals and/or accessing certain public spaces and roads. Both of these rights and freedoms are protected under the ECHR. For the purposes of this study, therefore, they should be regarded as basic and/or fundamental.

At first sight, the foregoing conclusion can be criticised for failing to take into consideration the purpose of the restrictions/obligations imposed on the perpetrators. It could be argued, for instance, that the imposition of certain restrictions on those who behaved in an anti-social manner should not be regarded as an interference with their liberty since their ultimate objective was to prevent further ASB and criminality. Although the purpose of these restrictions/obligations appears to be legitimate, we still need to be mindful of the impact of these measures on the perpetrators. Moreover, it should be remembered that in order for these restrictions to amount to criminal punishment, they also need to *publicly* and *purposefully* convey censure. Otherwise, these restrictions will simply constitute non-punitive sanctions.

### 6.4.2. Were the Perpetrators Publicly and Purposefully Condemned?

As seen before, the implementation of the ASBO was heavily criticised due to the 'naming and shaming' practices used by many local enforcement agencies in England and Wales in previous years,[133] which contributed significantly to the demonisation and social ostracisation of certain social groups, such as young people.[134] Nonetheless, in *Stanley*, the publication of the ASBO recipients' personal details along with the restrictions imposed on them was deemed

[133] See further, Brown, 'Punitive Reform and the Cultural Life of Punishment' (n 1) 96.
[134] P Squires and D Stephen, 'Rethinking ASBOs' (2005) 25 *Critical Social Policy* 517, 523.

compatible with the provisions of Article 8 ECHR, that is the right to 'private and family life'.[135] More precisely, it was held that the publication of this kind of information was essential for the effective enforcement of the ASBOs.[136]

A similar approach with regard to the publication of this kind of information is adopted under the 2014 Act with the Statutory Guidance emphasising the need to reassure victims and local communities 'that action is being taken'.[137] Although the publication of certain information can be necessary under certain circumstances for the effective enforcement of the requirements imposed, it was evident in some cases, such as in *Stanley* where colourful language was used against the perpetrators, that this could also be used as a means of *publicly condemning* the ASBO recipients. The pressing question, therefore, is whether the implementation of ASB measures *purposefully* resulted in the public condemnation of those against whom these measures were used.

In Site A, most of the participants stated that they would publicise information about the perpetrator and the restrictions imposed on them only to those 'affected' by their behaviour.[138] As one local practitioner explained,

> you have to be very proportionate as to how you ensure that people are aware of the order ... if a person is banned from going to [the] Co-op you do not need to inform the national press about it. You just let people who enforce it and the Co-op staff.[139]

This need for targeted publicity was further evident by a number of other testimonies according to which publicity should be limited only to what is *absolutely necessary* for the effective policing of the measures put in place. To illustrate this, one interviewee made reference to a case where 'local residents were given a photo pack. They all had to sign the Data Protection and they would have different photos of that person. Not giving their identities but showing them so people could report the behaviour that was going on'.[140]

Moreover, what was clear from the evidence collected is that for the majority of the participants it was important to ensure that 'each case [was] dealt with on its own merits'.[141] The following account given by one local practitioner is representative of most of the testimonies given in Site A:

> Every case needs to be risk-assessed ... there will be a multi-agency risk assessment that will need to take place. What are the risks to the individual if the public finds out about what they have done? You look at age. You look at personal circumstances. You look at the impact upon the victim ... It is not publicised in every occasion, but everything you do is revisited and reassessed in order to make sure that it is proportionate.[142]

[135] *Stanley* [2004] EWHC 2229 (Admin) [31].
[136] ibid [40].
[137] Home Office, *Anti-social Behaviour, Crime and Policing Act 2014* (n 10) 40.
[138] Int 19-PO-Site A.
[139] Int 26-LP-Site A.
[140] Int 3-LP-Site A.
[141] Int 21-PO-Site A.
[142] Int 9-LP-Site A.

The need to take into account the potential impact that the publication of certain information might have on the perpetrator was emphasised by many participants, especially in cases involving young people. As one local practitioner mentioned, publicising information about a young individual can be counterproductive because it is likely to 'increase the fear of harm and the negative views about young people'.[143]

The foregoing testimonies are consistent with the Statutory Guidance according to which '[e]ach case should be decided carefully on its own facts' striking a fair balance between the perpetrator's right to privacy and the effective enforcement of these measures.[144] Moreover, they reiterate that the administration of ASB in this site was mainly risk driven.

Although for most of the participants publicising information about the perpetrators and their behaviour should be confined only to those immediately affected by this kind of behaviour, many participants noted that under certain circumstances information should be shared more widely. They noted that this would only happen in cases where the 'victim is at real risk and any further ASB by the perpetrator ... can make them really suffer'.[145]

For three out of the 19 participants from Site A, however, it appeared that 'the norm is that if you are dealing with an adult, then you are going to inform the public'.[146] There was an impression that this seemed to be particularly the case with police officers when dealing with persistent offenders. One police officer noted the following:

> I think it is not necessarily a bad thing. I think that other people from the wider society have a right to know if somebody has breached the law in a sense and has certain conditions in order to safeguard and protect them.[147]

This officer then went on to explain that through this process the public are also made 'aware [of the conditions and] are able to notify the police that they breached' either their injunction or their CBO.[148]

In Site B, five out of the 10 participants mentioned that certain pieces of information were shared only with those affected or likely to have been affected by the perpetrator's behaviour. As one local practitioner explained:

> We will always consider [to] who we are telling about this. We do not publicise things ... so we told the estate what has actually been done because we obviously believed that everyone would have been affected because of the nature of the behaviour and because of where the behaviour was happening.[149]

[143] Int 2-LP-Site A.
[144] Home Office, *Anti-social Behaviour, Crime and Policing Act 2014* (n 10) 32.
[145] Int 29-PO-Site A.
[146] Int 23-PO-Site A.
[147] Int 21-PO-Site A.
[148] Int 21-PO-Site A.
[149] Int 16-LP-Site B.

As one interviewee noted, to publicise information to people who have not been affected by the perpetrator's behaviour 'would be a disproportionate' response.[150] Again, it was clear that the sharing of information was 'case specific'.[151] A risk-assessment was carried out in advance taking into consideration the impact of the perpetrators' behaviour and any personal issues they might be facing, such as 'mental health issues'.[152] One interviewee noted that in order for them to publicise the issue of an injunction the behaviour in question must have had a 'community impact'.[153] They stated, however, that their aim was to 'inform [the public] rather than to identify' the perpetrators.[154]

As far as the remaining participants were concerned, there was an impression that 'the public at large need to be advised as well because clearly that person has not changed from all the efforts you have put in beforehand'.[155] The following statement is illustrative of this approach:

> It is incredibly difficult to prove that somebody has breached the sanctions that have been placed upon them without the community taking ownership. It was never a particularly popular concept across the country. You know the old 'name it and shame it'. You know posting people's pictures. Did it breach their human rights? My personal opinion is that the rights of the victims should be held at a higher level than the rights of the perpetrator … they solely engage in [a] negative lifestyle which is having a bad impact upon everybody and people are getting frightened. So, I liked it when we could 'name and shame'. Put pictures on the internet, on a billboard or to the local press.[156]

The above testimony is not to suggest that these aforementioned 'name and shame' methods were used in Site B. Rather, it is to illustrate that half of the participants from Site B were in favour of a broader approach in terms of how information about the perpetrator and their behaviour should be managed. Moreover, the foregoing testimony is consistent with many other accounts which emphasised that these measures can hardly be monitored and for this reason local enforcement agents should 'rely on the community … to inform' them about any possible violations of the restrictions imposed on the perpetrators.[157]

In fact, it was clear from the evidence collected in both areas, that the limited availability of resources was one of the main reasons for publicising information about the perpetrators and their behaviour. As one police officer pointed out, 'unfortunately, there are not enough of us to police every single injunction or CBO. So, we rely upon whoever sees or if the victim sees to come forward with

[150] Int 17-LP-Site B.
[151] Int 8-LP-Site B.
[152] Int 8-LP-Site B.
[153] Int 8-LP-Site B.
[154] Int 8-LP-Site B.
[155] Int 22-LP-Site B.
[156] Int 9-LP-Site B.
[157] Int 17-LP-Site B.

the details of the breaches'.[158] According to one local practitioner, this cooperation between the public and the local enforcement agents was vital because 'once [the perpetrators] realise that they can get away with it they are not bothering'.[159] Hence, it was stated that in order for these measures to be effective 'you have to advertise' them.[160]

Although there was evidence to suggest that on a number of occasions information about the perpetrators was publicised to people who were not directly affected by their behaviour, this does not necessarily mean that the restrictions imposed on those individuals amounted to criminal punishment. As noted earlier, the purpose (or at least one of the purposes) of publicity must be the public condemnation of the individual at hand in order for the restrictions imposed on them to amount to criminal punishment. The fact that certain pieces of information about the perpetrator were publicised will not automatically satisfy the second prerequisite of the working definition of criminalisation.

To illustrate the distinction between the two, let us consider the following two testimonies. When one of the participants was asked to describe the circumstances under which they would let the entire community know about the issue of an injunction, their response was the following:

> [I]t is something that we try, not in a negative way, to say that this person has got this and get the feeling to the public that to let them know that action has been taken against that particular person.[161]

The foregoing account can be compared with the following one:

> With adults we have gone along further. We had *deliberately* put some articles in the [local newspaper]. That guy was extremely racially and homophobic abusive to a few people and this was not the first time he had done it and he had some previous convictions for racially aggravated offences ... We did a press release in the [local newspaper] when we got an ASBO for him because it was really important. Members of the community who had experiencing hate incidents were there.[162]

While both testimonies describe the circumstances under which information about the perpetrator was made available to the community at large, it is evident that only in the latter case the purpose or at least one of the purposes of publicising certain information was to *publicly condemn* the perpetrator and his behaviour. Conversely, in the first case it is clear that the purpose of sharing information was to reassure the public that the ASB had been dealt with.

Based on the data collected from both sites, in most of the cases information about the perpetrators was shared only with those *directly* affected by the behaviour in question as a means of facilitating the effective policing of the restrictions

[158] Int 13-PO-Site B.
[159] Int 1-LP-Site A.
[160] Int 10-LP-Site B.
[161] Int 27-PO-Site A.
[162] Int 1-LP-Site A (emphasis added).

imposed rather than as a means of publicly condemning those who behaved in an anti-social manner. There was evidence to suggest, however, that on certain limited occasions the main purpose (or at least one of the main purposes) of information sharing was to publicly condemn the perpetrators and their behaviour. In these *limited* cases, the implementation of the ASB tools and powers satisfied both prerequisites of the working definition and thus constituted a form of indirect criminalisation. The importance of this finding lies in the potential impact that 'name and shame' practices can have on those subjected to these measures. Such practices can result not only in the stigmatisation and social ostracisation of certain individuals, but in a 'risk-obsessed' society they can also be utilised to legitimise – by increasing the level of insecurity in society – more punitive methods of regulation in the absence of compelling evidence.[163] In the context of ASB, this might result in the extensive use of the injunction pre-emptively and the imposition of disproportionate restrictions on the liberty of those subjected to this measure. This not only highlights further the welfare–crime management tension that lies at the heart of practice, but it also demonstrates the need for robust procedures at a local level through which it can be ensured that the injunction remains a preventive rather than a punitive measure.

## 6.5. CONCLUSION

Based on the findings of this study, it would be unjustifiable to conclude that localised criminal codes were created through the implementation of ASB tools and powers. In both sites under study, the implementation of these measures *rarely* constituted a form of indirect criminalisation. Nevertheless, the study did expose the potential for indirect criminalisation in some cases. It is worth reiterating here, though, that the findings of this study should be approached with caution, since they do not necessarily represent how the ASB tools and powers are implemented across the country. The 2014 Act provides local enforcement agents with a considerable magnitude of discretion both in terms of the scope of the law and its implementation. Moreover, it should be borne in mind that this study examined the implementation of the injunction from a practitioner's perspective. Those against whom the ASB measures were used might feel that the requirements imposed on them were grossly disproportionate and that they amounted to a form of punishment.

Despite the (methodological) limitations of this study, its findings can be further analysed in order to identify those factors that contributed to the adoption of a more welfarist as opposed to enforcement-led approach, while

[163] P O'Malley, *Crime and Risk* (London, Sage Publications, 2010) ch 1; P Gray, 'The Political Economy of Risk and the New Governance of Youth Crime' (2009) 11 *Punishment & Society* 443, 445–47.

mitigating some of the concerns raised about the possibility of the injunction operating as a de facto criminal measure. I argue that these factors can inform existing ASB policies and/or assist in the formulation of new mechanisms as a means of preventing the injunction from operating as de facto criminal measure while securing a more consistent implementation of the law across England and Wales.

# 7

# *Conclusion*

THE MAIN OBJECTIVE of this book is to offer a detailed and interdisciplinary analysis of the issue of indirect criminalisation by scrutinising the implementation of the successor of the Anti-social Behaviour Order (ASBO) at a local level, that is the Part 1 injunction of the Anti-social Behaviour, Crime and Policing Act 2014. Simply put, the book examines whether the implementation of the injunction resulted in the indirect criminalisation of certain kinds of anti-social behaviour (ASB). To achieve this, the book engages with central questions within legal theory, such as the normative distinction between the criminal law and other forms of social regulation used by the state and mechanisms for distinguishing criminal from non-criminal rules, as well as by exploring how such questions can be tested and applied empirically. This enables the book to move beyond a purely theoretical analysis of the issue of indirect criminalisation and investigate whether non-criminal interventions have indeed been operating as de facto criminal measures. Although there is a substantial body of literature on the rise of the preventive state, this is the first book-length study on the issue of indirect criminalisation highlighting a different facet of the rise of the preventive state since the injunction formally lies outside the ambit of the criminal law.[1] Moreover, despite the concerns raised about the potential punitive nature of the ASB, this is the first study that investigates this issue empirically.[2] The importance of this analysis is heightened by the continuous proliferation of civil preventive measures in many Western jurisdictions since the beginning of the twenty-first century, such as the gang injunctions in the United States. What is problematic about civil preventive measures is not their stated objective, that is to prevent certain kinds of criminality and unwanted behaviour. As I argued before, the prevention of crime and other undesirable kinds of behaviour that can undermine the security of its

[1] For more on the rise of the preventive state see: H Carvalho, *The Preventive Turn in Criminal Law* (Oxford, Oxford University Press, 2017); P Ramsay, *The Insecurity State: Vulnerable Autonomy and the Right to Security in the Criminal Law* (Oxford, Oxford University Press, 2012); A Ashworth and L Zedner, *Preventive Justice* (Oxford, Oxford University Press, 2014).

[2] It has to be noted that a number of small and large-scale empirical studies have been conducted examining the implementation of the ASBO from different perspectives. That said, none of these previous studies focused specifically on the issue of indirect criminalisation.

citizens is a *legitimate* objective for the liberal state to pursue.[3] Rather, what is problematic about civil preventive measures is the *way* in which the liberal state seeks to prevent crime and other undesirable outcomes. That is, by introducing non-criminal interventions which are susceptible to indirect criminalisation as a means of (purposefully) circumventing the enhanced procedural and evidential protections afforded to those facing the prospect of a criminal prosecution. As a result of this, those subjected to civil preventive measures fall into a legal lacuna with limited legal protection compared with those facing criminal prosecution, notwithstanding the potential punitive nature of these interventions.

It is worth reiterating here that this book does not engage with whether and, if yes, on what basis civil preventive measures in general (or the injunction in particular) can be justified. I argue that in order to reach this point, that is to scrutinise the legitimacy of civil preventive measures, we first need to determine their true nature. What justifies the introduction of a punitive intervention does not necessarily justify a non-punitive measure and vice versa. In what follows, an overview of the main findings of this study and their implications is provided. Although the jurisdictional focus of this book is mainly England and Wales, as we shall see, its findings and the analysis made can be utilised by legislatures, policymakers, criminal law theorists, criminologists and law enforcement agents from across the globe who are interested and work in the fields of criminal justice and ASB, especially in jurisdictions where there has been an influx of civil preventive measures.

## AN OVERVIEW OF THE MAIN FINDINGS OF THIS STUDY AND THEIR IMPLICATIONS

One of the most important challenges faced by any contemporary liberal state is the protection of its citizens' interests from any unjustifiable interference by others while respecting their individual liberty and autonomy.[4] As I argued in chapter one, in theory, a totalitarian regime can be equally (if not more) effective in safeguarding the security of its citizens. What really distinguishes a liberal state, therefore, from other political orders is its promise to limit its interference

[3] See ch 1, section 1.5.

[4] As far as England and Wales is concerned, a particularly apposite example of the curtailment of suspects' rights in the name of victim protection is the introduction of ss 34–38 of the Criminal Justice and Public Order Act 1994 which, under certain circumstances, allow for the drawing of adverse inferences from the accused's silence. The rhetoric that underpinned the introduction of these provisions is encapsulated in a 1993 speech of the then Home Secretary Michael Howard according to whom: 'The so-called right to silence is ruthlessly exploited by terrorists. What fools they must think we are. It's time to call a halt to this charade. The so-called right to silence will be abolished. The innocent have nothing to hide and that is exactly the point the prosecution will be able to make in future.' See H Quirk, *The Rise and Fall of the Right of Silence* (London, Routledge, 2016) 44.

with personal autonomy to what it is *absolutely necessary* for safeguarding the security of its people and for the maintenance of those conditions within society that will enable them to realise their full potential. On this view, security and individual autonomy should be regarded as the cornerstones of each contemporary liberal society. In reality, though, since the late stages of the twentieth century, liberty and individual autonomy have been increasingly seen by both the legislature and the executive of many Western liberal societies as a threat to security. This trend is evident not only by the preventive turn in the criminal law (exemplified by the proliferation of pre-emptive crimes) and the curtailment of the suspects' rights, but also through the introduction and rise of civil preventive measures.

A key objective of this book is to problematise the increased reliance of liberal states on civil preventive measures by highlighting the possibility of them operating as de facto criminal rules and therefore constituting a form of indirect criminalisation. Apart from allowing for the imposition of criminal punishment in the absence of the enhanced procedural and evidential protection afforded to those facing criminal prosecution, indirect criminalisation is morally problematic because: (i) it poses a threat to liberty and individual autonomy by allowing the net of social control to be extended to the private sphere; (ii) it undermines the normative distinction between the criminal law and other forms of social regulation used by the state; and (iii) it is not subjected to certain rules and principles that are so important to restrict the punitive state.[5]

In order to investigate whether indeed the implementation of civil preventive measures could result in the indirect criminalisation of certain kinds of behaviour, I decided to use the ASBO's successor as my primary case study. The reason for this was threefold. First, ASB can be conceptualised very widely ranging from everyday neighbour disputes that can be regarded as part of daily human interaction to behaviour that already falls within the ambit of the criminal law, such as criminal damage. Hence, very few (if any) limits are imposed (at least based on how the law appears on the statute book) on the ability of local enforcement agents to utilise the injunction and the other ASB tools and powers. Second, not only does the law provide local enforcement agents and courts with a significant magnitude of discretion as to the scope of the injunction, but it also allows them to decide what kinds of restrictions can be imposed on the liberty of those against whom such a measure is issued.[6] In theory, the requirements imposed on the liberty of those against whom an injunction is issued can be so severe as

[5] See further, ch 2.

[6] This is not the case though with all civil preventive measures since some of them, such as the TPIMs, allow only for the imposition of specific restrictions on the liberty of those against whom they are imposed. In the case of the TPIMs, for example, only those requirements listed under Sch 1 of the Terrorism Prevention and Investigation Measures Act 2011 can be imposed on a suspected terrorist, such as a requirement to reside at a specified residence.

to amount to a form of punishment in their own right, regardless of whether breach of the injunction constitutes a civil contempt of court.[7] The importance of this is heightened even further by the fact that these restrictions can last indefinitely since there are no minimum or maximum duration requirements for adult perpetrators.[8] Third, of particular concern were the 2014 amendments through which the hybrid ASBO was repealed and replaced by what appears to be a purely civil injunction.[9] Although at first sight this shift towards a purely civil response appeared to mitigate against the well-founded concerns raised about the ASBO's hybrid nature,[10] following a more in-depth examination of the ASBO's successor it becomes immediately apparent that this shift to what appears to be a purely civil injunction should be approached with caution.[11] The reason for this is that the proximity of the injunction to the criminal law has been officially distanced, something which might mean that the implementation of the injunction attracts less attention and external scrutiny, albeit the injunction being potentially more liberty restrictive than its predecessor.

Examining whether indeed the implementation of the injunction resulted in the indirect criminalisation of certain kinds of ASB poses a number of normative and practical challenges. Initially, an account of criminalisation is needed based on which it could be examined whether non-criminal interventions operate as de facto criminal rules. Although there is rich academic literature on the unique nature of criminal punishment, none of these accounts was formulated with the intention of identifying (or even take into consideration) potential instances of indirect criminalisation. Rather, their objective was to provide a normative account of criminal punishment focusing on those characteristics that distinguish it from other types of legal sanction.[12] Similarly, a mechanism, that is the anti-subversion doctrine, was formulated by the European Court of Human Rights as a means of identifying and preventing instances of indirect criminalisation. That notwithstanding, after carefully scrutinising the anti-subversion doctrine, a number of problems have been identified, such as the vary narrow interpretation of the term 'liberty'.[13] It was argued that these problems necessitated the adoption of a more flexible definition of criminalisation that will truly enable us to look beyond the label attached by the legislature and examine

[7] Although here Duff and Marshall were referring to the restrictions that could be imposed on the liberty of those against whom an ASBO was issued, their argument is readily applicable in the context of the injunction as well since under the 2014 Act positive obligations were added to the list of requirements that can be imposed on those whose behaviour is regarded as anti-social. See A Duff and S Marshall, 'How Offensive Can You Get?' in A von Hirsch and A Simester (eds), *Incivilities: Regulating Offensive Behaviour* (Oxford, Hart Publishing, 2006) 80.

[8] For those under the age of 18, the injunction can last for a period of no more than 12 months. See ch 4, Table 4.1.

[9] Anti-social Behaviour, Crime and Policing Act 2014, Part 1.

[10] For more on the concerns raised by the ASBO's hybrid nature, see ch 1, section 1.4.1.

[11] See ch 4, section 4.2.2.

[12] See ch 3, section 3.2.1.

[13] See ch 3, section 3.2.2.

the actual nature of (allegedly) non-punitive interventions that are susceptible to indirect criminalisation. To this end, a working definition of criminalisation was formulated for the purposes of this book. To reiterate here, what distinguishes criminalisation from other forms of social control is the imposition (or the threat of imposing) criminal punishment. In order for a legal sanction to be regarded as a form of criminal punishment, the following two prerequisites must be satisfied:

(i) The implementation of the legal rule must result in the imposition of a sanction which interferes with the perpetrator's liberty.
(ii) The sanction imposed and/or threatened to be imposed on the perpetrator must *publicly* and *purposefully* communicate state censure.

Although the interference with the perpetrator's liberty does not have to be substantial in order for the first part of the test to be satisfied, it is worth reiterating that for the sanction imposed (or threatened to be imposed) to amount to criminal punishment, both prerequisites must be satisfied. Moreover, it should be borne in mind that this working definition of criminalisation cannot predetermine whether a non-criminal intervention is punitive in nature. Instead, it requires us to scrutinise the implementation of each measure on an individual basis in order to determine whether it satisfies both prerequisites.

The theoretical analysis of the injunction did expose the potential for indirect criminalisation,[14] but in order to examine whether indeed the injunction was operating as a *de* facto criminal intervention, it was imperative to scrutinise its implementation in practice in light of the working definition of criminalisation formulated for the purposes of this book. To this end, an empirical study using semi-structured interviews with local practitioners and police officers who had a daily interaction with ASB and were responsible for the use of the relevant tools and powers at local level was conducted in two sites in England. Some of the most important findings of this study included:

1. Despite the 'sweeping and vague' statutory definition of ASB,[15] it was evident that local enforcement agents' decisions to classify someone's behaviour as anti-social was informed by a number of factors, such as the limited availability of resources and the presence of both internal and external review procedures, that significantly narrow the scope of the injunction. As a result of this, in the sites under study the behaviour dealt with through the injunction and the other ASB tools and powers was *impactful* and in most of the cases *persistent*.
2. In line with the findings of previous studies, it was clear from the data collected that there was an overlap between crime and ASB, that is some

[14] See ch 4, section 4.3.2.
[15] A Ashworth et al, 'Neighbouring on the Oppressive: The Government's "Anti-Social Behaviour Order" Proposals' (1998) 16 *Criminal Justice* 7, 9.

kinds of behaviour that were deemed to be anti-social already fall within the ambit of the criminal law.

3. The procedure followed by local enforcement agents when notified about a potential incident of ASB was primarily risk-driven. Simply put, local enforcements agents' handling of each incident of ASB was determined by the level of risk posed by the alleged perpetrator to others.
4. Before applying to court for the issue of an injunction, local enforcement agents would utilise a range of informal interventions, such as sending warning letters and engaging those involved in a RJ process. Hence, the regulation of ASB was taking place primarily in the shadows without resorting to formal legal action against the perpetrators.[16] That said, if the level of risk posed by the perpetrator was high and the informal interventions used were not successful in preventing further ASB, then local enforcement agents would resort to enforcement without exhausting all informal interventions available at their disposal.
5. It was evident through the data collected from both sites, that there was a genuine belief amongst local enforcement agents that in order for any interventions to be successful in the long term, it is imperative to address the underlying causes of the perpetrators' behaviour. As mentioned by many local enforcement agents, people do not often behave in an anti-social manner simply by choice. Rather, their behaviour is often the product of deep-seated socio-economic issues.
6. Based on the data collected, on some occasions the ASB tools and powers were used as a means of diverting people, especially young perpetrators, away from criminality. Simply put, rather than prosecuting that person for the commission of an offence, local enforcement agents would seek to address the behaviour at hand by utilising the ASB tools and powers available at their disposal in order to divert the perpetrator away from the criminal justice system.
7. In most cases, the requirements imposed on those against whom the ASB tools and powers were used did satisfy the first prerequisite of the working definition of criminalisation that was formulated for the purposes of this book. That notwithstanding, the requirements imposed *rarely* satisfied the second prerequisite of the working definition of criminalisation and therefore their imposition did not constitute a form of indirect criminalisation.

Although the implementation of the ASB tools and powers in the sites under investigation rarely constituted a form of indirect criminalisation (based on the working definition of criminalisation formulated for the purposes of this book), three really important points should be noted here. First, it should be reiterated that the findings of this study should be approached with caution since the

[16] For more on the procedure followed, see ch 6, Figure 6.1.

implementation of the ASB tools and powers can *vary considerably* from one area to another. This is primarily due to the significant magnitude of discretion afforded to local enforcement agents and courts regarding both the scope and the implementation of the relevant tools and powers. Hence, the fact that in the two sites under study the implementation of the ASB tools and powers rarely resulted in the indirect criminalisation of the behaviour at hand, does not necessarily mean that this is the case across England and Wales. Second, it should be borne in mind that the implementation of the injunction was examined from the local enforcement agents' perspective without taking into account the views of those subjected to these measures. What this means is that those against whom an injunction (or any of the other ASB tools and powers) was imposed might feel that they were in fact criminalised for their behaviour. Finally, although only in some limited instances did the implementation of the injunction's first limb constitute a form of indirect criminalisation, the findings of this empirical study can be further utilised by the legislature, policymakers and local enforcement agents to formulate mechanisms through which the misuse of the ASB tools and powers can be prevented. To this end, through a more detailed examination of the findings of the empirical study, a set of factors can be identified that have contributed to the adoption of a more welfarist (as opposed to a more punitive) approach in these two sites. These factors included:

1. *The need to adopt a multi-agency approach*: In most of the institutions that participated in this study, there were a number of review layers (both internal and external) in place relating to the management of ASB. The presence of these internal and external review procedures not only laid the foundations for a more consistent implementation of the ASB tools and powers at a local level, but also enabled local enforcement agents to combine their knowledge, skills and expertise examining each incident from various different perspectives. Moreover, it was evident that the adoption of this multi-agency and multidisciplinary approach resulted in a more welfarist as opposed to enforcement-led stance towards ASB, thereby minimising the risk for indirect criminalisation.
2. *The need to address the underlying causes of ASB*: It was evident from the data collected that for most local enforcement agents a purely enforcement-driven approach is not a panacea since it cannot permanently address the behaviour at hand. This was due to the belief that on many occasions ASB was the product of a number of antecedent causes. On this view, the imposition of some bland prohibitions is unlikely to permanently address the perpetrator's ASB. This belief prompted local enforcement agents to work with perpetrators to address the underlying causes of their behaviour rather than resorting to formal legal action against them.
3. *Contemplating the impact of enforcement*: Based on the data collected, on most occasions local enforcement agents would contemplate what the potential impact of enforcement would be on the perpetrators. That is, whether the requirements local enforcement agents sought to obtain would

*unjustifiably* interfere with the perpetrators' liberty, such as preventing them from doing their grocery shopping. Moreover, most of the research participants were mindful of the need to keep publicity to what was *absolutely necessary* for the effective enforcement of the ASB tools and powers.

I argue that local enforcement agents who work in the field of ASB can utilise the aforementioned principles to inform existing practices adopted at a local level regarding the implementation of the ASB tools and powers as a means of adopting a more welfarist as opposed to a more enforcement-led (and possibly punitive) approach. The adoption of these principles can, for instance, be in the form of a code of practice that will provide local enforcement agents with specific guidelines as to how incidents of ASB should be managed.[17] The formulation of such a code would not only result in the more consistent implementation of the law across England and Wales, but it would also minimise the risk of indirect criminalisation. Moreover, despite the jurisdictional focus of this book on England and Wales, the principles laid out above can also be of use to legislatures, policymakers and local enforcement agents across the world when implementing ASB policies at a local level.

Apart from the implications that the findings of the empirical study can have for the implementation of the ASB tools and powers, attention should also be paid to the broader philosophical ramifications of this book. Although, for instance, the implementation of the ASB tools and powers rarely resulted in the imposition of punishment, it is evident that a proper discussion about how indirect criminalisation can be prevented and the proper limits of the preventive state is still needed.[18] The importance of this discussion is heightened by the increased reliance of legislatures, especially in many Western jurisdiction, on civil preventive measures that are susceptible to indirect criminalisation.

A discussion is also needed about the proper relationship between the criminal law and civil preventive measures. In particular, as seen before, there was evidence to suggest that on some occasions the injunction was used as a means of diverting perpetrators away from the criminal justice system. That is, rather than prosecuting someone for their conduct, local enforcement agents preferred to utilise the injunction and the other ASB tools and powers to address the perpetrator's behaviour. As a police officer pointed out, for example,

> if it is one off low-level then no we are no way near that … If there is a fifteen-year-old who does graffiti for a first time are we going to criminalise this person? Or is it better to make him face the victim and scrape this off the wall themselves?[19]

[17] For an attempt to do so, see S Demetriou and M Lukera, *Addressing Anti-social Behaviour: A Guide for Local Enforcement Agents* (2019), available at: sro.sussex.ac.uk/id/eprint/104249/3/Addressing%20Anti-social%20Behaviour%20-%20A%20Guide%20for%20Local%20Enforcement%20Agents.pdf.

[18] See further, Ashworth and Zedner (n 1) 11.

[19] Int 26-PO-Site A.

At first sight, using the injunction as an alternative to criminal prosecution appears to be a sensible (and defensible) strategy given the adverse consequences that a criminal conviction can have on someone, especially a young first-time offender.[20] That said, to use the injunction or any other non-criminal method of social regulation as a means of addressing behaviour which is criminal in nature raises a number of really important practical and normative questions for criminal law theorists. Initially, it has to be determined whether from a normative perspective such a diversion is permissible and on what basis. Even if it is accepted that such a diversion can be justifiable, it is imperative to decide under what circumstances, for what purpose(s) and for what kinds of behaviour this alternative route should be followed. Furthermore, clear guidelines are needed as to who should decide on each occasion if this alternative route is to be followed. Moreover, criminal law theorists should be mindful of the fact that those subjected to civil preventive measures fall into a legal lacuna with fewer rights and protections compared with those facing the prospect of a criminal prosecution. Consequently, it is essential for this process to be governed by a set of predetermined principles which provide safeguards that are necessary to prevent its potential misuse, such as using the injunction as a means of avoiding the enhanced procedural and evidential protections afforded to those facing criminal prosecution. Although it was not my intention in this book to engage with any of the aforementioned normative questions posed by the use of the injunction as an alternative to criminal prosecution, the preceding analysis of civil preventive measures (both at an empirical and a theoretical level) clearly highlights the need for such a debate.

## CONCLUDING REMARKS

ASB can be construed very widely depending on an individual's tolerance threshold, their personal circumstances and their socio-economic background. Although it can sometimes be dismissed outright as too trivial and/or as part of everyday human interaction (and therefore not warranting any kind of formal legal intervention), as the tragic case of Fiona Pilkington demonstrates, it can severely disrupt people's lives and lead to their repeated victimisation.[21] What can start as a minor dispute between two neighbours over parking, can rapidly

[20] Beyond the hardships of criminal punishment, such as the monetary impact that this can have on the offender, attention should also be paid to the collateral consequences of criminal convictions as well, such as voting restrictions. See further, A Corda and J Kaspar, 'Collateral Consequences of Criminal Conviction in the United States and Germany' in K Ambos et al (eds), *Core Concepts in Criminal Law and Criminal Justice: Volume II* (Cambridge, Cambridge University Press, 2022); Z Hoskins, *Beyond Punishment: A Normative Account of the Collateral Legal Consequences of Conviction* (New York, Oxford University Press, 2019) 4.

[21] See ch 1, section 1.4.3.

escalate to serious criminality with devastating consequences for both sides. For this reason, a flexible legal framework is needed through which local enforcement agents will be able to address behaviour that really has a negative impact on people's quality of life.

The need to address ASB (and crime in general) swiftly and effectively can hardly be disputed. As seen before, the prevention of crime and other undesirable kinds of conduct that can *unjustifiably* interfere with people's liberty lies at the heart of the liberal state's promise to its citizens. What is concerning about the current legislative framework, though, is that the ASB tools and powers can be implemented, at least in theory, in a manner that results in the indirect criminalisation of certain kinds of behaviour, albeit presented as measures the primary aim of which is to prevent ASB and low-level criminality. Although in most of the cases explored within this empirical study the implementation of the ASB tools and powers did not result in the imposition of criminal punishment, it seems appropriate to conclude this book by reiterating the need for legislatures, policymakers, legal commentators and local enforcement agents to be mindful of *how* and *at what cost*, in terms of individual liberty, the prevention of crime and other undesirable kinds of conduct is to be achieved. What really distinguishes a liberal state from other political orders is its promise to limit state interference with personal autonomy to what is absolutely necessary for safeguarding the security of its people and for the maintenance of those conditions within society that will enable them to realise their full potential.[22] Hence, liberty and security should not be seen as opposing values, that is that one should take priority over the other, but as the cornerstones of every contemporary liberal society.

[22] S Demetriou and N Partington, 'Criminalising Hate: The Need for Rationalisation and Reform' (2022) 6 *Criminal Law Review* 448, 460.

# Index

www.ingramcontent.com/pod-product-compliance
Lightning Source LLC
Chambersburg PA
CBHW071351220926
51613CB00008B/50
*9781509941438*